THE SUCCESSFUL MIDDLE SCHOOL:

A PLACE TO BELONG AND BECOME

DR. LAURIE BARRON AND PATTI KINNEY

Association for Middle Level Education

ISBN: 978-1-56090-085-6

Library of Congress Control Number: 2024938628

Contents

APPENDICES 263

Acknowledgments

Woodrow Wilson once said, "We should not only use the brains we have, but all that we can borrow," and we certainly took his advice to heart in writing both editions of this book. Far too many people to list were involved in helping us frame, reframe, write, rewrite, organize, reorganize, and then create a second edition of this manuscript, but we especially want to acknowledge the tremendous help given to us by the following individuals:

Neither this new edition nor the original book would have been completed without the amazing work of our editor, **Marj Frank**. She guided, encouraged, and challenged us from beginning to end and then took what we wrote, made it so much better, and helped us sound so much smarter! She has our most sincere thanks and appreciation—we couldn't do it without her.

Rick Wormeli wrote an outstanding foreword for the first edition—and then raised the bar even higher for this new edition. We are so grateful for his support over the years in the form of encouragement, comments, probing questions, and constructive feedback to help us refine our thoughts and focus even more closely on the importance of *belonging* and *becoming*.

A big thanks also goes to **Judith Brough** for giving us valuable feedback on our first (very) rough draft. Her questions, comments, and edits were instrumental as we continued to revise and improve upon our initial manuscript.

Our friend and colleague **Andrew Maxey** has long been an advocate of middle level education. His insights, candid thoughts, and reminders as we prepared the second edition of this book helped keep us focused on ensuring that this book provides current and meaningful support to all those working to support middle level students.

Our work over the years with the students, staff, and families at **Ashland Middle School** and **Talent Middle School** in Oregon (Patti) as well as **Smokey Road**

Middle School in Georgia and the **Evergreen School District** in Montana (Laurie) provided us with the knowledge, background, experience, and understanding of just how important the concepts of *belonging* and *becoming* are when it comes to providing the best education possible for young adolescents.

A book simply cannot be written without the support of **family and friends**. We thank all of you for understanding and putting up with the numerous hours spent writing that pulled us away from spending time with you. We want to give special thanks to our husbands **Dan** and **Dan** (they even have the same middle name) for all of their support along the way!

Finally, it would be heresy to write about the importance of student voice without incorporating it into this book! We are appreciative of Talent Middle School teacher **Sandra Tringolo** for sharing her students' writing with us, and a big thank-you goes to the many **middle school students in the Flathead Valley of Montana** who served as our sounding board and resident experts whenever we needed a student perspective. Much of the student work in the second edition represents submissions by **the finalists of AMLE's 2023 Middle School Student Sound Off Contest**. Although we can't thank all of them by name, we do give them our appreciation for sharing their voices and middle school experiences. We want to give a shout-out to Laurie's daughter, **Emma Barron**—who was in middle school when we wrote the first edition, is now in college, and still offering her thoughts—for her continued support and contributions.

Foreword

by Rick Wormeli

To be nobody but yourself in a world which is doing its best day and night to make you like everybody else means to fight the hardest battle which any human being can fight and never stop fighting.

— "A Poet's Advice to Students,"
***E.E. Cummings: A Miscellany Revised,* 1965**

A tree says: A kernel is hidden in me, a spark, a thought, I am life from eternal life. The attempt and the risk that the eternal mother took with me is unique, unique the form and veins of my skin, unique the smallest play of leaves in my branches and the smallest scar on my bark. I was made to form and reveal the eternal in my smallest special detail.

Herman Hesse, *Wandering: Notes and Sketches,* 1972

With deepening roots in the soil of their time and place, and on the cusp of all they are to be, young adolescents bend and twist in the rising breeze, ready to form and reveal the eternal in their authentic selves. We are lucky enough to bear witness—and wise enough, we hope—to provide a patient compass.

In his beautiful book, *The Hidden Life of Trees* (Greystone Books, 2015), Peter Wohlleben writes that, in times of stress, trees not only depend on the entwined nature of their roots to fortify them against the wind, but they also share with one another the nutrients and water for photosynthesis, ensuring that those with access to neither can yet thrive. The trees live in relationship, each with a role to play in nurturing the other. This is belonging.

For both our students and our adult selves, if we do not have ties or belong to someone else, we are perpetually in survival mode, rarely extending ourselves for fear of having nothing left on which to subsist. We are on guard, too, against our realness—for others knowing who we are makes us vulnerable to them. In an already fragile world, we cannot afford that. In our most vulnerable moments, we hope that we are known and valued by others. Just like the community of trees, if we do not belong, we do not thrive—we do not become.

In 2017, Laurie and Patti generously shared their insights in a book on how to help middle school students become and belong in their worlds. It was inspired and practical, and upon reading it, we had no choice but to step through the door it showed us. In this updated edition, you will find new, extended, and serious research (the appendices and endnotes are goldmines) as well as new student examples and voices, expanded sections on helping students cultivate their own executive function, and new discussions and insights on helping students navigate their digital lives and the influencers therein—ironically, participation in the online world is among the most daunting real-life challenges middle schoolers face, and they (and we) must be properly equipped for the landscape.

You'll also find new recommendations for Student Learning Profiles and Graduation Profiles, expanded collections of useful books and resources, and a super-helpful section in which Laurie and Patti make the connection between research and middle school practice, straightforwardly declaring: "Because we know this about young adolescents...schools and classrooms need to do this...," which goes a long way toward turning junior versions of high schools (junior highs) into true and effective middle schools. In all, the authors provide well-vetted insight gleaned over seven years of engaging with the first edition's content and educators around the world. Heck, almost every page has been revised to reflect the modern era as we accelerate toward 2030 and beyond.

I'd like to suggest that this be THE book we now hand out to all new middle level teachers or even to all teachers and leaders applying for open positions in our schools, be they novices to education or seasoned veterans. Hand them a copy of the book, and say, "This is us. Does your disposition and practice resonate with what you find here?" If the answer is yes, they're going to be wonderful additions to the faculty and administration, doing right by students and their learning.

As we look for books about what it really means for those of us teaching middle schoolers and how to do this great thing we do, *The Successful Middle School: A Place to Belong and Become* is right up there with *The Successful Middle School: This We Believe* (2021), *What Every Middle School Teacher Should Know, Third Edition* (2014), *Middle School Matters: The 10 Key Skills Kids Need to Thrive in Middle School and Beyond–How Parents Can Help* (2019) as well as *Middle School Superpowers: Raising Resilient Tweens in Turbulent Times* (2023). This a trusted compendium and candid mentor of what we find at the heart of middle level teaching.

The next five paragraphs have been gently revised and updated from the foreword I provided for the first edition. The descriptions still hold for this new edition—and indeed, even more so today, as the world has become ever more extreme, and the research and insights for our constructive roles in young adolescent teaching have grown more compelling in the interim between the two editions.

Laurie and Patti's insights are timely. Today's political, religious, sexual orientation, race, and economic rhetoric—and realities—are growing ever more divisive, while unhealthy fear of the other (xenophobia) is becoming progressively normalized. What's more, students—and many of their teachers, too—are increasingly reliant on external validations for mental and emotional balance, sliding toward paranoia, anxiety, or even anger if no one immediately responds to their social media posts: *What's wrong with me? Am I not worth at least one "like"? Did I do something wrong? Do I not matter?* When we don't belong, or when we lack a clear identity, feelings of abandonment, threat to life, anger, and loneliness are exacerbated.

Now, more than ever, we need skilled mentors like the authors of this exceptional book. As award-winning principals, Laurie and Patti made major contributions to both of their local communities as well as to the nation and the global profession at large, but theirs are the souls of classroom teachers—and *wow*, does that practicality shine through! There are plenty of classroom examples here as well as generous offerings of the sort of wisdom that accrues only to "seasoned veterans" who, over many years on the frontlines, have come to understand the unique nature of young adolescents and how to work with them. Reflecting the authors' commitment to practicality, their ideas are refreshingly actionable— and sensitive to budget constraints, offering workarounds when finances are an issue. Their combined experience is stunning: They've been there, done that, and now they're telling us what's what—and we're lucky to be in the room when they do.

Laurie and Patti are up to speed on the latest thinking in multiple fields, including executive function, self-efficacy, differentiation, special education, staff development, educational research, and reflective practices. All the helpful thinkers and doers of our profession are here, too: Kohlberg, George, Swaim, Deci, Ryan, Lounsbury, Rosenthal, Jacobson, Boaler, Hattie, Brooks, Berckemeyer, Crocker, Dewey, Dweck, Guskey, Kohn, Compton, Curwin, Eichhorn, and even Winnie-the-Pooh.

Readers will also appreciate Laurie and Patti looking at all of this through the eyes of a principal, organizing and structuring schools and programs so as to cultivate the school's deeply held values. We also get clear advice on how to sustain the middle school concept and all its pieces, even in times of political change as well as clearly explained elements that we can apply to develop such professional and effective practices.

I am further struck by how many of their insights in working with students also translate to leaders' work with teachers. Collectively, the sections on the characteristics of young adolescents and "Putting It Into Practice" would constitute a cogent focus for an entire course on middle level education, adequate in its own right for specialized certification programs. In addition, we can incorporate many of these strategies as we connect with one another as faculty, and as we aspire to improve our own instructional design. An easy "a-ha!" inspired by the book is to look at ourselves: How do we teachers and administrators learn to belong and actively help others belong? How do we become? And how can taking such journeys like those of our students make us better educators for them?

After reading this new edition, I'm on fire to pursue these ideas and to be the best version of my educator self. Let's not just leave these ideas posted as simplistic sound bites on the teacher's lounge wall and let them fade into the ceaseless din and drone of competing education reforms. No, the content here is worth the deeper dive, because it is the raw DNA of middle level success—the stuff of life, sparked by inspired teachers who shout, "Heck yeah, I'm in!" This book is that kind of oxygen.

So, who are we to disturb the universe, embracing the real and powerful role early adolescence plays in individual growth and our collective future? Who are we to nurture the unique and the eternal in our students, and to help them be nobody but themselves? We are middle level professionals who welcome the instructional vitality of students becoming and belonging.

What an honor it is to be given such responsibility, and what a relief it is to be given the tools to do it properly! Not all are called to such work, but with Laurie and Patti's insights here, we belong to our students and they to us; we become what our students need us to be, and our students become the world itself.

I look forward to that.

Rick Wormeli
Teacher, Teacher Trainer
Author of *Meet Me in the Middle*
July 2024

Preface

Two words sparked the creation of this book: *belonging* and *becoming*. Words that kept popping up in all our discussions of middle level students. Words so powerful that we quickly realized they had to be not only the key ideas of a book but the title as well! As we reflected on the students we have had the opportunity to know and teach, the schools we have led and observed, the teachers we have mentored and enjoyed as colleagues, the programs we have examined and developed—in a sort of "a-ha!" moment, we were struck by how often *belonging* and *becoming* were centerpieces of the conversation.

It reminded us of learning that handy trick for finding a common denominator of two unlike fractions—once you learn it, suddenly your eyes are opened to the value of the numbers: You see them in the same terms, you can compare them, you can work with them, and you can gain a clearer understanding of equivalencies. In much the same way, we have discovered a common denominator in our work—a thread that ties together the concerns of students, successful and effective middle level practices, and young adolescent development. **That common denominator is young adolescents' profound need and deep desire to find places and situations where they feel they can *belong* and where they can discover who they are—and who they want to *become*.**

The more we looked at the words *belong* and *become* (and the broad meanings behind them), the more we realized just how foundational these concepts are to the development of young adolescents—and therefore to the goals, passions, and purposes of our work with them. This brought us to the questions, "Why are *belonging* and *becoming* critical to the education of our students?" and "What can middle schools and educators do to help students *belong* and *become*?" And thus, to explore and share some answers to those questions, the first edition of this book was born.

In the six years following the publication of *Middle School: A Place to Belong and Become*, we watched as the world changed for our middle schools: We've seen students and staff isolated, healthy socialization interrupted, and learning time disrupted or lost—to the pandemic, to the proliferation of smartphones, to the growing influence of social media and the internet that looms over our students, and to the stress and anxiety triggered by an uncertain social climate beyond school. Because of the massive changes students undergo during early adolescence, middle school has always been a tough experience for students to navigate—but now the struggles may be even greater, and they are certainly more complex in some ways. We see that the topics of *belonging* and *becoming* are now more relevant than ever for young adolescents.

As we continue to explore the success of a middle school culture that promotes both *belonging* and *becoming* in these transitional years for young adolescents, we're reminded of a saying we've used in joint presentations: "Crustaceans are at their most vulnerable when they are between shells."

One summer I (Patti) was visiting friends in Maine where I found myself fascinated by the lobster pots in the bays. We even visited a "lobster pound" to buy some for our dinner. But I also learned a few new things about lobsters: Lobsters, like other crustaceans, must shed their hard outer shells in order to grow. As its body becomes too large for the shell that has protected it, a lobster finds a safe place—away from predators—to begin shedding the old shell that is now holding back its growth.

However, the new shell provides little protection until it hardens. Thus, the lobster is extremely vulnerable—and most likely feels somewhat awkward—in the new, larger shell, and is at great risk from the outside world. It is completely exposed to its surroundings. Yet, without the periodic shedding of its shell, the lobster could not grow.

Sounds like a middle school student, doesn't it? Middle school is a time of great change—physically, socially, emotionally, cognitively, and psychologically. In order to grow and flourish (*become*), young adolescents must live in a safe, protected environment (*belong*), and it is up to those of us who work with them to provide the encouragement and support they need in order to grow. (To help my teachers keep this in mind, I even brought back little rubber lobsters for them to put on their desks.)

Schools now have greater awareness of the importance of *belonging* and *becoming*, and many have brought focus to these topics—but there is still much work to be done. This reality has compelled us to update our book with a mission to expand the efforts for all educators in all schools and to understand *belonging* and *becoming* more deeply and to double down on building rich, effective cultures of *belonging* and *becoming* for all our middle school students as well as the adults who work with and care for them.

Cultivating a middle school where students can *belong* as well as where they can *become* what they are capable of being (both personally and academically) is a great challenge. We freely admit that we don't have all the answers. However, after nearly 80 combined years working with young adolescents, we can share stories and practices founded upon both effective middle level education as well as the development, needs, characteristics, gifts, and amazing possibilities of young adolescents. Our desire is for this book to give readers timely and practical information and strategies to help them establish and nurture an environment where the young adolescents entrusted to them can both *belong* and *become*. We wish you well on this journey.

Laurie and Patti

Part I

Foundations for Belonging and Becoming

If you have ever bought a house, had a house built, or even watched a TV home renovation show, you know the critical importance of the building's foundation. Without a solid base, the building will not support the remainder of the structure; it will sink, throwing other things out of alignment as you build upward. Houses built without foundations or with shaky foundations will eventually crumble and fall down. So it is with schools.

In the absence of a firm foundation, changes made, ideas implemented, and strategies used are likely to be temporary: They'll have only short-term or minimal impacts on the school's overall culture. Part I of this book lays the foundation needed for a middle school that promotes *belonging* and *becoming*—a school that embraces the essential attributes of being "responsive, challenging, empowering, equitable, and engaging," as articulated in *The Successful Middle School: This We Believe*, the Association for Middle Level Education's landmark position paper on best practice in the middle grades.[1] This includes the following elements for a lasting base. Each of them is critical, but none stands alone; they are interdependent and work well only when implemented together.

1. A common understanding of what *belonging* and *becoming* mean for your school.
2. School procedures and practices solidly based on the developmental characteristics, needs, and experiences of young adolescents—as a group and as individuals.
3. An organizational (school) structure that promotes respectful, inclusive relationships and that provides opportunities and support for students' personal health and development as well as academic growth and accomplishments.

Putting it into practice: At the end of each chapter in this book, you'll find a section that offers concrete strategies for engaging with the ideas presented in that chapter. Use these strategies to spark discussions, gather feedback, evaluate current practices, expand your skills with a process, set goals, and decide on action steps. Adapt the ideas as needed for individual self-reflection or for working in pairs with a colleague, as a team or other small group, or as an entire staff.

While important life lessons are learned from rules like *turn in your work on time, listen when the teacher is talking, always come to class prepared, and don't run in the halls,* middle school teaches even deeper, more personal lessons. We've come to learn when to hold our tongues and when to speak out, how to treat our friends and those we're not so fond of so that we can make it through the day, and how to show the people who we care about that we truly appreciate their friendship. We've learned what does and does not make somebody smile, the best things to say when confronted by a bully—if we need say anything at all—and that in the end, the easiest person to be is oneself. Without every up and every down that we have had at this school, surely none of us would be the people we have become.

—Calvin, Paty, Alexia, and America, Grade 8

Chapter 1

Build a Common Understanding of Belonging and Becoming

Belong | *verb* | *be·long* | *bi-ˈlȯŋ, bē-ˈlȯŋ* |: *to be a part of; to be connected with*
Become | *verb* | *be·come* | *bi-ˈkəm, bē-ˈkəm* |: *to come or grow to be, develop into*

Early adolescence has often been referred to as the "wonder years"—an appropriate label, because the developments during these years give students themselves (and the adults who live and work with them) plenty to **wonder** about! In this time, these youngsters experience some of the most profound physical, cognitive, social, emotional, and psychological changes in their lives—the most growth since birth to age three. But what's significantly different from previous growth spurts is that, at this stage, they are now able to recognize the changes in themselves.

And with that recognition come such concerns, fears, and questions as: "Am I normal?" "Why is my best friend more physically developed than I am?" "Why am I happy one moment and sad the next?" "Do I fit in?" "How do I fit in?" "Am I really accepted by my friends?" "Why do adults keep asking me what I want to be when I grow up when I don't have a clue?" "Why can't I understand what the math teacher is trying to explain?" "Why does my best friend from elementary school no longer talk to me?" "How can I be more independent yet still stay connected to important adults in my life?" "I'm too fat, too skinny, too tall, too short, too different. . ." And the list goes on and on and on.

Far too often, we adults get caught up in the busyness of schooling—covering the curriculum, collecting homework, filling out paperwork, meeting state standards, administering state tests, etc. In doing so, we often forget to take time to listen to and address **real** student concerns. If we do stop to examine their worries, we find that at the heart of the apprehensions is a compelling need to *belong*, to be accepted, and to discover who they are and what they are capable of doing and *becoming*. As middle grades educators, we simply are not doing our jobs if we fail to help our students address these needs in safe, positive environments. We have been entrusted with the care, nurturing, and education of young adolescents. To honor that pledge, we must work to provide a climate where every student can feel a secure sense of *belonging*. In addition, we must offer many tools and supports to help them discover (and move toward) the individuals they are capable of *becoming*. To begin to accomplish these goals, we must agree on a shared understanding of what is meant, in our own schools, by *belonging* and *becoming.*

BELONGING

All human beings want to *belong*; this is a basic human need. We each have a deep-seated need to feel connected to others and to be a valued and accepted member of a group—whether it be family, friends, a community, a class, or a school. Young adolescents are at a time in their lives when this need is particularly strong. They desperately want to *belong* and figure out how they can fit in, for better or worse.

In her seminal study of students' sense of *school belonging*, Carol Goodenow defined *school belonging* as students' sense of "psychological membership in the school or classroom, that is, the extent to which students feel personally accepted, respected, included, and supported by others in the school social environment."[1] Roy Baumeister and Mark Leary, pioneers in *belonging* research, noted *belonging* as an innate motivation—a universal need to form and maintain long-lasting, positive, and significant interpersonal relationships.[2] Heather Libbey, author and psychologist, has studied students' relationships to their schools for three decades.

She describes ***school belonging*** as a situation in which students "feel close to, a part of, and happy at school; feel that teachers care about the students and treat them fairly; get along with teachers and other students, and feel safe at school."[3]

Others, including Kelly-Ann Allen, researcher and author of *The Psychology of Belonging* and many other books and articles focused on adolescent or adult *belonging* and *school belonging*, have broadened the understanding of *belonging* to encompass the need to be a valued part of a place or experience—such as a school, family, workplace, community, culture, environment, land, or the world.[4] Paul Kuttner, who explores broad aspects of *belonging*, some of which have been underemphasized in views of *school belonging*, argues that because children spend so many hours of their lives in school, *belonging* in the school setting is a **human right** and thus a core responsibility of educators.[5]

Students who *belong* at school:

- Feel a sense of identification with a group.
- Feel safe at school—physically, psychologically, socially, and academically.
- Believe that they have a voice in school on things that matter.
- Feel respected.
- Believe in their own indispensability to the group.
- Feel the freedom and safety to be themselves.
- Trust their teachers and their peers.
- Believe that they have as much value as anyone else.
- Are confident that others see them as valuable.
- Feel securely connected with others in their school and classes.
- Feel wanted and needed.
- Feel like individuals, not stereotypes.
- Perceive and trust that the *belongingness* they feel is likely to continue.

Students who experience school as a place where they *belong* might say:

- *There is mutual respect here.*
- *Everybody matters.*
- *This school is committed to every student.*

- *I feel solidarity with my class (team, school).*
- *People are not left out.*
- *I feel trust, and I feel trusted.*
- *I have something to contribute.*
- *I do not feel threatened.*
- *We don't put each other down here.*
- *Students here are connected.*
- *I feel comfortable interacting in my classroom.*
- *We help each other belong.*
- *There are no kids here who are excluded.*
- *We have each other's backs.*

Why Does *Belonging* Matter?

A wide body of research supports a multiplicity of positive benefits that accompany students' feelings of connection to their school as well as the adults and peers in it. In several meta-analyses of research on school *belonging* and school connection (including a focus on middle school and high school settings), it has been found that *belonging* is **positively associated** with psychological, social, and academic functioning in school across a range of variables.[6]

It has been found that *belonging* is *positively associated* with psychological, social, and academic functioning in school across a range of variables.

These **benefits** of *belonging* include **positive** indicators of self-esteem, self-belief, optimism, social competence, identity development, trust of others, building relationships, emotional stability, attachment to peers, cognitive performance, academic work, attitudes toward learning, expectancy of success, intrinsic motivation, participation, effort, positive interactions with others, classroom engagement, autonomy, physical health, academic self-efficacy, and general life and school satisfaction. In addition, students with a strong sense of *belonging* take greater advantage of learning opportunities and do better in school. Compared to students who have little sense of *belonging*, they are more fully and enthusiastically engaged in learning, more likely to see classes as interesting and useful, more likely to persevere, more open to feedback, more resilient to trauma, and more able to respond in healthy ways to situations of adversity. They exhibit less disruptive behavior, fewer negative emotions in class, less stress, fewer behavior problems, and lower absenteeism.

Many students do **not** enjoy a sense of *belonging* at school. In her 2022 article, *The Science of School Belonging,* researcher Kelly-Ann Allen reports that "Although belonging is a fundamental human need, one in three students worldwide do not experience a feeling of *belonging* to their school. As a result, a student's school experience is impacted."[7] The failure to feel a sense of *belonging* is **negatively** associated with emotional distress, loneliness, increased anxiety, boredom, and depression as well as with frustration and sadness in situations of academic engagement. Disconnected students can feel out of place or rejected. They experience increased self-consciousness, social isolation, deteriorating motivation, anxiety, and depression. They are more likely to exhibit withdrawal or commit acts of vandalism, violence, harassment, aggression, and other disruptive behaviors at school than students who feel they *belong*.[8]

Sadly, a common thread among much of the violence that has occurred in schools is that the perpetrators were isolated—not included in social groups—and often felt harassed or bullied. When we wrote the first edition of this book, the negative impacts of harassment and exclusion were already noticeable. However, during and since the global pandemic, when the majority of students experienced some form of remote education, quarantines, isolation, and increased connection to smart phones and social media—along with increased internet exposure to disturbing national and worldwide events—student mental health has been clearly impacted, and school leaders report an even greater prevalence of these anti-social behaviors in today's schools.[9]

In addition to missing the benefits of *belonging* described in the lists and paragraphs above, students who **don't** feel they *belong* are at risk for a variety of academic, social, or behavioral problems. When examining the connection between school relatedness and academic engagement, researchers Carrie Furrer and Ellen Skinner explained that "children who feel unimportant or rejected by key partners are more likely to become frustrated, bored, or alienated from learning activities, which in turn interferes with their academic progress; poor performance coupled with disaffection erodes social support, leading children to feel further estranged."[10] These findings give us more reasons why *belonging* matters.

Not all students are solidly on one or the other end of the *belonging* spectrum. There are some who might say they are confident that they *belong*—but even for these students, that confidence can fluctuate depending on the time of day! There are others who are seriously disengaged, feeling like complete outsiders. But there are many more (perhaps the majority) who are in the middle and fit the following description: "When students are uncertain about whether they *belong*, they are vigilant for cues in the environment that signal whether or not they *belong*, fit in, or are welcome there. This hypervigilance and extra stress uses up cognitive resources that are essential for learning, diminishing their performance and discouraging them from building valuable relationships."[11]

About two decades ago, the Johnson Foundation funded a conference at the Wingspread Conference Center in Wisconsin, sponsored by the U.S. Centers for Disease Control and Prevention's Division of Adolescent and School Health. A group of key researchers and representatives from the education and health sectors focused on the state of school connectedness and its effects on health and education outcomes for students. After a detailed review of research and in-depth discussions, the group issued the *Wingspread Declaration on School Connections.* This set of insights and strategies, they stated, "should form the basis for creating school and classroom environments where all students, independent of academic capacity, are engaged and feel a part of the educational endeavor."[12]

The *Wingspread Declaration* and other research on *belonging* showed that schools need greater awareness of the relationship between *belonging* and academic success, psychological health, and physical health. This declaration impacted awareness and contributed significantly to the increased emphasis on *belonging.* Along with other burgeoning *belonging* research, it fueled practices and initiatives that got schools **actively working** to develop and support students' connections at school.

But the work on *belonging* is far from finished: Current research continues to affirm that a sense of *belonging* has long-term associations with individual well-being and that the "positive impact of school belonging can last decades, impacting future mental health and even employment."[13] Building and maintaining a sense of *belonging* is a continuous process, and even after a few decades of strong awareness of its importance, many students struggle daily to *belong*. So this is ongoing work for our schools. Every day of every year, our students deserve the security of authentic *belonging*—the assurance that they are valued and genuinely have a place in the school community, not for what they can do but just for who they are.

BECOMING

Just think of all the things we want our middle grades students to be and ***become***—all the qualities we hope they'll develop; the academic content, skills, and processes we think they need to master; the personal and interpersonal behaviors we believe are healthy for them to acquire; and the understandings we're convinced they need to internalize! *Becoming* is a complex concept—a lifelong process with oh-so-many facets and meanings.

A major part of *becoming* is navigating the journey of growing up, of maturing, of *becoming* an older teenager and an adult. But that doesn't happen overnight or in one fell swoop; it's a process with many facets, variations, and bumps along the way. Most importantly, it is unique to every individual. When asked what it means to grow up, many middle grades students describe it as living on their own, going away to college, starting their first real job, finding a career, and being financially independent. But *becoming* is not all about what happens for students in their futures. They are *becoming* every day: One way or another, they are developing, learning, growing, gaining autonomy, taking more charge of their own lives, and changing. We must tune into (and appreciate) this reality—that their *becoming* is in the present. And we must help them **right now** to develop such critical components of maturity as making good decisions, taking responsibility for their actions and their commitments, and accepting the consequences of their choices and actions—understanding that what they say and do can affect others and can shape their own futures.

Of course, part of *becoming* for our students is learning academic skills, honing various processes for continued learning, and building a necessary base of knowledge. Yes, we know that students need to be critical thinkers and must learn to find, process, evaluate, and use information. We want them to take on challenges and strive for mastery. We want them to *become* active listeners, competent writers, proficient readers, and capable mathematicians. We want them to be articulate and able to express themselves clearly and to engage productively in discussions. We want them to be able to reflect on actions and ideas—to think about and process their own thoughts and behaviors. And we certainly want them to be able to make reasoned evaluations about the messages from peers, pop culture, social media, and numerous other internet sources that constantly bombard them—telling them what to think, who to be, and how to act—and to develop skills to filter out and cope with what is untrue, unhealthy, irrelevant, harmful, or inappropriate.

However, it is not only the task of middle schools to promote academic skills and future success. *Becoming* encompasses and transcends the academic realm. It is also a school's mission to provide students with opportunities to explore, to make choices, to take risks, to grow in autonomy, to learn to interact with others, to take good care of themselves physically and emotionally, to be curious and inventive, to try new endeavors, to be able to recover from failure, to be exposed to the world beyond their community, to dream big, to set goals, and to discover what their futures may hold.

If we are to prepare our students to participate productively in a democratic society (and in all the groups of which they are a part within their society), we must think far beyond content knowledge. We wish for our students to **be** and *become* young adolescents, older adolescents, and adults who are kind, caring, compassionate, and inclusive—with hopeful, optimistic attitudes toward learning and life. We wish to see them *become* seasoned problem solvers and independent, lifelong learners.

We want our students to understand how to develop and maintain positive relationships, cope with peer pressure, demonstrate tolerance and acceptance of others, and develop the people skills needed to learn, work, and interact with others. They need to recognize the developmental changes that are happening within them and appreciate how these changes can impact their emotions and actions. They must learn to handle anger, cope with disappointment, channel their emotions in positive ways, and both understand and deal with all the stress that the roller-coaster ride of young adolescence can bring. We want them to develop resilience and perseverance. Students must also be helped to realize that *becoming* is not just a destination but rather a life-long process that continues throughout adulthood. Yes, we want so much for our students! And, yes, it is an overwhelming task.

One growing trend in education today is supporting schools with the processes and strategies for helping students ***become*** personally and academically. Many districts across the country are developing "learner centered model(s) based on a shared vision of learner attributes that students should have when they graduate."[14] These models, commonly referred to as Graduate Profiles or Learner Profiles, are being developed (jointly, by representative groups of stakeholders in schools or districts) to set guides for the agreed-upon competencies students should have when they graduate—in other words, what they want students to *become*. The profiles include such components as specific **cognitive skills** (e.g., critical thinking, problem solving, creativity, digital literacy and discernment, metacognition); **personal qualities and behaviors** (e.g., self-direction, personal power, self-awareness and self-control, confidence, self-advocacy, self-care, resilience, responsibility, autonomy, academic tenacity, flexibility, initiative, ethical values); and **interpersonal-social skills** (e.g., communication, kindness, tolerance, acceptance, honesty, empathy, collaboration).

But middle schools cannot afford to wait for students to develop these competencies by the time they graduate high school; accordingly, many are beginning to develop their own Middle School Learner (or Graduation) Profiles. To help with this process, middle schools should consider articulating competencies that their students should possess by the time they are ready to move on to high school. For example, my (Laurie's) school district is a K–8 school district; we developed a learner profile to help identify the primary skills and competencies students need for high school and post-secondary success. We want to make sure students are equipped to be successful *in* high school, not just *after* high school.

Research indicates that the middle grades play a critical part in graduating students from high school and preparing them for college, careers, and future life. These are "make it or break it" years for keeping students engaged in school, increasing their chances of success in high school, and decreasing their likelihood of dropping out. Robert Balfanz, professor at Johns Hopkins University School of Education and director of the Everyone Graduates Center, along with other researchers, asserts that early warning signals can be identified as early as sixth grade. Any of the following—and in particular, a combination of two or more—greatly reduce the likelihood of academic success beyond the beginnings of middle school: attendance rates of less than 85%, repeated behavior problems, or a failing grade in an English language arts or mathematics course.[15]

Middle level students often come to us with hopes and dreams for what their futures hold. Some of their dreams are realistic, whereas others could be called "fairy-tale" thinking (i.e., if you want it and wait long enough, then magically, it will come true, all will be well, and you will live happily ever after).

When I (Patti) taught sixth grade, I kicked off a unit of study on lifecycles with an activity where students created their own life timelines. They were to choose important events that had already happened in their lives and then predict events in their future. Students illustrated their timelines on long strips of paper and displayed them on the classroom walls. I remember a conversation with a student who was examining the predicted lives of his classmates. I had noticed a common thread among most of the boys' lifelines (his included): They were going to be NBA or NFL stars. So I asked him whether he thought that was a reasonable prediction, and I'll never forget his response: "Mrs. Kinney, we know it's not likely to happen, but just let us have our dreams!"

It's a fine line that educators must walk. We don't want to belittle or impede our students' dreams, but we also need to help them discover just what they will need to do to realistically accomplish their dreams, to *become* what they dream of *becoming*. Fortunately, unrealistic dreams and ambitions usually change with maturity, so we must help our students develop their skills and see the options and possibilities beyond those potentially unrealistic dreams. We owe it to our students to do the best we can to prepare them for adulthood, regardless of whether that sixth-grade dream comes true.

Why Does *Becoming* Matter?

The list of what we hope (and work) for our students to *become* is long. You could add many skills, qualities, and behaviors beyond those mentioned here. It is important to realize that the *becoming* process is not something we **do** for our students. Certainly, families, schools, and others in society can nurture aspects of *becoming*, and many factors in students' lives (such as peers and pop culture) contribute to the process for better or worse. But inevitably, willingness to learn, effort, engagement, integration, self-determination, and healthy choices flow from the individuals themselves.

It may seem strange to even ask the question, "Why does *becoming* matter?" The answers seem so obvious. *Becoming,* after all, is what human life is about—and it is the focus of all schooling (and parenting)! One look at the aspects of *becoming* that we've already described gives an answer—just notice how important all those qualities are! We can encapsulate what is at the heart of *becoming* with the term *self-determination*: the ability to make choices and decisions and to set and achieve goals based on one's own intrinsic motivation and volition (and not dependent upon outside influence). All the facets of *becoming* we've described, and the many more that we did not, need the student to be a full participant. We educators must nurture that intrinsic motivation and volition to give each of our students the best chance at *becoming*.

> ***Becoming,* after all, is what human life is about—and it is the focus of all schooling (and parenting)!**

According to self-determination theory, there are three innate psychological needs: autonomy, competence, and relatedness. (Note that "relatedness" (aka *belonging*) is an integral part of this triad of basic needs!) When these needs are met, the individual moves toward self-motivation, self-regulation, constructive social development, and overall personal well-being. Through extensive research into conditions that foster or impede self-determination, authors Richard Ryan and Edward Deci found that self-determination flourished in social contexts (such as school) that supported and encouraged those three needs.[16] On the other hand, conditions that included "excessive control, nonoptimal challenges, and lack of connectedness," undermined the growth and expression of self-determination.[17]

Ryan and Deci recognized the power of the social contexts in which growing humans are embedded. They emphasized that the natural tendencies toward positive cognitive development, personal development, and well-being do not develop automatically; they need ongoing nurturing in social settings. The authors of the self-determination theory adamantly entreat all practitioners who work with growing human beings to integrate practices that address those three psychological needs—autonomy, competence, and relatedness—in order to facilitate the development of these natural tendencies.

Consider social contexts. Think about how much of students' lives are spent at school! As educators, then, we must become very knowledgeable about the conditions and practices that enhance (rather than undermine) *becoming* in positive ways. As our middle level colleague Andrew Maxey, author of *Elephant in the Classroom: Tracing the Complexity of Teaching by Exploring 13 Competencies and Practices*, regularly reminds us: When we ignore these psychological needs in favor of academic goals, we virtually ensure that neither will be achieved.

IMPLEMENTING THE BELONGING-BECOMING PARTNERSHIP

Becoming is closely entwined with *belonging*. Young adolescents need a place to *belong* so that they are free to *become*—to develop skills, knowledge, and character, determine strengths, discern potential, and discover passions. Paired together, *belonging* and *becoming* can be described as a powerful interdependent relationship. When students feel that they *belong* to a school community, their chances for deeper personal and academic growth (*becoming*) improve; when students are more academically and personally successful (aspects of *becoming*), their senses of *belonging* increase.

Next to families, schools are the settings with the greatest potential to help children in these two foundational processes. When we, the authors, look at this powerful combination of needs in the lives of our students (the needs to *belong* and *become*), we:

1. Are adamant that schools be aware of them and the dynamic interaction between them.
2. Feel the urgency of schools to make addressing these needs a priority.
3. Are invigorated by the possibilities of what can happen for middle level students when we take deliberate actions to address them together.
4. Are cognizant of the reality that *belonging* and *becoming* are also foundational for the adults in the school community—because adults are the models for developing and sustaining these processes. Also, and just as importantly—the adults' own growth and maintenance of **both** processes are critical to a high-quality education for students and to a healthy middle school culture.

What students do (and how they feel about themselves and their lives) in middle school matters. The habits that young adolescents develop socially, emotionally, and academically equip or hinder them throughout their future education. During these years, they form their beliefs about themselves, set the course of their life values, and build the foundations of their character. The National Academies of Sciences' pivotal 2019 report, *The Promise of Adolescence*, describes early adolescence, due to the plasticity of the teenage brain, as "a window of opportunity"—a chance to set students on a solid path for their remainder of their education.[18]

Paired together, *belonging* and *becoming* can be described as a powerful interdependent relationship.

In her landmark book, *Our Last Best Shot: Guiding Our Children Through Early Adolescence*, Laura Sessions Stepp (mother and Pulitzer Prize-winning journalist specializing in covering teenagers) argues that the middle-level school years offer us what is truly "our last best shot" at making a difference in the future success of students.[19] Middle level educators will likely agree with Stepp, recognizing that the middle school years are a critical period for students to establish patterns, skills, and self-beliefs that enable present and future academic and post-high school success and for adults to have a strong influence on their direction. This is because most of them are still young and impressionable enough to allow us to help them travel through the maze of early adolescence and find the path that leads to healthy, responsible present and future lives.[20]

Effective middle level educators understand this urgency, recognizing that young adolescents need an environment focused on their unique requirements. They also recognize that these students deserve to be with adults who understand them, appreciate them, and who will work to meet their needs both in and out of the classroom.

Creating a place where students can *belong* and *become* is a challenging proposition with no easy answers or silver-bullet strategies. Middle level students are often more interested in *belonging* to a friendship group than to their school. They tend to be more concerned about impressing their friends than their teachers. They may be more worried about wearing the right brand of clothing than turning in their homework. They may be more focused on *becoming* professional athletes, famous pop singers, or social media influencers than *becoming* accomplished students.

The Successful Middle School: This We Believe identifies 18 characteristics of a successful middle school, the second characteristic being that "The school environment is welcoming, inclusive, and affirming for all."[21] For this to grow into a reality, plans and actions to help young adolescents *belong* and *become* must be infused into all of the structures, policies, practices, programs, and relationships in a school and in its classrooms.

We know that schools struggle with budget issues, staffing cuts, and over-emphasis by lawmakers and the public on state test scores. As well, we know that schools sometimes struggle with a general misunderstanding from outsiders of middle level education. Additionally, schools are still feeling the impact of the pandemic in both the academic and mental health arenas. Academically, they are still working hard to make up for lost time and remedy lagging growth in math and reading. Perhaps even more disconcerting is the increase in students reporting that they feel more anxious, depressed, fatigued, or distressed than before the pandemic.

Those issues and others may be reasons why the task seems insurmountable at times—but they can't be used as excuses for not trying. And, thankfully, increases and successes in nurturing *belonging* and *becoming* contribute significantly to addressing the academic losses and mental health difficulties of recent years. Also thankfully, many effective ideas for increasing *belonging* and *becoming* can be incorporated into school and classroom practices without additional costs or staffing. We urge you to make your lists of components, qualities, and skills related to *belonging* and *becoming* (as recommended at the end of this chapter) and keep them visible at all times.

In their book *The Life-giving Home*, authors Sally and Sarah Clarkson suggested ways to create a home that is foundational to life. We think their introductory words apply equally to creating a life-giving school:

> All people need a place where their roots can grow deep and they always feel like they belong and have a loving refuge. And all people need a place that gives wings to their dreams, nurturing possibilities of who they might become.[22]

PUTTING IT INTO PRACTICE

As an individual, team, small group, or entire staff, use these activities to spark discussions, reflect on your current practices or situations, listen to others, or set goals.

1. Use a 1, 2, 4, 8 process to define what *belonging* and *becoming* mean at your school. Ask each person to write a personal definition of *belonging*; next, pair up with a colleague to combine definitions into one agreeable to both; then combine pairs into groups of four and repeat; and once more have groups of four combine to form groups of eight. Have each group share its definition and look for commonalities among the groups. Repeat the process using the word *becoming*. Even if you and other staff members in your school or district are already committed to enhancing *belonging* and *becoming*, it will be a valuable exercise to find commonality in your understanding of the concepts. In addition, this will set the stage for sharing of successful practices, broadening your efforts, and brainstorming how school staff can coordinate efforts in the best interest of students.

2. Divide the staff into six groups and set up six stations around the room for a gallery walk. Stations 1–3 each should have butcher or sticky-back paper with one of the following questions on it. (For stations 4–6, use the same questions—and the same paper—with *becoming* substituted for *belonging*.)

   If students felt a strong sense of *belonging* at this school, what might we hear them say?

   If students felt a strong sense of *belonging* at this school, what would teachers be saying about student performance and behavior?

   If students felt a strong sense of *belonging* at this school, what outcomes would we notice?

   Place one group in front of each station and ask them to write down what they see as answers to the qustions. After a set amount of time, rotate groups. The next group reads what has been written, stars important ideas, puts a question mark by something that needs more clarification, and adds its own ideas to the list. Rotate through until each group arrives back at its first station. Have them read through the answers and choose a few items to share with the entire group. Lists from each station can be saved and used later for further discussion.

3. Repeat the gallery walk activity described in #2 above, replacing those questions with the following questions. Remember to use the idea of *belonging* for the first three stations and *becoming* for the last three stations.

    If students felt they did **not** *belong* in this school, what might we hear them say?

    If students felt they did **not** *belong* in this school, what things have we seen, heard, done, or said that might be impeding that from happening?

    If students felt they did **not** *belong* at this school, what outcomes would we notice?

4. Hold focus groups with students to discover their thoughts and experiences on *belonging* and *becoming.* Ask them: "What does it mean *to belong*? *To become*?" "What's happening at school that makes you feel as if you *belong*? That you can *become*?" "What improvements are needed at this school to help students *belong* or *become*?" As a part of such exploration, you might use student-ready surveys such as those shown in Appendices F-1 and F-2 on pages 280-283. Be sure that the groups are heterogeneously mixed across grade levels, genders, abilities, social groups, ethnicities, etc.

5. Use the "Brainstorming Guide: What You Already Do to Help Students Belong" from our ASCD book *We Belong: 50 Strategies to Create Community and Revolutionize Classroom Management* and included in this text as Appendix G. Identifying what you already do can help you continue those practices and envision new ones that will enhance *belonging.*

Middle school is a point in time where adults tend to perceive teenagers differently than how we actually are. Adults do not always understand us or our actions, but I think that in order for them to understand us we have to teach them.

— Marley, Grade 8

99.9%

I like me.
I rate myself a nine-point-nine.
(It isn't a perfect score)
I'm doing quite fine.

I have a schedule
It's set in stone.
Get up at eight,
work myself to the bone.
I check my grade 7 out of 7 days.
If I have a hundred, I laud myself with praise.

My grades have dropped four times in the past six hours.
I turn off my phone
And set it on the table.
I can't look at it anymore. I am unable.

One day, we learned about figurative language.
I like hyperbole.
My workload is killing me.
I've said this a million times.
I like me.
I rate myself a 9.9
It isn't a perfect score.
(I'm doing quite fine.)

— Dhwani, Grade 7

Chapter 2

Understand Young Adolescents and Their World

At no other time in the life cycle are the chances of finding one's self and losing one's self so closely aligned.

— Erik Erickson

When educators set out to create settings where *belonging* and *becoming* can flourish for middle level students, we must first understand just who the students are and where they are in the course of both processes. It has long been recognized that young adolescence is a developmental stage distinct from both childhood and full adolescence. In *The Successful Middle School: This We Believe*, young adolescence is identified as the period from "ages 10 through 15."[1] It is also critical to recognize that **each young adolescent has a unique set of characteristics**—and it's no secret that one of the prime markers of this stage is the wide variation among these individuals in the timing and manifestation of those characteristics! This means that we must know our students **both** as a developmental group and as individuals. The stronger an educator's understanding of the physical, cognitive, social-emotional, and psychological development of students, the better are the chances of helping them grow academically and personally—in all the aspects related to *belonging* and *becoming*.

In our memories, it was during those years between elementary and high school that we most struggled to *belong* and to discover who we were and what we might *become*. I (Laurie) watched the same process when my daughter was in middle school and saw that many of her peers (who were 13 but physically appeared to range from 10 to 16—or even older) struggled to "fit in" and to get clear senses of their abilities, talents, and goals. And in our many years, jointly, as middle school educators and leaders, we have lived amid thousands of young adolescents with these same struggles and needs to *belong* and *become* as they've navigated their worlds.

EMBRACING YOUNG ADOLESCENT DEVELOPMENT

Effective middle level teachers have learned how to appreciate and make the most of their students' developmental characteristics rather than fight against them. For example, they understand well that young adolescents have strong needs to socialize. They know that young brains learn best in concert with other brains! So, they don't expect students to sit quietly for long periods of time without interaction. They know that one of the most effective ways to increase students' senses of *belonging* is to get them to work together. They want students to cooperate and communicate; they know how many academic, social, and emotional needs this strengthens. Therefore, they build learning activities around this need to socialize. (Teachers also realize that thwarting this need is guaranteed to lead to classroom management issues!)

Teachers need to make plans and choices about what can foster *belonging*. But we can't do this unless we know the specifics of behaviors, attitudes, and situations in which our students do and do not experience *belonging*. Only when we understand just where they are in the process of those many aspects of *becoming* (academically, cognitively, socially, emotionally, and psychologically) can we catch clues as to what procedures to use, what skills to teach, and what opportunities to offer. As we deepen our awareness of various aspects of their development, we get better and better at seeing specific actions we can take in our classrooms to help our students *belong* and *become* in many ways. It is imperative that all educators who work with young adolescents have keen knowledge and understanding of their developmental characteristics and needs (as a group and as individuals) as well as of the shape and content of the world they navigate.

Effective middle level teachers have learned how to appreciate and make the most of their students' developmental characteristics rather than fight against them.

The need to socialize is just one of many characteristics to incorporate into our learning plans. What follows on the next two pages are some examples of ways that the understanding of students' development can inform and direct choices for our schools and classrooms. For a broader discussion and more ideas about incorporating understanding of young adolescent development into our plans for students' school life and learning, consult the section on "Young Adolescent Development and Implications for Educators" in *The Successful Middle School: This We Believe.*[2]

Physical Development

Because young adolescents . . .

- Are experiencing rapid, irregular physical growth;
- Are undergoing bodily changes that may cause poor motor coordination;
- Are developing sexually;
- Experience mood swings, abrupt transitions from alertness and high energy to fatigue and lethargy;
- Need plenty of healthy food choices, rest, and sleep (and tend not to get enough); and
- Need frequent and somewhat continuous movement,

Schools must . . .

- Vary the pace of lessons and incorporate movement;
- Assure individuals they are not the "only one" experiencing difficulties;
- Develop a comprehensive health and physical education program relevant to students' specific needs and capabilities;
- Plan opportunities for all students to succeed at physical accomplishments;
- Encourage adequate sleep, nutrition, and hydration; and
- Help students understand their personal talents, skills, proficiencies, and inadequacies.

Cognitive Development

Because young adolescents . . .

- Have a wide range of intellectual abilities;
- Are curious, especially about the things that interest them;
- Are more willing to learn material they consider useful and relevant;
- Are increasing in their ability to think abstractly and metacognitively; and
- Tend to be egocentric and can have difficulty seeing another's viewpoint,

Schools must . . .

- Build lessons from concrete to abstract;
- Ask questions that require higher levels of thinking: "What if . . . ?" "How do you know . . . ?" "What led you to that conclusion?" "Can you describe your thinking about this?" "How is this valuable

to you?" "How does this make a difference?";

- Create an environment where taking cognitive risks is encouraged, supported, and safe;
- Involve them actively in the learning—have them show AND tell AND do;
- Give them time to **think**—to process, to let ideas "gel," to explore different ideas; and
- Be prepared for off-the-wall responses.

Social Development

Because young adolescents . . .

- Are concerned with acceptance and seek approval from peers;
- Do not flourish in uncompromising settings;
- Can be argumentative;
- Experience flashes of social consciousness;
- Are self-conscious in social settings;
- Often reject adult standards or viewpoints on social issues;
- Follow social trends and fads;
- Are highly influenced by social media and pop culture;
- Can demonstrate extremes of social shyness or extroversion; and
- Spend a great deal of time on smart phones connected to friends and to social media and other internet sites,

Schools must . . .

- Design appropriate school-based social activities;
- Promote and model acceptance by adults and peers;
- Help students understand how they fit into the complex roles society expects of them;
- Allow students to work in groups and teach one another;
- Provide opportunities for students to work and interact with others from different social, economic, and academic groups and backgrounds;
- Plan situations in which they can identify and evaluate messages and influences from social media and pop culture;
- Help students build skills to manage and cope with

the pressures and reality of the bombardment of digital information and messages;

- Include community involvement and service learning in the curriculum;
- Understand and respect students' need for social self-definition; and
- Help students understand how to set limits for themselves and to recognize the possible dangers of online interactions.

Emotional Development

Because young adolescents . . .

- Experience chemical and hormonal changes and imbalances;
- Often overreact to seemingly minor issues;
- May look like adults but emotionally resemble children;
- Are increasingly aware of themselves, individually and in comparison to others;
- Tend to be unrealistically self-critical;
- Are easily offended;
- Have a strong need for privacy;
- Have emerging senses of humor; and
- Are basically hopeful,

Schools must . . .

- Understand and accept the typical behaviors of the age group. (Is the person being "appropriately" inappropriate or defiant?);
- Be honest, available role models;
- Be attentive listeners;
- Avoid sarcasm (which is not always seen as humor);
- Help students feel skilled and competent;
- Use praise and reinforcement in appropriate ways; and
- Create an environment of acceptance, both with peers and adults.

UNDERSTANDING EXECUTIVE FUNCTION

Due to the rapid growth and multiple changes they are experiencing, middle level students are "in process" in just about every facet of their development—and one cognitive aspect is still very much "under construction." How often do you notice students:

- Finding it difficult to transition between lessons, classes, or tasks?
- Getting easily distracted from their own work by anything happening around them?
- Not knowing where to begin to tackle three homework assignments?
- Making unrealistic plans?
- Having a hard time breaking a project down into manageable pieces?
- Struggling to finish what they start?
- Rarely resisting the impulse to trip someone walking by?
- Forgetting something they learned and practiced yesterday?
- Drawing a blank when asked to summarize what they just did?
- Seeming to not have learned anything from a repeated mistake?
- Leaving all homework tasks to do until the last minute?
- Blurting out inappropriate comments without thinking?
- Sitting down to do a project without having thought to gather supplies?

Each of these is an indication of the incomplete development of the prefrontal cortex portion of the brain (which normally does not finish developing until early adulthood). This is the part of the brain that controls what is known as *executive function*—the set of complex mental control mechanisms and skills that enable us to:

- Make and follow through on plans.
- Filter distractions.
- Juggle multiple tasks.

- Move from one cognitive focus to another.
- Set and work toward goals.
- Curb impulses.
- Maintain attention.
- Solve problems.
- Consider the consequences before making decisions.
- Regulate behavior.

In addition, research supported by the National Institutes of Health has found that executive functioning helps humans to develop resilience and "plays a role in protecting against risk factors that worsen symptoms of depression and anxiety during stressful, uncertain times," particularly for children and adolescents.[3]

We use (and need) executive function to manage ourselves so that we can successfully navigate through life. According to the Center on the Developing Child at Harvard University:

> In the brain, the ability to hold onto and work with information, focus thinking, filter distractions, and switch gears is like an airport having a highly effective air traffic control system to manage arrival and departures of dozens of planes on multiple runways. Scientists refer to these capacities as executive function and self-regulation—a set of skills that relies on three types of brain function: working memory, mental flexibility, and self-control. Children aren't born with these skills—they are born with the potential to develop them. The full range of abilities continues to grow and mature through the teen years and into early adulthood[4]

Understanding executive function allows us to realize that, regardless of what they look like physically, we are working with students whose brains aren't yet fully developed, who are not fully capable of thinking and acting the way (well-adjusted) adults might think and act, and who aren't always (thank goodness) *deliberately* trying to drive us crazy. In fact, we were once just like them. (And because executive function develops at different paces, needs a certain quality of experiences and interactions to emerge, and can change due to aging of the brain or outside influences, some adults are still like these young adolescents at times!) Yes, many of the habits or behaviors that seem irresponsible, intentionally annoying, or just "out to lunch" are perfectly normal for young adolescents.

Even students themselves often don't understand why they do what they do. If you ask them, "Why did you do that?" or "What were you thinking?" often they will be genuinely confused, tell you they know it was a poor decision, and say they just aren't sure why they behaved the way they did. And although we can't let them use "lack of brain development" to excuse inappropriate behaviors, students need to know that their still-developing brains may explain why it is sometimes difficult to control their actions, even when they know better.

Even students themselves often don't understand why they do what they do.

These skills are critical to every aspect of *belonging* and *becoming* that we've identified and will continue to explore in this book. "When children have had opportunities to develop executive function and self-regulation skills successfully, both individuals and society experience lifelong benefits."[5] These benefits include successful school achievement, positive behaviors, good health, and increased potential for success at work.[6]

The good news is that executive function tends to improve with time—especially if children are offered specific strategies that teach, practice, and strengthen its development. Such executive function training is particularly needed and helpful for young adolescents and high-risk teens, but it is an important component of education for all students.[7]

Executive function is enhanced by interactions and observations with adults who model the functions. It is also boosted by experiences that help guide kids toward autonomy, protect them from chaos and harmful stress, reduce access to distractions, and increase social connection and physical exercise. In addition, executive function is strengthened by engagement in activities that break tasks into small chunks; practice problem-solving, creativity, and exploration; and motivate by rewarding periods of consistent effort.[8]

As we focus on helping young adolescents *belong* and *become,* we see how important it is to help our students develop the full range of executive function capacities. Educators must move beyond understanding the importance of executive function and the fact that these are still developing for our students. We must plan and take informed, specific actions to provide experiences and relationships that teach and strengthen these skills. In upcoming chapters, you'll find recommendations for practices that focus on such strategies as those described above, and others, that develop aspects of executive function.

We recommend the following resources on executive function for your reading: Rick Wormeli's article "Looking at Executive Function" available at amle.org;[9] the book *Smart But Scattered Teens: The "Executive Skills" Program for Helping Teens Reach Their Potential* by Guare, Dawson, and Guare;[10] and the article "Executive Function" available at psychologytoday.com.[11]

EXAMINING AND HONORING INDIVIDUAL DIFFERENCES

Those who work with young adolescents are aware of the contradictions that occur within the age group, but we don't always remember to consider the differences that occur among individual students. It is often far too easy to think of them, relate to them, or teach to them as one group: "those middle schoolers."

In his essay "Understanding and Appreciating the Wonder Years," John Lounsbury (one of the founders of the middle school movement) made this observation:

> The dramatic physical changes do not occur at the same time or at the same rate. The fact that girls mature a year and a half to two years ahead of boys is widely recognized, but the tremendous variation in the rate and timing of the developmental processes of both boys and girls is not so well known. Some boys have achieved puberty before some girls have started. And what one child accomplishes in growth in 18 months may take up to three or more years in another. **As a result, a seventh-grade class is likely to include** (physically) **men, women, and children.** It is virtually impossible for young adolescents to keep their chronological age in conformity with their social age, physical age, intellectual age, and/or social/sexual age.[12]

As examples of Lounsbury's observation, let's use two students who were classmates when I (Patti) taught sixth grade:

Kevin was about 5'6" when he started sixth grade. He was a sensitive student, concerned about how he fit in with the rest of the class. He struggled quite a bit in math, primarily because he had not yet begun to make the cognitive leap from concrete to abstract. By the end of the school year, he was nearly six feet tall, broad-shouldered, and deep-voiced. But he was still sensitive, concerned about fitting in, worried about *belonging*—and still struggled with abstract mathematical concepts.

When **Will** started sixth grade, he was somewhat socially immature, and his physical appearance was like that of a fourth grader—and not much had changed by the end of the school year. But he was brilliant; he could grasp a concept that had just barely been presented and fly with it. One Friday afternoon he asked, "What can you tell me about trigonometry?"

"Well, it has something to do with triangles," I answered.

On Monday morning he reported he'd read his dad's college trigonometry book; then he proceeded to give an overview of the field and ways trigonometry is used in the world.

Even though both boys were 12 years old, they had vastly different developmental profiles, and if I wanted to help each of them (as well as all the other students in the classroom) *become* successful, I had to see each as a unique individual. It would not help either of them feel as though he *belonged* among his peers if I had simply "taught to the middle."

The Association for Middle Level Education (AMLE) has long identified responsiveness to the significant growth and changes in young adolescence as a hallmark of middle level education since the field's inception. Their landmark articulation of the middle school concept, *The Successful Middle School: This We Believe,* offers a generalized description of developmental traits of young adolescence—presented in the categories of physical, cognitive, social-emotional, and psychological development.[13] (See also Appendix A in this book, pages 263-267).

Be aware that the authors of this information on young adolescent development point out (emphatically) that educators "must exercise caution when discussing young adolescents holistically"[14]—that any general list of characteristics should not be seen as uniform attributes. They remind us that there can be great variation among individuals (and even variance within a given individual) and that characteristics may fluctuate depending on the time and situation. They also caution educators to understand that viewing young adolescents holistically with a developmental model can "constrain our understanding of young adolescents."[15] Thus, although it is helpful to understand generalized characteristics of young adolescents, it is also imperative that we be aware of the uniqueness of each of our students individually.

One way to look closely at the distinct developmental path of a particular student is to construct a profile of that individual's development in several aspects, including physical growth and cognitive growth as well as social and psychological development. Our interest in this concept was sparked by John Swaim, a colleague of ours (also a luminary of the middle school movement) who devised a matrix for his Otterbein University pre-service students and graduate students (many of whom were middle level teachers) to help gain a better understanding of individual students. His matrix was a tool for examining physical and cognitive development. He used a scale for each of these aspects—drawn from reliable, well-researched sources on growth and development—and plotted points on the matrix to represent characteristics in each aspect. For example: Physical growth ranged from pre-pubescent to adolescent (adult-like), whereas cognitive growth ranged from pre-concrete information-processing and thinking (literal, surface thinking) to abstract thinking (dealing with complex mental processes). Eventually Swaim added such other aspects as social and psychological development to the matrix.

If we were to place Kevin and Will on such a matrix for physical and cognitive development, it would be easy to see that Kevin falls on the high end of physical growth but more in the pre-concrete to concrete range cognitively. Will would be the opposite: early pubescent in physical growth—but cognitively, clearly an abstract thinker.

A tool such as this matrix can be cumbersome, but this process of examining different aspects of an individual's development is more than just an academic exercise. We have experienced firsthand the many benefits that can be gained when teachers engage in such a process. Inspired by Swaim's matrix, we have developed an adapted tool in the form of a table—a tool that gives teachers flexibility to consider various categories of development, using reliable scales or describing students with observations rather than scales. See the Individual Development Profile, (Appendix B) on pages 268-270 and below for a sample tool that can be used to create individual profiles and for more information about using the tool and scales.

Individual Development Profile (Template)

Student Name ***Date*** ***Teacher(s)***

Developmental Category	Scale Rating, Descriptors, Comments
Physical	
Cognitive	
Social	
Emotional	
Psychological	

Note: Add other categories, such as sense of belonging, executive function, academic tenacity, academic patterns, demonstration of competence, self-determination, and autonomy.

We think you'll be amazed by what you learn when you take the time to ponder and record what you know about a student. The exercise will push you to find out things you hadn't paid enough attention to! Admittedly, it would be difficult to analyze each student in such great detail, but we encourage you to try this—even if with just a few students for starters. It will take you a long way toward seeing students not as a mass but as individuals. It is valuable to repeat the review of a student's developmental characteristics later in the school year to observe changes (because, as we all know, things change fast for middle level students).

Yes, we must use the best research and information available to us to create conditions, programs, and lessons to help our students, as a group, to *belong* and *become.* But those plans must make room for (and meet the needs of) Kevin and Will and every other individual student as well. All students have their own unique set of features, gifts, needs, complications, assets, barriers, and skills in relatedness (*belonging*) and aspects of *becoming* (such as autonomy, competence, and self-determination). Our plans and strategies can fit individuals within the group **only** when educators are proficient at ascertaining where individuals are in different aspects of development.

Not only must we ascertain the profile of each student, but we must also respond to them as individuals; we must value and celebrate their uniqueness. AMLE specifies five essential attributes of an appropriate education for young adolescents; one is that the school is responsive to the "distinctive nature and identities of young adolescents as the foundation upon which all decisions about school are made."[16] (Note that the attribute says **all decisions are made on this foundation!**) Understanding the development of young adolescents allows us to be appropriately responsive to their needs.

The five attributes of successful schools and the 18 essential characteristics exhibited by successful middle schools are presented in this book in Chapter 3, Figure 3.1 on page 46. This information is also available at amle.org/smssummary.

TUNING INTO THE WORLD OF THE YOUNG ADOLESCENT

As this chapter title states, a fundamental requirement for nurturing *belonging* and *becoming* is that middle level educators thoroughly understand young adolescent development. All our decisions about curriculum, instruction, assessment, school structure, programs, mission, and goals should be based on this rock-solid foundation. Part of understanding our students' development is having an accurate view of the wider culture in which they live and the pressures, influences, and demands that they must manage in their daily lives—and that they bring with them to school every day.

Yes, we can observe, assess, and attend to our students' general and individual academic progress and personal development (*becoming*) that we see evidenced at school. Also, we can perceive signs of the state of their *belonging*. We can do our best to keep in close contact with their families and to understand the situations in which they live. But even the most caring, astute educators cannot be with each of their students every minute of their day. We cannot be present in all their interactions in the hallways, buses, courtyards, bathrooms, and off campus. We don't observe every syllable of what they hear, read, write, and post on their screens. We can no longer **be** young adolescents ourselves! Much of their lives are not available for us to see or readily know.

To understand young adolescents, we must be on a fast learning curve to find out everything we can about the world they navigate that is beyond what we see. This means putting aside assumptions and deeply exploring the complexities of young adolescents' lives, including their digital lives. It means listening to the kids themselves—hearing their challenges, fears, experiences, joys, frustrations, worries, wishes, questions, mistakes, hopes, and viewpoints. If we don't truly "get" where our students are right now—at their specific stages and within the complex world in which they live—we may stunt, rather than nourish, their chances of *belonging* and of *becoming* self-determined persons and learners.

As we shape the cultures of our middle schools and strive to give students the best environments for *belonging* and *becoming,* we can craft structures, policies, and practices that are responsive not only to developmental stages but also to their development within a fast-paced, ever-changing, challenging—and often scary—world. But these must be based on what is truly going on for the kids, and we can only learn that from the kids themselves (and good research that includes listening to young adolescents). As educators, we must scramble (if that is what it takes) to catch up and keep up with the realities of students' lives. Schools and the adults in schools can and must play an important role in helping these young people navigate their complex world.

PUTTING IT INTO PRACTICE

As an individual, team, small group, or entire staff, use these activities to spark discussions, reflect on your current practices or situations, listen to others, or set goals.

1. As a team, design some questions (or sentence starters) and a process for listening to students talk about the realities of their lives as young adolescents. Listening to students in small groups or pairs can be a way to start. You might consider such questions as:

   What do we (teachers) not know about young adolescents' lives that you think we should know (i.e., where are we clueless)?

   What are some of the best things about being 12 (or 13, 14, or 15) in today's world?

   What are some of the hardest things you face?

   What worries you about the digital world and your digital lives?

   How does social media affect you?

   Who do you feel really knows you?

   Listen to the students' answers and discussion of questions. Take notes if doing so doesn't seem to intimidate the students. Or ask the students to give a few summarizing statements at the end of the session.

   Ask students to suggest ways for adults in the school to understand the students' world a little better. Also, ask students to contribute questions and topics for discussion.

2. Divide into groups according to the decade when participants were 12 years old (or 13 or 14). Those on the margin between two decades may choose either one. Ask them to draw a picture or make a list of what it was like to be 13 in their decade. What major events happened in the world? What

was important to them? How did they dress? What music did they listen to? (And so on.) What were their joys, accomplishments, concerns, etc.? Share the pictures or lists, and then discuss how today's 13-year-olds are different from how they were at 13. Then discuss how today's 13-year-olds are the same as they were when they were 13. Consider repeating this process with students present. The commonalities may surprise you and the students, too!

3. As a team, choose four or five students whom you've found challenging to get to know or to reach. Use the Individual Development Profile (Appendix B) on pages 268-270 to describe where you see those students falling in each of the categories. Share your results with one another, and look for areas of agreement and disagreement. Discuss how you might use that information to help each of those students increase in *belonging* or in an area of *becoming*.

4. Access AMLE's "Developmental Characteristics of Young Adolescents: Research Summary" by Kathleen Brinegar and Micki Caskey at amle.org/YAD. Read the article on your own, and then, in small groups, discuss how developmentally responsive your school is to the needs of your students.

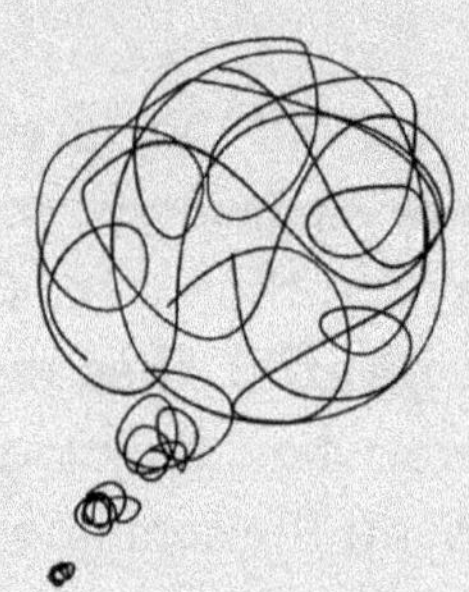

What is it like to be in middle school in 2023?
Get home from school late afternoon
Do lots of tough homework
Sports practice
Club practice
Therapy
Crap, another school shooting
Mom restricted my video games
Police brutality on the news
Will China start a war?
What is trending on YouTube?
I like her
More therapy
I don't like her anymore
Big fight in the cafeteria
Teacher calls my parents
Thought I did good on the test but I failed
Got pizza with my parents
7th grade will be even harder.

— Amari, Grade 6

Chapter 3

Organize to Promote Belonging and Becoming

Organizing is what you do before you do something, so that when you do it, it's not all mixed up.

— Winnie-the-Pooh

"If you don't know where you are going, you will end up somewhere else." No, Yogi Berra wasn't thinking about schools when he said this. But his axiom does remind us that the first step in becoming a high-quality middle level school is knowing and articulating where you are now and where you want to go. To realize such a goal for your school, the larger school community must collaboratively build a vision around a set of core beliefs so that the vision becomes understood, expanded, nurtured, owned, and supported. And Winnie-the-Pooh is right: We've all experienced the "mixed-up-ness" of things (everything from one lesson to whole programs and structures) when someone didn't plan and organize well enough before getting started!

The organization of a school **makes a difference** for how the two fundamental concepts of *belonging* and *becoming* are embraced and addressed.

Certain basic structures promote one or both of these processes; other structures inhibit them. For example, students are more likely to develop a sense of *belonging* and feel secure to develop many aspects of *becoming* in small, personalized learning environments (e.g., teams or advisory classes) than in the vast learning environment of the whole school. A smaller number of students assigned per teacher (i.e., 90 versus 120) helps teachers build relationships with students (*belonging* and *becoming*). Classroom arrangements where students can collaborate on tasks together increase both academic and personal growth (*becoming*) as well as positive relatedness (*belonging*). Academic settings with time and space for students to initiate learning, explore topics in depth, and experiment (as opposed to those with short, rigid time periods) give students better opportunities to gain competence, autonomy, and knowledge (aspects of *becoming*). A schedule that provides time for teachers to collaborate as a staff or in grade-level groups or teams increases chances for true implementation of shared goals.

> **The organization of a school *makes a difference* for how the two fundamental concepts of *belonging* and *becoming* are embraced and addressed.**

Time dedicated to professional development enables teachers to enhance their ability to understand developmental characteristics and to teach students skills they need for such things as self-determination, self-regulation, and management of academic tasks—all aspects of *belonging* and *becoming*. (One of the 18 characteristics of successful middle schools describes the importance of "relevant, long term, job embedded" professional learning for **all staff** as a critical component of the school structure.)[1]

AMLE's 18 characteristics of successful middle schools also define foundational leadership and organizational structures as "absolute musts" that lead to excellent education and positive culture for young adolescents and that have critical implications for furthering *belonging* and *becoming* for all students.

These are:

- Policies and practices are student-centered, unbiased, and fairly implemented.
- Leaders are committed to and knowledgeable about young adolescents, equitable practices, and educational research.
- Educators are specifically trained to teach young adolescents and possess a depth of understanding in the content areas they teach.
- Comprehensive counseling and support services meet the needs of young adolescents.[2]

The conditions are just some of the structures that affect student success, but all are features of an optimal middle level environment. We believe, and research supports, that the middle school concept is uniquely suited to cultivating conditions that help young adolescents *belong* and *become*.

IMPLEMENTING THE MIDDLE SCHOOL CONCEPT

A good starting point for considering school organization and the benefits of the middle school concept is a review of the fifth edition of the AMLE's position statement on middle grades best practice, *The Successful Middle School: This We Believe*. This text, which we have mentioned in previous chapters and will mention in future chapters, builds a foundation for a school's design by defining five essential attributes and 18 characteristics of a successful middle school.[3] See also Figure 3.1 (page 46) for a graphic of these attributes and characteristics (a downloadable version is also available at amle.org/smssummary).[4] Take time to focus on each aspect, as they form the core organization of a middle school that makes possible the *belonging* and *becoming* we espouse for students. Watch for those places throughout the book where we note "an essential attribute of the successful middle school" or "one of the 18 characteristics of successful middle schools."

The Successful Middle School: This We Believe

Essential Attributes

AMLE affirms that an education for young adolescents must be:

Responsive

Using the distinctive nature and identities of young adolescents as the foundation upon which all decisions about school are made.

Challenging

Cultivating high expectations and advancing learning for every member of the school community.

Empowering

Facilitating environments in which students take responsibility for their own learning and contribute positively to the world around them.

Equitable

Providing socially just learning opportunities and environments for every student.

Engaging

Fostering a learning atmosphere that is relevant, participatory, and motivating for all learners.

From **The Successful Middle School: This We Believe**, *published by the Association for Middle Level Education. Build your own professional development plan with the Successful Middle School program.*

Visit **amle.org/sms**

Characteristics

Successful middle schools exhibit the following 18 characteristics:

Culture and Community

— Educators respect and value young adolescents.
— The school environment is welcoming, inclusive, and affirming for all.
— Every student's academic and personal development is guided by an adult advocate.
— School safety is addressed proactively, justly, and thoughtfully.
— Comprehensive counseling and support services meet the needs of young adolescents.
— The school engages families as valued partners.
— The school collaborates with community and business partners.

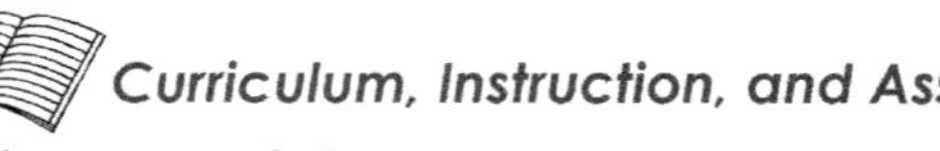

Curriculum, Instruction, and Assessment

— Educators are specifically prepared to teach young adolescents and possess a depth of understanding in the content areas they teach.
— Curriculum is challenging, exploratory, integrative, and diverse.
— Health, wellness, and social-emotional competence are supported in curricula, school-wide programs, and related policies.
— Instruction fosters learning that is active, purposeful, and democratic.
— Varied and ongoing assessments advance learning as well as measure it.

Leadership and Organization

— A shared vision developed by all stakeholders guides every decision.
— Policies and practices are student-centered, unbiased, and fairly implemented.
— Leaders are committed to and knowledgeable about young adolescents, equitable practices, and educational research.
— Leaders demonstrate courage and collaboration.
— Professional learning for all staff is relevant, long term, and job embedded.
— Organizational structures foster purposeful learning and meaningful relationships.

Figure 3.1

Another source has offered guidance for years about critical elements for successful middle schools: *What Makes Middle Schools Work*, a report resulting from close examination of higher-performing middle level schools to identify common elements and practices. "Higher-performing" was defined by the comparative level of academic performance of a school's students on New York State's eighth-grade English language arts and mathematics assessments over a three-year period. Identifying these elements, the study reminded readers that no single element stands alone—**all** must be present and implemented simultaneously. If even one of the five elements is missing or lacking, it is far less likely that a middle level school will show high academic performance or that it will genuinely meet the needs of its students.

- **Trusting and Respectful Relationships**
  Relationships based on mutual trust and respect among administrators, teachers, students, and families are fundamental to every common element in the findings. Nurturing these relationships provides the backbone for successful learning.

- **Students' Social and Emotional Well-Being**
  Higher-performing schools recognize that creating a sense of security for middle school students provides them with a support network and a connection to their school, removing significant barriers to learning.

- **Teamwork**
  Higher-performing schools establish a collaborative environment and organizational structure that supports teamwork between and among teachers, school leaders, and administrators. Groups of teachers, administrators, and specialists meet frequently and focus on specific instructional strategies and student performance within and across grades.

- **Evidence-Based Decision-Making**
  Sharing and using data from a variety of sources to make decisions is critical to helping schools achieve success. Data are frequently gathered, analyzed, and used to inform decision-making regarding the impacts of new programs, instructional practices, and interventions.

- **Shared Vision of Mission and Goals**

  When teachers and administrators collaboratively build a vision of success and shared goals, this leads to better communications, mutually agreed-upon expectations, and more long-term success.[5]

Both of us have read, used, taught, and interacted with the two abovementioned documents many times. Now, since taking on the mindset that *belonging* and *becoming* are key foundations to the whole picture of what we believe young adolescents need, we can't help but notice the prominence (direct or inferred) of these two concepts in both resources! Look back at Figure 3.1 (attributes and characteristics of successful middle schools) in this chapter and above at the five bulleted common elements of highly successful schools—and see whether you don't have the same revelation!

MAINTAINING FLEXIBILITY

Particular structures, schedules, and factors of school organization certainly contribute to students' well-being in a range of areas. Yet what matters even more than the specific details is what happens within the organization. In AMLE's *The Successful Middle School Schedule,* author Ann McCarty Perez asserts the importance of longer and more flexible time blocks to address the developmental needs of middle school students:

> Across time, we know to be true that there is great power in the schedule and leaders should use this tool thoughtfully and strategically to best meet the needs of the students they serve. The schedule is one of the most useful and impactful tools that a leader can use to address student needs, implement new initiatives, and drive progress.[6]

But McCarty Perez also reminds us that a schedule is as unique as the students it serves and that schools must follow their own culture and shared beliefs in creating a schedule that works for educating their young adolescents. Her book outlines a research-based and practice-based process recommended for middle schools to consider before embarking on setting schedules.[7]

Ron Williamson, coach to school and district leaders, and author of *Scheduling to Improve Student Learning,* explained:

> There is no perfect way to organize a school. And there are no schedules that fit every school or every need. What's clear, however, is that the way you organize your school is a reflection of your school's values and priorities and can either support achieving your vision or become a barrier to its success. Without a clear vision and agreed upon goals, the schedule is merely a plan for organizing teachers and students. But when guided by goals the schedule becomes a powerful tool to positively impact teaching and learning.[8]

The best organization for middle level schools has long been considered to center around interdisciplinary teams within a flexible schedule that also includes a built-in advisory time. Such teaming can be a crucial element for the success of a middle school. (For extensive advice on the process of interdisciplinary teaming, see AMLE's *Successful Middle School Teaming.*)

There is no perfect way to organize a school. And there are no schedules that fit every school or every need.

For a variety of reasons, at my former school, my staff and I (Patti) were unable to implement traditional teaming. But we still wanted to create a framework that addressed the needs of young adolescents that are met through teaming. After trying a few variations, we created a structure in which students were placed on two teams—one for language arts and social studies and a second for math, science, and health. Teams were multi-graded, and students generally stayed on the same team for more than one year.

We knew this was not the "ideal" organization for a middle school, so the staff continued to explore ways to move to complete interdisciplinary teaming. We had the good fortune to enjoy a visit from Dr. Paul George, a noted middle level scholar and author, who spent a day at the school to observe and give feedback on our program. In his summary report, he described the school's structure as "fresh, different, and effective." He felt the organization was a "workable alternative to traditional interdisciplinary team organization [and that] it [would] be hard to improve upon the attention individual students receive in this arrangement."

Because the staff had kept the focus on creating a school for the students, we were able to think outside of the norm to create an organizational structure that worked for the school. Teachers valued this feedback, appreciated that developing an organizational structure that benefited students didn't mean having to adopt a "canned" program, and were reaffirmed that they were doing what was best for students.

The multi-graded structure provided students with additional support from adults they knew and trusted; it gave them a sense of security and allowed them to be themselves while having a place to *belong*. Once students felt comfortable and had a sense of *belonging* at the school, they were able to *become* more successful academically and personally. The schedule described above was difficult to create and challenging to implement; it worked because it was designed around the school's specific needs and resources. It was risky, required thinking "outside of the box," and would be hard to replicate—but it worked for our school.

Sadly, the check-off mentality is still alive in some middle schools today. Such elements as flexible block schedules, shared students, common planning time, proximity of classrooms, and student advisory are still considered by many to be requisite components of an effective middle school. Some even suggest that a school can't practice a middle level concept unless these components are present! And although those structures are good and have been shown to be effective, it's far too easy for a school to check them off the list and then believe that it has created a school where students feel they *belong* and can *become* all they are meant to be.

But that's not the case. A school may have integrated teams with common planning time, but all the teachers talk about in team meetings is student behavior—never about how to connect their curriculum and instruction, develop and consistently use common protocols, or pursue professional development as a team.

The school may have a schedule that can be flexed, but all class periods remain the same length of time, month after month, year after year. An advisory period may be present but is used as a time to work on homework and do school "business" rather than addressing social, emotional, psychological, and cognitive issues and needs. Structure alone does not guarantee an effective school. The bottom line is that "organizational structures (must) foster purposeful learning and meaningful relationships" (one of the 18 characteristics that AMLE identifies as indicators of a successful middle school).[9] Therefore, structures must be designed to further the identified goals and vision of the school for fulfilling those purposes.

SUSTAINING MIDDLE LEVEL PRACTICES IN TIMES OF CHANGE

There is no question that dwindling resources, combined with more stringent accountability standards, have had significant impacts on middle level schools across the country. In most locations, educators and school boards grapple with such realities as reductions in staff levels, pressures to increase instructional time in reading and math, and shrinking budgets. These have led many schools to move away from established middle level structures that included advisory periods, teaming, individual and team prep time, and block schedules. An additional issue facing schools today is the widespread shortage of teachers and support staff.

Yet when faced with these dilemmas, some schools rise to the challenge and look for creative ways to keep the middle level concept alive, regardless of the constraints of a less-than-ideal schedule (or budget). The first step in accomplishing this is to determine the "why" of structures such as teaming, advisory, flexible schedules, and exploratory classes. To illustrate, here are examples of reported and research-backed outcomes for common middle level structures.

Structure	***Outcome***
Teaming	*allows for* smaller and more personalized learning communities.
Advisory	*contributes to* building relationships and *belonging.*
Block schedule	*provides* for flexibility in learning practices.
Common planning time	*makes it possible for* teachers to collaborate.
Interdisciplinary organization	*facilitates* connections between content areas.
Elective classes	*increase* student exposure and exploration within different topics.
Team-leader councils	*builds* collaborative leadership.

Once staff members agree upon the purposes of these structures, it's possible to think creatively to find ways to meet those needs that do not rely on a particular structure. To help with this process, schools must first clarify what they are trying to accomplish. For example, are you compensating for loss of staff? Looking for ways to reduce expenditures? Trying to provide additional instruction time in a content area? Be sure you don't fall into the trap of "we've always done it this way." We visited one middle school where staff members were able to accomplish their goals once they realized that not every class had to meet every day for the same amount of time and that teachers did not have to have the same prep period every day.

When a middle school team in North Carolina was faced with the loss of their advisory period, team members decided that the benefits of the program were far too important to abandon. So they searched for ways to infuse advisory activities throughout the day. The team's advisory program had been built around 12 character traits and actions that formed the basis for their team's core values. Because the team strongly believed in the importance of the program, each teacher committed to using 10 to 15 minutes of class time, three days a month, to introduce the concepts to students. They continued to infuse this program into all aspects of classroom and team meetings, classroom discussions, reflections when behavioral issues arose, goal setting for conference time, recognizing and celebrating individual accomplishments, and more. This team, convinced that the well-being of each child is at the core of what good middle schools do, was not about to abandon this belief over the loss of advisory classes. Instead, they put their heads together and launched an alternative plan to ensure that the same benefits remained available to their students.

Here's one caveat: Changes in a school's program can evoke strong emotions from a variety of sources, so be sure that any process to create or modify a school's organizational structure is collaborative and inclusive. Gather thoughts and suggestions from a variety of stakeholders, including students.

To design a school structure that best advances the processes of *belonging* and *becoming*, start with a shared vision of what those processes are, what your beliefs are, and what you want to happen for students. Tools like AMLE's Successful Middle School Assessment, or conducting a book study of *The Successful Middle School: This We Believe*, can help support that work (learn more and access resources at amle.org/sms). Next, take seriously the reality of how your school's structure impacts its ability to meet the academic, personal, and developmental needs of your students. Then, after asking "How can we meet our goals for students in ways that satisfy our vision and beliefs?" agree on what to do. Identify the kinds of specific programs or classes that will focus on strategies for *belonging* while keeping a balance with a strong focus on academic learning as well. Set programs and schedules that can reasonably lead to meeting your goals and addressing your students' needs.

Once your plans are underway, don't forget to keep continuously reexamining the structure. Don't shy away from being flexible enough to make needed adjustments to the structure over time—or to completely revamp it. And even when you're forced to lose or change part of the structure, be creative enough to find ways to ensure the outcomes you believe to be critical for your students.

For more information and strategies on elements of successful middle school structure, consult these AMLE companion texts to *The Successful Middle School: This We Believe:*

- *The Successful Middle School Schedule* by Ann McCarty Perez (2022)
- *Successful Middle School Teaming* by Jack Berckemeyer (2022)
- *Successful Middle School Advisory* by Todd L. Brist (2023)
- *The Successful Middle School Counseling Program* by Ann McCarty Perez and Elise Kenney-Coldwell (2023)
- *The Successful Middle School Leader* by Cedrick Gray (2023)
- *Successful Middle School Instructional Technology* by Ryan Ruggles and Tim Schigur (2023)
- *Successful Middle School Student Voice* by Sandy Cameli (2024)

Putting It into Practice

As an individual, team, small group, or entire staff, use some of these activities to spark discussions, reflect on your current practices or situations, listen to others, or set goals.

1. As a group, examine and discuss AMLE's list of essential attributes and characteristics of a successful middle school (Figure 3.1) shown on page 46. What evidence can you give that all or some of these elements and characteristics are implemented in your school? Which do you see as your strongest areas? What areas need improvement?

2. Questions for group discussion: What do you see as the structural elements of an "ideal" middle level school? Which are in place at your school? Are they effective? Which are missing or could be improved? Are there elements at your school that are implemented in name only? Do any areas need more flexibility? Have you given up important aspects that should be reconsidered using a more flexible method?

3. Examine the list of structures and outcomes on page 52. Do you agree with the outcomes for each structure? What would you change? How would you address those that are missing?

4. Download the article "Reimagining School – What Should It Look Like and Who Is It For?" from this link: amle.org/reimaginingarticle. Read it individually or as a team, and discuss the implications for your school and classroom structure as well as for your instructional practices.

5. Consider purchasing and using AMLE's "The Successful Middle School™ Assessment," which comprises 134 research-based exemplars that assess implementation of the 18 characteristics of successful middle schools. For more information, visit: amle.org/sms.

Part II

Practices for Belonging and Becoming

Once a strong foundation has been laid, it's time to build the rest of the house. With that process come multiple decisions that will lead to a unique design. Each school will choose (and decide how to implement) policies, practices, and programs to promote *belonging* and *becoming* within its own unique context. Some decisions will be influenced by policies and legal requirements, but for all decisions that are within the control of the staff and other stakeholders, start from the base of your school's shared mission, vision, beliefs, and goals. Although the environment you shape for your students to *belong* and *become* may be patterned after other successful models, it must depend heavily on the unique needs, preferences, and characteristics of **your** students, staff, families, and community. No two schools are exactly alike, and the choices made for your school will work only if they address your unique situation. Don't feel pressured to be a mirror image of someone else's school.

In Part II, we share practical strategies and examples to help students and other members of the school community experience their schools as places where they can *belong* and *become*. The chapters offer suggestions for creating and sustaining the conditions and skills that cultivate various aspects of those processes through:

1. Creating a culture of connection throughout the school.
2. Believing in students.
3. Fostering academic competence and autonomy.
4. Facilitating personal development, including self-determination and self-regulation.
5. Inviting, hearing, nurturing, and acting on students' voices in the school.

6. Offering students many choices in all aspects of their school lives.
7. Teaching leadership skills and providing leadership opportunities for all students.
8. Celebrating students' successes at *belonging* and *becoming*.

Friends at this age really play a vital role in who you are and what you've become so I recommend finding the people who are best for you and help you work towards becoming a good person. Being a middle schooler in today's day and age comes with its ups and downs, but you have to find the people, adults and peers, who are really going to be there for you throughout the whole thing.

— Laila, Grade 7

Chapter 4

Create Connections and Community

The most important things in life are the connections you make with others.

— Tom Ford

Many young teachers, particularly at the middle and high school levels, enter the education field believing they've been hired to teach a specific subject. They are often passionate, eager, and ready to change the world—in short, they arrive burning with those attitudes we hope to find in new teachers! But the idea that teachers are hired to teach a specific subject is not quite right; in fact, they are hired to teach *students*. And there *is* a difference between the two. Certainly, a school needs capable, skilled teachers with strong preparation for their content backgrounds. But all practitioners must realize that students' sense of well-being and experience of connectedness (*belonging*) influences everything else we hope for them to be, to accomplish, and to *become*.

What do we mean by *community*? For decades, extensive research and debate in the social sciences has centered on the meaning of community. The *Stanford Social Innovation Review* defines it this way:

> **It's about people.** First and foremost, community is not a place, a building, or an organization; nor is it an exchange of information over the internet. Community is both a feeling and a set of relationships among people. People

form and maintain communities to meet common needs. Members of a community have a sense of trust, belonging, safety, and caring for each other. They have an individual and collective sense that they can, as part of that community, influence their environments and each other.[1]

In Chapter 1, we outlined many of the critical benefits of *belonging* as well as some effects of **not** *belonging*. It was the research of sociologist Karen Osterman, published and widely embraced in the early 2000s, that alerted educators to the need for attention to *belonging* in the school community. She noted that even after years of recognizing that students' needs extend beyond the academic realm, many schools still paid too little attention to students' social and psychological needs, had structures or practices that contributed to isolation or alienation for some students, and operated on beliefs that academic achievement is more important than needs for relatedness.[2] A large percentage of schools, she found, held a pervasive view of *belonging* as a "reward for compliance and achievement" rather than a "precondition for engagement."[3]

Sadly, current researchers (such as Kelly-Ann Allen, lead author on a meta-analysis of what schools need to know about fostering school *belonging*) find that, more than two decades later, these attitudes and conditions are still far too pervasive in schools—including middle schools, where *belonging* to a school community is "an essential aspect of psychological functioning" for adolescents and wherein there are unique opportunities to improve *belonging* for school-age children.[4]

There are many who believe academic achievement is more important than other needs—but they must come to understand that academic achievement simply is not possible without addressing other essential needs as well. Allen and her research colleagues are adamant (and hopeful) about the unique opportunities schools have to improve *belonging* for their students.[5] This is good news: Research shows that specific school policies, instructional practices, and aspects of school climate—even short programs focused on *belonging*—can help students feel accepted in their school and classrooms. These can also "acknowledge and normalize students' worries about *belonging* and explain how these concerns can lessen with time."[6] In addition, efforts to build community in a school lead to increased academic motivation, improved social and emotional competencies, and lower rates of violence—all aspects of the kinds of *becoming* we wish for our students.[7]

A note of caution: When designing specific practices and programs to increase *belonging,* take care to reach the *belonging* needs of **all** students. It is critical to realize "that an increased sense of *belonging* for some students at the exclusion of other students may lead to detrimental outcomes for some students, such as greater levels of perceived social rejection and greater reports of problems at school."[8]

SHAPING THE COMMUNITY

Being aware of the meaning and benefits of *community* is just the first step. Beyond that, **all school personnel** must share in the belief that students' success includes social and emotional well-being in addition to (and with equal importance to) academic well-being—and that these aspects are interdependent. All students must participate in planned experiences that focus on community—in their schools and in their classrooms. **All staff members** (and volunteers) in the school must put effort into developing a culture that helps students feel included, important, equally valued, and safe. In addition, all staff members must contribute to the connection with, and valuing of, other adults in the school community. **All parents, caregivers, and family members** must hear the message about the importance of social and emotional well-being in combination with reaching academic goals. They must consistently be invited to participate in creating this supportive community.

Even short programs focused on *belonging* can help students feel accepted in their school and classrooms.

One of the 18 characteristics of successful middle schools, identified in *The Successful Middle School: This We Believe,* is that "health, wellness, and social-emotional competence are supported in curricula, school-wide programs, and related policies."[9] In light of the mental health crisis impacting today's young people, it is imperative to help them develop competencies in aspects of social and emotional health, even if this occasionally comes at the expense of academic learning.

One might even argue that a student who struggled academically but had strong social-emotional skills may become a better-adjusted and more employable adult than a peer who was academically successful but never developed social-emotional competence. Research consistently shows that social and emotional learning is essential to academic growth and success—that without social and emotional skills, even the strongest academic skills won't be enough. In short, they are better together.[10]

Even though we don't have control over such things as state mandates and district budgets, many of the programs, strategies, and attitudes that build the kind of community needed by middle level schools **are** within the control of educators. And many of them do not involve budget increases or more staffing! Based on evidence from current research, the most effective practices and conditions for helping students feel connected (*belong*) to their school and that have the greatest chance to drive their personal and academic *becoming*, include the following:[11]

- Prioritization of the value of *belonging* in the school setting for all members of the school community
- Active creation and nurturing of a supportive and caring learning environment, strongly anchored with trusting, caring relationships among students, teachers, school staff, and students' families
- Common values and practices across the school focused on such qualities as respect, care and inclusion for others, cooperation, personal responsibility, and good character
- Identifying, teaching, and reinforcing specific social and emotional skills, including those that enhance one's own *belonging* as well as the *belonging* of others
- Regular examination of the status of *belonging* and *becoming* for students
- Sensitivity to students' needs, emotions, points of view, and interests
- Strong availability of social and emotional support, advocacy, and counseling
- Prioritization of positive, consistent classroom management that does not diminish the sense of *belonging* or inhibit students' best chances for *becoming*

- Commitment to (and expectations of) respect for everyone and from everyone
- Removal of any roadblocks to learning and offering academic support to all students
- Frequent opportunities for students to develop and exercise autonomy—including taking part in school situations where they make or influence decisions
- Equity in expectations for and treatment of all students; visible respect for differences
- Intentional strategies to ensure that every student feels close to and known by at least one adult in the school
- Regular opportunities for students to cooperate and collaborate with one another
- Intentional, planned conversations between the school (staff and students) and families as well as school-wide community-building events and strategies that connect the school with students' families, designed to increase *belonging* for the families
- Professional development for staff in *belonging*, social and emotional well-being, and interpersonal skills, including competencies for *belonging*
- Leaders who take clear actions to create a community of connection

Additional effective middle school practices and conditions for boosting *belonging* and *becoming* include:

- "Comprehensive counseling and support services [that] meet the needs of young adolescents"[12] (AMLE's fifth characteristic of a successful middle school. See also *The Successful Middle School Counseling Program*.)
- A school policy on *belonging*, crafted specifically for the individual district or school and judiciously followed. (In the endnotes for this book, see the link for a school *belonging* policy that outlines the shared responsibility of *belonging* for the entire school community. If the school is part of a multi-school district, a *belonging* policy would be crafted at the district level.)[13]

- School-wide, concerted efforts to ensure students' physical and psychological safety (See AMLE's fourth characteristic of a successful middle school: "School safety is addressed proactively, justly, and thoughtfully.")[14]

In this book we have focused on strengthening *belonging* and *becoming* for our young adolescent students, but this goal cannot be reached if these processes are limited to students alone. If you want to build a culture of connection (*belonging*) and mutually supportive growth (*becoming*), **begin with the adults**; this is the advice of many researchers who study communities and cultures within schools and organizations. We know the importance of *belonging* for our students—both the key benefits when it is present and the negative consequences when it is absent. It is no less important for the adults in the workplace of schools to feel connected, accepted, and respected. Indeed, it is critical for them not only as individuals, both personally and professionally, but also as adult leaders in the school. This is because adults cannot fully demonstrate and teach the skills of *belonging* and *becoming* if they do not experience these themselves. They cannot fully demonstrate and teach the skills of *becoming* if they do not consistently participate in professional and personal growth and development themselves. We adults are the best models of the entire partnership of the two processes.

If you want to build a culture of connection (*belonging*) and mutually supportive growth (*becoming*), begin with the adults.

Many organizations in the worlds of business and education are aware of significant research about the importance of *belonging* in the workplace. This research tells us that when workers feel they *belong*, their work satisfaction and work performance dramatically improve. Also striking is the reduction in turnover and employee sick days. Other benefits of increased *belonging* are increased resilience and reduced effects of burnout. On the flip side, the absence of *belonging* increases isolation and diminishes employees' feelings of inclusion, security, and being valued. Indeed, lack *of belonging* is a major cause of people leaving their jobs.[15]

Thus, every school community, when planning to support *belonging* and *becoming*, must also consider ways to support those processes for adults. In their series of studies on *belonging*, the Coqual research group identifies these elements of *belonging* in the workplace:

- Being seen at work—recognized, rewarded, and respected by colleagues
- Experiencing real connections at work—with positive, authentic social interactions with peers, including leaders
- Being supported at work by peers, including leaders
- Pride in the purpose, vision, and values of your own work and the work of the organization[16]

Other research on *belonging* for adults includes these as factors that build a community of connection:[17]

- Plenty of opportunities for socialization and building social bonds
- Leadership that establishes a shared vision and purpose for the organization and the workers
- Equity and inclusion in decision-making and work processes
- Sharing knowledge, wisdom, experience, and challenges
- Affirmation of workers' importance, value, and competence
- Regular positive feedback from one another, especially leaders
- Planned, regular professional development with colleagues
- An environment of giving and receiving gratitude
- Discussions about the status of adult *belonging* and personal and professional development (i.e., *becoming*)
- Strong, compassionate leadership in the belief and implementation of *belonging* competencies

BUILDING RELATIONSHIPS

Belonging cannot be mandated. It emerges when relationships are nourished in climates of shared expectations and mutual trust. This is also true of *becoming*—expanding the skills, confidence, and competence that make up personal, professional, and academic growth. Students, their families, staff members (including leaders), and volunteers all flourish in a school environment where no one feels out of place—where everyone feels necessary and valued.[18] And, as we noted in Chapter 3, successful middle schools weave meaningful relationships **into the very structural fabric** of their school cultures (see the 18th characteristic).[19] In *The Successful Middle School Leader,* author Cedrick Gray notes the hundreds of relationships in a school that flow "all day long in all directions between individuals and among groups,"[20] each of these relationships affecting people deeply. He goes on to remind leaders (including all adults who staff the school) that there is "simply nothing a school leader does that does not involve relationships."[21]

At the end of my (Laurie's) daughter's fifth-grade year in middle school, families were informed that all sixth-grade students would be required to take either band or orchestra as a full- year, every-other-day class. Emma was asked to choose an instrument. I'm a strong supporter of music education and its impact on student achievement. However, as a family we struggled with her having to take a class that required a good deal of at-home practice because she was already committed to many other out-of-school activities. But it was just for one year, and we knew it would be good for her, so we rented her a viola (albeit begrudgingly) for the next year.

Throughout sixth grade, there was rarely a week when Emma didn't come home with a story to share about her orchestra teacher. Emma loved how she taught class, how she involved students, and how she made her feel special. When Emma was honored with the monthly orchestra award, it was as if she had won the World Cup. When her class performed their Christmas concert, my husband and I were amazed at how much she enjoyed playing and how beautifully she and her peers played together.

At the end of the year when it was time to return the rented viola, Emma informed us that she would need to purchase a new, larger one, because she was

choosing to take orchestra as a daily year-long class in seventh grade. She saw our surprise—after all, it had been a bit of a fight to get her on board for the obligatory sixth-grade year. She explained simply, "I **have** to be in her class. I don't care what she teaches." Although the class was a requirement (and might not have been Emma's choice originally), the relationship she developed with her teacher made all the difference. Emma continued to play viola through high school graduation and even played first-chair viola during her junior and senior years!

Outside of their families, schools provide the most important set of relationships that young adolescents can experience; there are so many possibilities for relationships within small and large groups. School is the ideal place—if the climate is right—for developing healthy relationships that increase their sense of *belonging*; at the same time, they contribute significantly to many aspects of academic and personal growth and success for students (i.e., *becoming*).

Resilience research shows us that the single most common factor in children who develop resilience is at least one stable and committed relationship with a supportive parent, caregiver, or other adult. "These relationships provide personal responsiveness, scaffolding, and protection that buffer children from developmental disruption. They also build key capacities that enable children to respond adaptively to adversity and thrive."[22] Because *belonging* plays a significant role in building resilience, we must help students experience a sense of *belonging* by helping them build multiple relationships.

We want our students to be resilient and bounce back from whatever life throws at them. The middle grades can be an especially difficult time for many young adolescents as they struggle to meet increasing academic demands and avoid new social pitfalls—all while adapting to monumental physical and psychological changes. As a result, they often look to teachers, friends, and families to make them feel safe and help them find where and how they fit in.

Our colleague Andrew Maxey, author of *Elephant in the Classroom: Tracing the Complexity of Teaching by Exploring 13 Competencies and Practices*, calls it "layers of belonging." He contends that young adolescents have a need to *belong*—yet at the same time, they also have a need to explore and discover who they are and how they fit in with others. If we wish to increase young adolescents' potential for success, we need to help them build multiple layers of *belonging* within the school; that way if one of those connections sours or fails (even temporarily), other connections will still be in place.

Relationships within a school form the cornerstones for a culture of trust and respect where students want to *belong* and meet the expectations in **their** school (part of *becoming*). If we want students to believe that they are valued, respected members of the school community—and that the school has been designed to meet their needs as they grow and develop—then we must believe it, too, and we must show that it is true. This belief must actively and continuously infuse the atmosphere of the school.

Teacher–Student Relationships

A recent meta-analysis of dozens of research studies on *belonging* examined multiple individual and social factors that improve school *belonging*; the results consistently showed that teacher support and student–teacher relationships were the strongest predictors of school *belonging.*[23] In a follow-up study, "School Belonging: The Importance of Student–Teacher Relationships," Kelly-Ann Allen and her colleagues share this research finding: Strong teacher–student relationships enable both the assessment of students' levels of *belonging* and the increase in school *belonging*—particularly for adolescents. Importantly, all of these benefits are heightened when the senior school leaders passionately support an inclusive sense of *belonging* across the school community while actively supporting (and providing time and structures for) the teachers' relationship efforts.[24]

Teachers who form secure, meaningful relationships with students—relationships that enhance *belonging* and *becoming*—share these characteristics and actions: They are warm, caring, sensitive, and affirming. They actively welcome students daily—meeting students at the door and leaving them with personal send-off contact. They work to get to know students as individuals and chat to share similarities. They are attentive and emotionally available to students. They are trustworthy, fair, equitable, and consistent. Students can rely on them to be even-tempered. They don't yell or threaten. They don't alienate students by embarrassing or belittling them or by shaming them with lectures about their shortcomings or misdoings. They don't discipline or scold a student in front of others; instead, they confront students in private and give them a way to save face in front of their peers. They do not show biases or favoritism. They're honest and direct and are not afraid to enjoy and use humor. They set high standards and help students reach them. They affirm students' efforts and talents; they honor each student's unique qualities. They are obvious and passionate advocates for students. Students can see that these teachers enjoy their students and work hard to help every student succeed. These teachers treat **all** students equally and with respect at **all** times.

There is no precise relationship formula that works with every student. Middle level students come in all shapes and sizes, and all have their own unique stories to tell that bear hearing. If we don't take the time to listen and look beneath the surface, we will fail at truly understanding that student; we won't be able to build an authentic relationship. When we pay close attention, we'll learn things we didn't know—for example, the student with hair dyed black and wearing baggy clothing is one of the school's honor students. The student who sits in the corner, not saying much, delivers food to the homeless in the park on weekends. The popular kid chatting animatedly with friends is battling an eating disorder. The student being reprimanded for a third tardy is responsible for getting younger siblings off to school each morning.

When we pay close attention, we'll learn things we didn't know.

Do we expect Sasha to be as academically proficient as her older sister? Do we think, "Well, Jerry is doing the best he can, given his home life"? Do we unintentionally favor Bella because her mother is head of the PTO? Do we have a preconceived notion of Curt's behavior because of what we were told by last year's teacher? Do we make judgments about Jana because of rumors we hear about her out-of-school relationships with boys? We must get past our first impressions and confront any prejudices we may have, especially those that may be hidden.

Even when a student doesn't initially show interest in establishing a relationship with a teacher, it's the teacher's responsibility to take the lead. Speaker and author Rick Wormeli cautions teachers **not** to put the responsibility for a teacher–student relationship onto the student: "A lot of teachers hide behind that 50/50 notion. Like the kid has to meet me halfway. No! After 25 years of teaching, it's much more 60/40, and the one kid who sits in the back of the room and never interacts, it's 90/10."[25]

Skilled educators know (and years of research confirm) the value of having caring relationships with students and the effects on many aspects of *becoming*: classroom disruptions are minimized; motivation, student engagement, academic tenacity, and achievement increase; self-belief soars and self-control matures; academic confidence and attitudes improve; and students *become* more satisfied with school and grow in a variety of personal aspects, including physical and mental health.[26] Additionally, the teacher's positive, consistent, friendly attention to students needs and concerns gains their trust and increases their senses of *belonging*, and positive student–teacher relationships ultimately lead to better teaching.[27]

Teacher Relationships with Others

Young adolescent students may appear uninterested in the adults in the school. But make no mistake—they are always watching! They notice what teachers and other adults do. They notice how you talk to and treat other students. They notice your attitudes and preferences. They are keenly aware of your facial expressions and body language. They notice how you relate to your colleagues. They notice how your voice changes when an adult enters the room. They notice when you roll your eyes about something another teacher says or does. They overhear your conversations.

The relationship behaviors of adults are perhaps the most powerful lessons for students. Intentionally or not, all the adults in the school are models for how to conduct relationships—how to treat others, how to be trustworthy and loyal, how to handle conflicts and frustrations, and how to handle one's own emotions in relationships. To be secure in their relationships at school, students must see the adults around them operating with the same care, respect, compassion, and self-control that we try to teach to them.

Being aware of how others see us, what others see in us, and how we positively model behaviors, attitudes, and actions is much less challenging when we—as adults in the school—feel that we *belong* as well. All of us, regardless of age, have a need to feel valued, heard, welcomed, included, and that we matter. When we don't, no matter our age or role, it's much more challenging for us to carry ourselves in a way we want to model and others want to emulate.

Student–Student Relationships

As all middle level educators well know, relationships among students play a large part in individual well-being at school. Yes, the teacher–student relationship is powerful and sets a model for young adolescents to emulate. But how their peers see and interact with them (or what they say about them to others) is what middle level students notice and worry about the most. Students can truly feel that they *belong* **only** when they are at ease with **both** the adults and other students in their school.

Heather Libbey's landmark analysis of school connectedness found peer relations to be a key component of *belonging*.[28] The benefits gained from trusting teacher–student relationships extend and multiply when students feel they *belong* with peers. In their overview of research on the effects of student relatedness at school, Carrie Furrer and Ellen Skinner found that peers are a potent influence on many aspects of *becoming*—affecting one another's self-concept, educational goals, and day-to-day behaviors and satisfaction at school.[29] Kelly-Ann Allen and Terence Bowles concluded that social *belonging* and satisfying peer relationships positively affect classroom engagement, student motivation, and academic performance. Fostering healthy relationships among students is a critical part of the teacher's role.[30] Here are some ways to do that:

- First and foremost (at the risk of sounding repetitive), **model** caring, respectful, unbiased relationships.
- By your actions and reactions, show that you honor differences and appreciate the uniqueness of each individual.
- Set strong expectations for students respecting one another, and hold students to them.

- Give students responsibilities for increasing *belonging* in the class. Let them make and implement plans to do this.
- Define *respect*. Define *disrespect*. Have students define these terms as well, and talk about them with students. Let them give examples of what both of these concepts look like in action. Get them talking about how it feels to be the recipient of respect, disrespect, disregard (or ignoring), esteem, and value.
- Notice and celebrate examples of respectful, caring, and uplifting behaviors.
- Do not ignore incidents of disrespect (of any magnitude).
- Teach students skills for actively and respectfully listening to one another.
- Teach students to give respectful, useful input and responses to one another.
- Get students involved in lots of interactive activities, such as cooperative problem solving, group discussions, joint research, and group projects.
- Mix up groups so that students dialogue and work with everyone in the class.
- Give meaningful tasks that enable students to succeed at group efforts.
- Plan opportunities for peer tutoring.
- Constantly validate students' opinions, ideas, and feelings.
- Ask for input from all students. Honor the input you receive.
- Help **all** students succeed. Let their peers see their successes.
- Find opportunities to showcase each student's skills, ideas, interests, and competencies.
- Teach and practice such interpersonal skills as communication, listening, decision-making, self-control, and conflict resolution.
- Emphasize and practice pro-social behavior (students helping others).
- Emphasize and practice non-exclusionary attitudes. Let students identify what these are, and discuss behaviors that show evidence of non-exclusion.

I (Patti) am reminded of a group of about five girls in my sixth-grade class who were locked in a seemingly never-ending conflict. (Anyone who has worked with middle level girls—or boys, for that matter—who are having "friendship issues" knows that it can be a treacherous experience.) Finally, I decided to meet with the group to see whether the problems could be settled once and for all. I first asked them to state the issue in their own words. Then I gave them the standard teacher "chat" on getting along, forgiving and forgetting, etc.—a lecture I'm sure we've all used a few times. When I had finished, there was silence. After a while, Heather spoke up: "So what you're telling us is that we don't have to be friends, but we do have to be friendly. I think we can do that." Heads nodded; conflict resolved! (And, in the manner of sixth graders, they were all friends again a week later!)

MAKING INDIVIDUAL CONNECTIONS

This chapter is about building a connected environment—and as we've emphasized, there are a host of practices that schools and individuals in them can do to foster connectedness for all students. But here's the thing: We can't connect with students we don't know. We can't be models of connection if students don't **see** us getting to know them and other students—not just knowing on the surface but also knowing and valuing what's inside. So commit yourself to getting to know students as individuals. Find out what's important to them. Hold conversations with them about their out-of-school interests. Notice what drives and inspires them. Pay attention to what discourages them. Keep your senses alert to nonverbal signs of distress, delight, withdrawal, anxiety, etc. Discover what's on their minds, and they will begin to see you as someone who is genuinely interested in them.

We can't connect with students we don't know.

Finding out (and honoring) what students value is a strong component of getting to know them. Teachers need to be tuned in to the interests and activities of the whole group of young adolescents. This means paying attention to the fads, fashions, events, heroes, music, media, social media sites, topics, and games to which they choose to give their time and energy. But to know students more deeply, we must also home in on their passions as individuals.

From my time as a middle school principal, I (Laurie) recall a student who really struggled in one teacher's class. (In fairness, Michael struggled in all of his classes, but his other teachers had found some common ground and were able to help him make some progress.) But in this one class, he and the teacher just couldn't seem to connect. Looking for something to break this cycle, the teacher stayed after school to watch Michael play in a school basketball game. He cheered on this talented player (although not so obviously that it would embarrass the student). The next day in class, he used something from Michael's basketball performance as an example of a lesson concept. Suddenly, it was almost as if they had never had a problem—and from then on, they rarely did! This change had a significant impact on the entire class: There were fewer disruptions, and classroom management was much less challenging for the teacher. Michael also got the message that his teacher valued this very important part of his life. As a result, he was more open to the values the teacher was trying to teach (a win-win for both—but most of all for Michael).

What we adults see as important in education may not hold the same significance for our students. Regardless of whether our values jibe with theirs, our goal is to reach and educate the whole student. Therefore, we must recognize the parts of their lives that are as important (or possibly more important) to them as academics: school-sponsored or out-of-school arts, athletics, clubs, volunteer activities, family responsibilities, or even jobs. We must also recognize that their participation in the ventures they value can have a major impact on their academic achievement. When we honor what other individuals value and show our enthusiasm, we deepen our trusting relationships with them. These relationships, in turn, make it easier for us to contribute to shaping other values related to aspects of *becoming* productive, well-rounded learners and citizens. Thus, it's good for each of us to ask ourselves: "Do I see math class, cheerleading practice, being part of the football team, practicing for a skateboard competition, building a babysitting business, helping clean up the city park, writing songs for a garage band, coding a video game, and scoring well on a state science test **all** as equally important for students?"

You may be thinking, "We all know it's critical to build relationships with students. I want to get to know my students individually, but I have so many students!

How can I do this?" First of all, consider that you may know more about your students than you think. Take the time to make a quick list of what you know about each one. Start this list early in the year, and continue jotting down other things as you learn them. Plan some quick activities (such as those below) that help you learn more in a short amount of time. Learn more things about students from colleagues or other adults who work with them. Then, make brief "check-in" contacts with each student at least once a week—find time to make a comment about something you know or have observed about him or her, follow up on something the student has shared, or encourage one of the student's interests or ventures.

Here are some strategies you might try to get to know individual students more closely:

"About Me" Letters: Ask students to write you a letter detailing what they think you should know about them.

Student Inventories: To get a close-up look at individual students, ask them to share their likes, dislikes, hobbies, interests, worries, passions, accomplishments, and personality traits. They can complete such sentence prompts as:

What I value most is . . .
My most burning interest is . . .
What teachers usually don't know about me Is . . .
I prefer to spend my time . . .
I'm really good at . . .
The best school assignment I have ever had is . . .
Something fascinating about me is . . .
The place where I feel most myself is . . .
The best quality of a true friend is . . .
I worry about . . .
I'm proud of . . .
My biggest concern at school is . . .
If I could trade places with anyone for a day, that person would be . . . because . . .

Get-to-Know-Me Lists: Ask students to make lists such as: My Top Ten Interests, My Top Ten Hopes, Ten Words that Tell About Me, Top Five Ways I Learn Best and Five Things that Keep Me From Learning, and Five Things I Wish Would Happen at School.

Family Input: Give parents or caregivers ways to tell you what they'd like you to know about their child, what they're proud of, and what they hope will happen for their child at school this year. These may take the form of letters, surveys, student interviews with family members, questionnaires, or even just sentences on note cards.

Extracurricular Activity Check-Ups: Investigate the extracurricular involvement of each student in your class. Every student in a middle school should have some outside activity as a chance to pursue an interest and interact with more peers in satisfying experiences. If you find that a student has no such involvement, work with them to find the right activity. (This should be done throughout the school so that every student has a chance for connections beyond classes. It can work only if the school offers some opportunities during the school day so there will be no reason why a student can't participate.)

Visits to Students' Events: Drop in on events that students care about—sports games, concerts, debates, recitals, clubs, and other places where they share their talents. Even if the student is not a performer in an event, you can show your interest in what the student values by showing up to see what it's all about. A nice side benefit of attending events is that you have more chances to engage with families, who often attend events to support their children's interests. Being a part of an event shows families that you believe in non-academic participation and support what the student values. This strengthens your relationship with students and families alike.

Building positive connections with individuals is like depositing money in the bank. If the time comes when you have to confront a student or get down to the hard stuff of dealing with a big problem, you want to be sure there is a balance in the account that you can draw from. You'll already have established the trust that helps students see that you are an advocate for them.

ENSURING THAT EACH STUDENT IS KNOWN

In most cases, middle level teachers have dozens of students rotating through their classrooms in a day. Even though teachers are working hard to know each student, individual students at this level may not feel closely connected to, or completely secure with, any one adult. A student may not know where to turn for a consistent listener or advocate. One of the 18 characteristics of successful middle schools, as identified by AMLE and supported by research, is "Every student's academic and personal development is guided by an adult advocate."[31] To give our students the best chance to *belong* and *become*, we must ensure that every student is well known and feels close to at least one adult in the school—and preferably more than one.[32] That adult does not necessarily have to be a teacher. This could be the custodian, a secretary, a classroom paraprofessional, a lunchroom worker, the principal, a counselor, the librarian or media specialist—any caring adult who can connect with the student and who takes responsibility for being that child's advocate. This adult is alert to the student's successes and struggles, keeps track of the student's academic behaviors and processes, and stays tuned in to whether the student has a sense of *belonging* and how the student perceives progress and abilities in the personal and academic processes of *becoming*. The advocate can connect the student with services, programs, other adults, other students, organizations, and opportunities that enhance progress and address needs for the student.

To give our students the best chance to *belong* and *become*, we must ensure that every student is well known and feels close to at least one adult in the school—and preferably more than one.

A school organization that includes teaming and advisory classes has long been considered an indicator of an effective middle school. A deeper look into the "why" reveals that these practices diminish anonymity—no student should feel lost or anonymous and especially not during the difficult time of young adolescence. Teaming creates smaller learning communities, and advisories help develop strong student–adult and student–student connections. If your school is not able to implement teaming and advisory programs, it's important to look for other strategies to fill the same functions for creating the culture of connectedness in the school.

At the middle school where I (Patti) was principal, we did not have a formal advisory program. Yet the staff knew the importance of ensuring that each student was closely connected with at least one adult. So, we posted a list of all our students on the wall of the staff room: All school employees (not just teachers) were asked to read over the list and star the names of students with whom they had a strong, personal relationship (for example, the student would initiate conversations, the adult knew the family, or the adult had connection with the student in some extracurricular activity). In addition, each adult put a checkmark by the names of students with whom they felt they had some relationship (but not as strong as those they had starred). After everyone had left their stars and checkmarks, a group of us examined the list. (Interestingly, those with the most markings by their names tended to be both the "top" students as well as the "disruptive" students.)

Unfortunately, there were also student names with no stars or checkmarks. The staff read through the list of those without any marks, and individuals stepped forward to commit themselves to developing a relationship with one or more of those students. Generally, it was along the lines of "Oh, she's in my second period class; I'll make a point to speak with her each day," or "I see him sitting by himself at lunch each day. I can ask him if he'd help me with something."

I remember one student I had chosen. I made sure to initiate a conversation with him several times a week while doing lunch duty. It was my last year as principal, and the following year I received a wrong-number phone call from the student's father. I recognized the name on the caller ID and told him that I'd been his son's principal. He immediately told me how much his son missed me because I was "really nice" and "talked with him a lot!"

My anecdotal experience was just one among many examples showing how effective this process was for learning about our students' connections to adults in the building and making a change for those who had no clear adult advocate.

It also served as a compelling reminder to staff about just how important it is to reach out to all students. AMLE's *The Successful Middle School Advisory* and *Successful Middle School Teaming* texts provide a wealth of advice, strategies, and understandings for ensuring that each student is known. The ideas can be adapted to your school and classrooms regardless of whether you have a formal advisory program or teaming process.

We'll note also that the book *The Successful Middle School Advisory* presents a broad definition of *advisory* as "regularly scheduled times when young adolescents have the opportunity to interact with a small group of peers and a teacher-advisor to discuss school and personal concerns."[33] For its part, *Successful Middle School Teaming* describes a range of configurations for teaming processes that enhance connection and promote close-up knowledge of individual students.[34]

RESPECTING DIFFERENCES

Schools are centers of diversity—in race, ethnicity, socio-economic status, religion, language, capabilities and disabilities, cultural patterns and values, gender, and sexual orientation or identification. *The Successful Middle School: This We Believe* states that all such social identities "equally contribute to who young adolescents are and to their experiences in and out of school."[35] As we work to forge a connected school community, we must remember, respect, welcome, and value the differences among us. This means that we must examine our own attitudes about—and responses to—such differences, teach our students to value differences, and require behaviors that show acceptance and respect of all people.

Unfortunately, student responses to differences can become roadblocks to a sense of *belonging* for other students. At the middle grades level, in addition to the diversity factors listed above, a host of physical, emotional, social, and personal-choice differences distinguish students and can lead to further stereotyping, mocking, exclusion, or criticism. These include weight, height, body type, emotional vulnerability (e.g., someone who cries easily), the sound of someone's voice, hair style or color, clothing choices, friend choices, popularity (or lack thereof), activities engaged in (or not engaged in), or even just being new to the school. An 11-year-old girl feels ostracized if she isn't included in a "cool" or "popular" peer group or clique. For an unathletic 13-year-old boy, not making the basketball team can be a devastating exclusion from a group to which he so desperately wants to *belong*.

Student responses to differences can become roadblocks to a sense of *belonging* for other students.

As middle level educators, we must watch for such instances. We can help connect the 11-year-old girl with other friends, and we can structure middle level athletic programs to be inclusive with opportunities for all students to participate. We can establish an environment where students understand that differences are part of the human race—where they feel they *belong* as whole persons because of who they are.

A group of researchers conducted a 15-year intervention (known as the Child Development Project) to create a sense of community in schools. The outcomes of this project led them to conclude that promotion of non-exclusionary attitudes was one of the key ways to increase a sense of *belonging* among students.[36] In this vein, we must help students identify exclusion and inclusion, understand the importance of inclusion, and practice inclusive behaviors. Whether there is a new sixth grader sitting alone at lunch with no friends, an eighth grader of a faith that doesn't celebrate Christmas who feels uncomfortable during a hallway discussion of the holiday (which other students would consider harmless), or a fifth grader who feels excluded because of race, a critical part of our role as educators is helping guide students through what it means to see life from someone else's perspective and to honor all humans equally.

How well we do (or don't do) in teaching the life lessons of respect and inclusion will make a difference in whether students can realize that actions they see as innocent, light-hearted jokes or gestures may be felt by others as demeaning, harassing, or bullying. Here are a few of the many possible ways to help students embrace and honor differences:

- Define *diversity, stereotype, inclusion, tolerance, intolerance, bias,* and *worth.* Discuss these terms and have students offer examples of them (without using names).

- Together, brainstorm, discuss, and role-play ways to show inclusion in the school community.
- Encourage and practice open-mindedness about people who look, act, celebrate, or think differently.
- Watch yourself, and listen to yourself! Examine your own attitudes and (even subtle) manifestations of bias, prejudice, exclusion, or stereotyping. Work with colleagues to reflect these to each other. Know that your students will pick up on them! Let your own behavior be an example that shows them what it looks like to embrace and celebrate differences.
- Notice external messages that students see and hear—from media and other sources in society. Teach students to be alert to these, and teach skills for evaluating and responding to them.
- Help organize (and participate in) professional development to further equity and inclusive behaviors in your school.
- Make sure the stories you read, activities you do, lessons you plan, foods you share, units you cover, field trips you take, and art you show are deliberately chosen to expose students to many cultures and viewpoints.
- Have students explore and share their own cultural histories, values, and traditions.
- Encourage students to try to put themselves in another person's shoes.
- Discuss courage as it relates to standing up to prejudice, intolerance, or exclusion.

INCLUDING AND COLLABORATING WITH FAMILIES

The African proverb *"It takes a whole village to raise a child"* is certainly true of middle schools as well. If we want to create schools where students *belong* and can develop their potential for many of the qualities of *becoming*, we must have the help and support of families. One of the 18 characteristics of successful middle schools is that "the school engages families as valued partners."[37]

Research has repeatedly confirmed what educators know from experience: Family involvement and support make a difference for students! Collective trust between school staff and parents or caregivers is a key ingredient in creating conditions for young adolescents' academic and social-emotional growth. Studies have found that students with involved families, no matter their income or background, are more likely to:

- Earn higher grades and test scores.
- Experience increased motivation and greater belief in themselves as students.
- Be promoted, pass their classes, and earn credits.
- Attend school regularly.
- Have better social skills, show improved behavior, and adapt well to school.
- Graduate and go on to postsecondary education.[38]

The above list shows some of the qualities, habits, efforts, and attitudes that are a part of our own lists of what we want students to *become*. Ongoing positive relationships between teachers and families greatly boost a student's sense of *belonging* as well. Imagine the messages you send to students about "having their backs" or being their advocate when you reach out to affirm students to their families. (And be sure that most of your contacts with families **are** for the purpose of reporting progress, improvements, compliments, and other positive messages!)

As a superintendent in my current district, I (Laurie) recently saw firsthand the power of positive outreach to families. One of our middle school students had really been struggling in school, primarily with behavior. Numerous meetings, phone calls, and interactions with the family over the past year had been especially difficult and stressful for everyone involved (student, family, and staff). The beginning of this year presented similar challenges, particularly in one class, which resulted in continued difficult communications with the family. At a recent school event, the student's parent approached me to tell me about a phone call received from the teacher of the specific class where the child's challenging behavior and consequences had been a persistent problem. That teacher—the one whom the student had most disrespected—had taken the time to call the family and share something uplifting about the student, who had recently had a positive experience in class. It wasn't just the phone call with unexpected positive information, the parent said, that made an impact: In fact, it was the *only* positive phone call the family had ever received in the student's entire school career. The parent teared up; I teared up. And just like that, the baseline for positive communication with this family has been set. What a powerful reminder of the need to share the positive with families!

Unfortunately, many parents and caregivers feel a need to back off from school involvement during the middle years (and yes, that decision is often instigated or supported by their student). Other parents and caregivers do not recall their days at the middle level fondly and do not care to revisit them by coming to school. Still others avoid the school because of language or culture issues. In recent years, a lot of media attention has been directed toward what some are labeling the "parents' rights movement." Some families have negative perceptions of schools and feel disconnected from them. Others generalize an isolated, undesirable event in one school as pervading all schools. Now, more than ever, it is critical to proactively and accurately inform, involve, and partner with families to build relationships and trust to better support and improve student outcomes.

It's great to have families participate in groups such as a PTA or PTO, help with fundraisers or carnivals, or serve on short-term committees. Yet, if we truly want to make schools into places where students feel they *belong* and where they can *become* what they want now and in the future, we must work to develop deeper partnerships with families. This begins each year with the establishment of a strong two-way communication process.

- Make positive contacts with each student's family at the beginning of the year. Tell them something you value about their child. (This shows that you have already made an effort to get to know the child as an individual.)
- Set up a workable system to keep parents or caregivers well informed about classroom procedures, events, and homework.
- Set up a consistent way to communicate with families. Establish the best way for them to receive information or make contact.
- Be accessible. Let them know how to reach you. Be sure to find ways to accommodate language differences. Respond quickly to any attempts parents or caregivers make to contact you. Make sure they know how they can share their worries or concerns with classroom teachers.
- Keep in regular contact with families about the accomplishments, progress, and needs of their child.
- Be sure that all communication to parents and caregivers reaches **all** families—and that it is always inclusive and effective. Consider whether some of your communication approaches or platforms may cause challenges for some families.
- Compliment students to their families several times a year—with a text, note, email, or call for the sole purpose of sharing something positive.
- Always be warm, kind, and respectful to students' families. Ask parents or caregivers for their ideas and concerns. Listen to what they tell you. (Listen as much as you talk—or more.)
- Whenever there is a problem or concern, contact parents or caregivers personally (phone or face-to-face), and make a plan together. (We encourage you not to use email to share concerns. It may be quicker, but it is often far less personal and effective. In particular, it is difficult to interpret tone via email, and you may inadvertently send the wrong message—making the situation worse, not better.) Always follow up to discuss how the plan is working and to give affirmations of the student.
- Build relationships before focusing on academics. Plan events that are non-academic in nature, family-friendly, free, and fun—to break down walls between school and home and to initiate goodwill.[39]

- Make academics transparent. Once school has been in session for a few weeks, hold small grade-level events to describe homework and academic expectations and explain opportunities and avenues for help and support. Invite students along with their parents and caregivers.[40]

To further build authentic connections with families that support *belonging* and *becoming*, explore additional ways to engage them. It's wonderful when families initiate involvement with school, but it's the school's job to reach out to them—to see that there are intentional practices that offer numerous and creative ways for families to support their child's learning experience. Teachers and school administrators should ask questions such as these:

"Are parents or caregivers fully functioning members of the school's leadership council?"

"Does the school regularly seek out feedback on current policies and practices?"

"Has the school taken the opportunity of a school event (such as a concert, movie night, or sports activity) to intersperse a short informational talk about how families can support their children at home?"

"Does the school hold transition meetings for incoming students? (If there are multiple feeder schools, have we considered holding the meetings at their neighborhood school?)"

"Do parents or caregivers who do not speak English feel comfortable at our school?"

TOP 8 WAYS TO BUILD RELATIONSHIPS WITH STUDENTS' FAMILIES

- Learn their names. Always greet them warmly whenever you see them—even briefly and even outside of school.
- Arrange to visit students' homes, particularly when students enter the middle grades.
- Have students take the lead at conferences when parents or caregivers are present.
- Invite parents or caregivers to join the class for parties and presentations.
- Host a family cookout or picnic during school lunchtime.
- Ask parents or caregivers to write you a letter telling you what is wonderful about their child.
- Thank families for their help and support. Do this both privately and publicly—and often.
- Trust (and treat) parents and caregivers as equals. Let them know that you value them and the insights they provide about their child.

A powerful way to engage families is through student-led conferences, a process that has families coming to school to hear students sharing a portfolio of classroom work samples, articulating strengths and weaknesses, and using a goal-setting process for future accomplishments. This kind of conference makes significant contributions to the student's process of *becoming*—it increases confidence and independence, strengthens the student's voice, and boosts the sense of competence and maturity in the eyes of parents and caregivers. In addition, it deepens the sense of *belonging* for both students and families. (We recommend Patti Kinney's book *Fostering Student Accountability through Student-Led Conferences* for more about this process.)

In their book *Reducing the Risk, Increasing the Promise,* Sheryl Bergman and Judith Allen Brough offer one clear caution about family involvement: that teachers "don't give up on kids because of the actions or inactions of the parents!"[41] We would add that teachers who value students' families also do not show favor to students whose families **do** take an active part in supporting the teacher, class, or school.

Find many more ideas to spark family involvement in these books by Phyllis Fagell: *Middle School Matters: The 10 Key Skills Kids Need to Thrive in Middle School and Beyond—and How Parents Can Help* and *Middle School Superpowers: Raising Resilient Tweens in Turbulent Times.*

For all that educators have learned in the past two decades about the value of building school communities, researchers have detected a disparity between the understanding of the importance of school connectedness *(belonging)* and the actual day-to-day practice of it. Authors of *The Social Cure: Identity, Health, and Well-Being* refer to this as a persistent "blind spot" to the critical importance of satisfying social relationships. The value of social connection, they argue—and we heartily agree—cannot be underestimated.[42]

Regardless of whether your school (or some of the folks in it) may have any such blind spots, there are workable, effective steps that you can take right away to move your school closer to a culture of connectedness in which your students reap the benefits of increased *belonging* and *becoming.*

PUTTING IT INTO PRACTICE

As an individual, team, small group, or entire staff, use these activities to spark discussions, reflect on your current practices or situations, listen to others, or set goals.

1. Work alone, with your teammates, or with a few colleagues to answer this question: "How do students experience being members of this school (or my classroom)? How can I (we) tell?" Then identify practices that are already working to create a connected community in your classroom or school. Identify other practices or areas that you'd like to add or improve. Set time-frame goals for putting these to work.

2. Group discussion: What methods does your school have in place to ensure that every student knows and has access to at least one adult advocate on campus? Are the methods working for each student? If nothing is in place, in what ways can you ensure that each student is known and feels valued?

3. Hold a focus group with students from all social groups. Ask them such questions as: "Do students in our school have a way to let adults know they have a need?" "If you or a friend had a problem, how likely would you be to seek help at school? Why or why not?" "Which adults would you or other students be most likely to approach?" "How can we do better at giving students a safe way to ask for help?"

4. For the adults in the school, explore the experiences and conceptions of your own *belonging* and *becoming*. Use "Reflection: What Does Belonging Mean to You?" from our ASCD book *We Belong: 50 Strategies to Create Community and Revolutionize Classroom Management* included as Appendix H on page 285 at the end of this book. Complete this reflection individually,

and share insights with your colleagues, discussing how your own sense of *belonging* intersects with the ways you help students *belong*. Repeat the process for the *becoming* concept by re-using the reflection—replacing the word *belonging* with *becoming* throughout.

5. Download, read, and discuss with colleagues the article by Leila Kubesch: "From Home Visits to Parent Academies: Transforming Engagement in Middle Level Education." What ideas does the article spark as to how your school might look to engage families in new and creative ways? (You can download this from amle.org/homevisitsarticle).

6. Use a student survey to gain insights from your students about student-teacher relationships in your classroom or on your team. You can design your own survey, or ask students to design one. AMLE also provides companion student and family/caregiver surveys to its Successful Middle School Assessment that help schools compare their perceptions of the school's effectiveness to those of staff.

   In writing our ASCD book, We Belong: 50 Strategies to Create Community and Revolutionize Classroom Management, we created an example of such a survey. This is called "Student Survey on Teacher-Student Relationships." It is included at the end of this book as Appendix J on page 288. Pay attention to your students' reflections, and find ways to address the concerns and suggestions they provide. Let them know you have listened to them and are responding to their opinions and experiences.

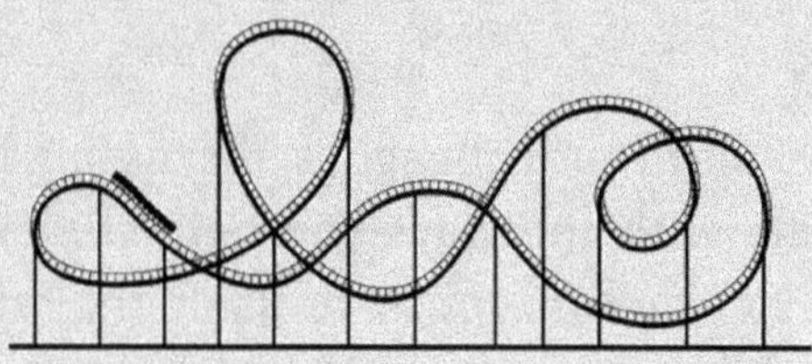

My middle school has an abundance of incredible educators that make all the difference in not just my life, but in thousands of other students.

Many students are very thankful for these opportunities that our parents have given us, but I don't believe that the incredible teachers get as much recognition as they could. All of the teachers here deserve to be recognized because they help all of the middle school students so much through the very aspect of day-to-day school life.

Being a middle schooler can be like riding a roller coaster—blindfolded.

You don't know what's going to happen, and you can't predict the twists and turns that could happen. However, teachers do an incredible job of keeping everyone less stressed. Truthfully, a lot happens in middle school. Parents divorce, puberty happens, letter grades come into play, and friendships change.

Teachers, though, stay by a student's side the entire year, making sure that student has someone in their corner at all times. They make navigating the rapids of middle school so much easier than it could be.

— Madison, Grade 8

Chapter 5

Believe in Students

You can be the person who turns things around for students and liberates their learning path. It usually takes just one person—a person whom students will never forget.

— Jo Boaler

Sometimes a person will defy all expectations by graduating from high school or college in the face of adverse life circumstances or after turning around a seemingly hopeless trajectory of scholastic failure. When you ask these people, "What happened that enabled you to do this?" often their response will begin with, "There was this teacher . . ."

Few educators get through teacher training without reading the landmark book *Pygmalion in the Classroom: Teacher Expectation and Pupils' Intellectual Development,* which detailed Robert Rosenthal and Lenore Jacobson's research study on how teacher expectations influence student performance.[1] The two researchers administered tests of intelligence and ability to students across six grades and gave each teacher a list of students in their classroom who, according to the test results, had great potential for academic growth. Unbeknownst to the teachers, however, the students ostensibly identified as having the greatest potential were in fact chosen at random. Their inclusion on the lists had nothing to do with their abilities reflected on the tests. At the end of the year, the researchers retested the students and found that those who had been identified to teachers as "ready to bloom" showed greater gains than those not identified as such.

The results of Rosenthal and Jacobson's experiments have been used to demonstrate the power of a "self-fulfilling prophecy" (also known as "the Pygmalion effect"): that students achieve as much—or as little—as their teachers expect of them.

In a more recent study, teachers gave hundreds of adolescent students in their English classes helpful, specific feedback to written essays. On half of the papers, an extra sentence was added to the end of the feedback. The teachers did not know which students' papers had the sentence. Even a year later, students who received that sentence still had higher grades. (There were no other differences between the two groups of students.) That one sentence was: "I am giving you this feedback because I believe in you."[2]

Education researcher John Hattie's landmark research on effect size (on various influences related to learning outcomes) strongly supports the power and impact of believing in students. Hattie found that average effect size of the examined influences was 0.40, "a marker that represented a year's growth per year of schooling for a student. Anything above 0.40 would have a greater positive effect on student learning."[3] His findings also show that any influence with an effect size of 0.70 or higher has "potential to considerably accelerate student achievement."[4] Of the more than 250 influences on student achievement documented, only seven of them have an effect size greater than 1.0 (which would predict two and a half years of growth when implemented effectively). Two of those influences with an effect size greater than 1.0 are collective teacher efficacy at 1.57 (the collective belief of teachers that they have the expertise to be able to positively impact students' learning) and teacher estimates of achievement at 1.29 (the teacher's belief about the level a student is able to achieve based on past experiences

Students achieve as much—or as little—as their teachers expect of them.

and teacher observation).[5] In essence, teachers' sincere and collective belief that they can help students succeed, as well as their belief about what students are capable of achieving, can have lasting impacts on student achievement of three years or more.

Such studies, along with the experiences of thousands of educators, attest to a powerful phenomenon: The beliefs that teachers hold about students—combined with the words, nonverbal messages, and actions through which they communicate those beliefs—have powerful, long-lasting effects.

This may seem obvious—that we should believe in our students. But if any of us look closely, we'd likely have to admit that we often **do** have preconceptions about students. Some seem to constantly struggle, lag in engagement, or just be stuck in "not getting it." Others appear more motivated, work harder, and learn faster. It's hard to look past students' behaviors, backgrounds, or attitudes and see them all as having equal chances of achieving. But because the messages we convey about individual students' possibilities for success make such a difference, we **must** pay close attention to our assumptions. Each adult in the school must do everything possible to show belief in **every** student.

GIVING STUDENTS THE GIFT OF YOUR BELIEF

The first of AMLE's 18 characteristics of successful middle schools is: "Educators respect and value young adolescents."[6] What better way to demonstrate this than by showing your students that you believe in them? Believing in every one of your students is one of the greatest gifts you can give. Let's look at what this means and why it matters.

Believing in students means understanding and acting as if every student has the capability to achieve and grow in all aspects of *belonging* and *becoming.* The speed with which someone "gets" a concept, skill, or process is **not** indicative of the individual's ability or potential.

There are many well-documented reasons for differences in performance (reasons that have nothing to do with inborn ability): Brains mature at different speeds; some students have had repeated experiences of failure or negative messages; some may not have had nurturing, stimulating pre-school environments; some have lives outside school that inhibit their best performances; some have deep anxieties about social situations or peer relationships. When you believe in students, you don't equate performance with potential. Instead, you trust that the possibilities for high performance in academic and personal development are there for all students.

Take some time to go back and look at the lists you made for *belonging* and *becoming* as a task at the end of Chapter 1 (or review Chapter 1). Look carefully at each item on your lists or in the chapter while considering the concept of teacher belief in all students. Think about how letting students know you believe in them (or allowing students to feel that you don't believe in them) would affect each factor.

When you believe in students, you don't equate performance with potential.

In simple terms, the strongest effect of believing in students is this: Your belief helps students believe in themselves. In more technical terms, it increases their *self-efficacy* (i.e., the belief that they are capable of achieving goals and meeting expectations). John Hattie's research (mentioned earlier) also finds that student self-efficacy has an effect size of 0.71, indicating that students believing in themselves has the "potential to considerably accelerate student achievement."[7] This self-belief leads to outcomes such as the following—**all** of which build students' sense of *belonging* and skills and progress in *becoming*:

- Building intrinsic motivation
- Developing performance criteria that students use to reflect on their work
- Understanding that, as individuals, they matter
- Strengthening courage to take risks, to push beyond what they thought they could do
- Boosting their confidence
- Increasing the quality of student–teacher relationships
- Positively enhancing peer relationships

- Helping them trust themselves more
- Approaching challenging tasks with reduced anxiety
- Decreasing anxieties about their abilities
- Elevating empowerment—helping them feel more competent and independent
- Igniting creativity
- Increasing students' belief in (and thus, regard for) one another
- Inspiring them to be persistent
- Setting higher expectations for their next performance
- Increasing resilience
- Building passion, energy, and fun in learning

Students' beliefs about themselves develop through their social interactions, and their social interactions with—and assessments of—peers mirror their teachers' beliefs and preferences.[8] The impact of your belief in students ripples out far beyond boosting their belief in themselves: It helps them see one another's worth and potential, and as they believe more in one another, the *belonging* and *becoming* benefits increase.

How do you let students know that you believe in them? Not just by telling them!

How do you let students know that you believe in them? Not just by telling them! Of course, encouraging words will be part of your ongoing messages to students. But your actions must **show** that you believe in them. All of us **want** to believe in students, and most of us feel that we **do** believe in students. But how often do we review last week's unit test and wonder in amazement at why so many students did poorly—and then place the blame on the students for their lack of preparation?

Students have built-in fraud detectors. They will know if you are faking belief. (And by the way, the benefits of believing in students manifest only when you actually **do** believe.) You demonstrate that you believe in students when you:

- Set high expectations while teaching specific skills and giving clear guidance and support for meeting them.
- Offer them lots of techniques and tools for succeeding at specific personal and academic tasks.
- Support, coach, and scaffold to help students succeed in academic and personal growth.
- Stay with them every step of the way as they tackle obstacles and pursue goals.
- Expect that they will achieve in different ways and on different timelines.
- Do not expect any students to fail—but when they do, help them recover.
- Use the word "yet," as in "I know this is hard because you haven't learned how to do it 'yet.' Let's try it again in a different way."
- Minimize competition among peers; help students see that they're competing with themselves.
- Encourage students not to impose needless limitations on themselves (e.g., assuming that they can't do, learn, or change something).
- Encourage students to develop a growth mindset, not a fixed one.
- Give positive, specific feedback as encouragement—not as judgment.
- Let students know you believe that they **can** do an assignment or pass a certain test.
- Give frequent messages to students' parents or caregivers that show you recognize the students' skills, efforts, talents, and progress—and that you believe they can achieve.
- Refuse to take part in conversations that complain about, label, or predict failure from individual students. (Yes, this means not whining about students in the teacher's lounge.)
- Model persistence and academic tenacity. Share examples or let students see you try something that is challenging for yourself. Let the students teach you something (such as a new technical skill) and watch you push past your fears or awkwardness, working hard to master it. They can watch you believe in yourself!

- Share stories of your "difficulties" and how you overcame them or are overcoming them.
- Encourage students to share goals and self-belief with one another and to encourage one another to believe in themselves. When students see someone else struggle and succeed, it strengthens their belief that they can do it themselves. This is particularly true if they have similar characteristics (age, gender, ethnicity) or interests.

MAKING FIRST IMPRESSIONS

As students settle into their first class with you, let your belief in them be their first impression. During the opening day of school, begin solidifying the message that this is a classroom and a school where each one of your students **can** gain the skills of *belonging* and *becoming*. Let them know right away that this is a place with high expectations for knowledge and skills with many opportunities to grow academically and personally—and that you will be there to provide the support needed when learning gets difficult.

Reflect on your own days as a student. Perhaps your typical first day of the school year was like this: Come in. Find your seat. Do not talk. Copy your schedule. Listen to the rules. Hear the consequences for breaking the rules. Read the syllabus (always scintillating reading). Fill out an information sheet with every piece of contact information short of giving a DNA sample. (After all, a teacher has to get that correct phone number before a misbehaving student does something wrong and then gives them a fake phone number!) Bell rings. Repeat the same cycle five or six more times that day.

Do you remember what the dinner-table conversation was like after your first days of school? Did anyone have anything exciting, fun, engaging, or positive to share about what happened? Or did you spend most of the evening hounding your parents or caregivers to sign a bunch of paperwork that was due the next day to rescue you from lunch detention? If you are a parent or caregiver now, is the cycle still the same? (Except that you are now the one being hounded to fill out all of that paperwork, read the handbook, and sign multiple pages of legalese you don't really read.)

Things have probably changed since you were in school. Today, most schedules, parent or caregiver contact information, forms to read, and other details are completed digitally, ahead of time and online. But is the most important task in your school still making sure that students know and follow the rules? If so, you will probably spend the first day of school talking to students about procedures, guidelines, rules, and consequences. This approach does not create a warm, inviting, or stimulating first impression—and it definitely doesn't give your students the impression that you believe in their capabilities to *become* or that they truly *belong* in your classroom.

But if the most important aspects of your school and classroom are *belonging* and *becoming*, then break the pattern! Make your first impression as someone who is focused on believing that students can learn (this includes personal as well as academic learning) and promising that you will help them all learn. Don't start your relationships with students by going over rules or procedures, and don't threaten consequences and punishment for failure to follow said rules and procedures. Let's face it—most students do the right thing most of the time, so let's treat them as if this is what we expect, rather than as if we expect them to step out of line or fail at any moment.

On top of making a bad first impression, this approach often backfires in other ways. For the student who is prone to disregard guidelines, going over the rules (such as "Don't be tardy to class" or "Don't skip class") simply makes the student think, "So, a bunch of people must be tardy or skip class, or the teacher wouldn't be going over this in such detail. I'm glad it's not just me. I'll skip class when I feel like it."

For the student who has considered skipping class—but hasn't, for fear of possible consequences, giving the specific detailed consequences for each broken rule may incline them to suspect that the consequences aren't really that bad. That student might think, "Hey, it's only one day of in-school suspension for skipping class? Cool! I'm in!"

Then there are the students who would never dream of breaking the rules. They might think back to a time last year when they were slightly late because they were sick or because a parent had a flat tire on the way to school—and they feel so terrible that they write you letters of apology all these months later. By going over rules and consequences, you've only made it more comfortable for misbehaving students to misbehave—and more uncomfortable for students who are already doing the right thing. For much more on this idea, see Todd Whitaker's book *What Great Teachers Do Differently*.

Instead of the usual going-over-the-rules-and-procedures approach, make the first day of school an 'A' Day for you and your students. (We thank our colleague Bill Bond, a former principal, for this idea.) Right out of the gate, teach your most engaging, thought-provoking, student-involved lesson of the year. Imagine a first day of school with 90 eighth graders outside learning about velocity by flying paper airplanes they just made in class, or getting first-hand experience of the concept of gravity when they float helium balloons, or understanding math by playing a game of cards with their friends (in groups), or dissecting a rat, or measuring shadows to learn the heights of the schoolyard trees, or exploring social studies concepts with a round-robin cooperative learning structure in a big circle outside on the grass. (For an explanation of this learning structure, consult the article by Gavin Clowes, "The Essential 5: A Starting Point for Kagan Cooperative Learning," found at www.KaganOnline.com.)

In addition to getting them up, moving, and doing, make sure students leave that first class feeling believed in, trusted, and capable. Your expectations as a teacher set the stage for the level of belief they feel. So ignore the labels you may have heard from others. Youki Tereda, *Edutopia* editor, advises teachers: "The first day of school, give every student a chance to start with a clean slate. It's a crucial step in establishing and repairing relationships" that may have been rough for students in the past.[9] Then, include strategies that invite them to work together, gain competence, use critical thinking skills, make independent or group decisions, create something, express their own opinions or reflections, receive positive feedback, and have fun. Now *that* is fodder for great dinner-table conversations! 'A' Day lets students see the very best **you** have to offer on the first day of school. It also lets them see the best **they** have to offer as students. You've let them know that you trust them to learn. You've let them know that they'll be learning from experiences that are lively and engaging and that this is what they can expect all year. Students will leave your class with a sense of anticipation; they'll be eager to return.

SOLIDIFYING FIRST IMPRESSIONS INTO LASTING IMPRESSIONS

One middle school student described her early days of the school year this way: "Our teachers start out giving us trust, and it never goes away unless we break trust with them."[10] How great to begin the school year with the model and promise of trust! Of course, this can't just be about the first day. The atmosphere, energy, dynamic learning, and belief you set on day one need to become the status quo for the whole year.

With a much more engaged audience after a great day of learning on day one, you can begin the business of collecting information and introducing guidelines during the days that follow. Involve students in decisions about classroom processes, guidelines for behavior, and consequences. Find ways for them to gain ownership in classroom procedures and expectations. Help them state guidelines in positive (rather than negative) terms. Regardless of when you choose to discuss codes of behavior, resist the urge to fall back into the "what-not-to-do" approach that leaves students feeling threatened, diminished, and untrusted.

The atmosphere, energy, dynamic learning, and belief you set on day one need to become the status quo for the whole year.

Over the first week or two, gradually review the school-wide expectations that have been established. Teachers can do this in individual classrooms, or they may host grade-level or team meetings. Approach this positively, making sure to send students the message that members of the school-wide community believe in them, expect the best of them, and do not expect them to make poor decisions. (On this last point, avoid emphasizing what happens if, or when, students do make bad decisions.) Student handbooks and word of mouth will take care of that! Here are some thoughts for a positive approach to the topic of school-wide guidelines:

Share the mission and commitment at the heart of the school. Sometimes a school's foundational beliefs, missions, and goals are shared only with adults. But young adolescent students are capable of interacting with this kind of information, and they deserve to know what's behind the structure, programs, and practices of their school. Also give them an overview of teachers' preparation, degrees, and certifications. Introduce the concept of professional development—to let them know about the continued commitment to learning and improvement of skills and programs. (Some students don't realize that teachers hold teaching credentials and may even continue "going to school" to learn more.)

Let students teach some of the specifics of school rules. For example, students can demonstrate the school dress code. Instead of you telling students what they can't wear, have them put on a fashion show to exhibit appropriate dress. (They love this, by the way.) They'll also enjoy bringing inappropriately dressed or misbehaving staff-member "models" before a panel of student "judges." They could even use adult models for makeovers, showing them how to do a better job of dressing. (This works for other elements of school procedures as well.) Give a group of students responsibility for planning a grade-level or school-wide assembly to share protocols and rules. They will be much more creative than adults, and the audience will pay much closer attention when their peers are running the show.

Give credibility to school-wide procedures. Let students in on the "why" of school-wide practices. Explain the reasons for things such as the school's grading scale, mastery-based assessment model, final exam policy, discipline policy, dress code, required standardized assessments, or grade promotion requirements. This shows students that you believe they are mature and smart enough to understand the needs and reasons for a school-wide approach. In doing so, these procedures become important parts of their learning, rather than things "done to them for no good reason." When students see the purposes and understand that all teachers will consistently use these approaches, they might just tone down their complaints and give a little more support to their teachers—who are themselves required to implement the requirements.

Emphasize the value of good decisions. Most schools have some sort of school-wide expectations (along with affirmations) for making wise choices. The bottom line is that we want students to make good decisions—not because they are afraid of getting in trouble if they don't and not because they want to please adults—but because they recognize that such decisions are healthy for them as individuals and for the school community. Focus on the intrinsic rewards of decisions that are helpful, respectful, safe, and growth-producing for self and others. Students' sense of *belonging* is bolstered when they realize that the wise choices they make for themselves also benefit the others in their class and school. In short, expect the best of students. Expect good decisions, not foolish ones, and give plenty of attention to the positive outcomes of "smart" decisions. If your school has a positive behavior support model, review the expectations (emphasis on what is expected instead of what is forbidden), and then review how students will be supported and recognized for good decisions.

Recognize and build students' power in the school. Students may not see themselves as powerful in the school. Help them realize the many ways they make a difference to the spirit, well-being, and success of others in the school community. Let them know how they can affirm others (including adults) and contribute to practices that help peers *belong* and meet their own goals (*become*). Review the ways they can develop and use leadership skills (see more on this in Chapter 8), be involved in school clubs, organizations, sports, arts, and activities, and take part in solving problems and making decisions that affect situations beyond themselves. Enthusiastically communicate the benefits of getting involved in school activities outside the classroom.

Share school-wide successes. We often share information about school-wide accomplishments with staff and families, but students need this information, too. Describe the various school improvement efforts underway in the school. Tell them about results of school improvement efforts, and let them in on the future goals for improvement. Share your school's successes in academics, athletics, activities, arts, and community service. Let students know how great their school is! Consider creating a display to highlight the accomplishments of former students (whether in high school, college, the military, or the workforce) with news articles, letters, photos, etc.

PROMOTING AN OPTIMISTIC OUTLOOK

Optimism—the tendency to focus on favorable characteristics and possibilities and to expect the best possible outcome—is at the heart of believing in students. In an atmosphere of optimism, students will be more likely to trust that you believe in them. In addition, their belief in themselves, belief in their peers, sense of *belonging*—and real hope for *becoming* what they want to be—can **all** flourish.

Optimism is deeper and more active than just thinking positive thoughts or having generally good feelings about life. According to Martin Seligman, a clinical researcher who has studied optimism and pessimism for decades, every individual has an "explanatory style" or a way of explaining to themselves why things happen. According to his findings, optimists see causes of bad events as temporary and causes of good events as permanent. They can contain a bad event to a particular situation (seeing it as temporary) but believe good events to be broader. Optimists take credit for good outcomes and ascribe bad outcomes to external forces or chance; they do not see them as indications that they are undeserving or worthless.[11]

Seligman also found that children's explanatory styles is influenced by the style of their caretakers (they mimic those adults most prominent in their lives) and by the kind of criticism they get from those adults: "You'll never be able to learn this" versus "You can get this if you practice more."[12] To be sure, both of these influences have implications for teachers!

Optimism has been associated with benefits such as those below—all of which we can recognize as characteristics that will help satisfy our students' needs for *belonging* and *becoming*:[13]

- Better relationships
- Less self-blaming, depression, and helplessness
- Less likelihood of giving up on challenges
- Greater ability to accept disappointments along with successes
- More hopefulness

- Increased confidence
- Better physical health
- Improved coping skills
- Greater persistence
- Increased productivity
- More feeling of control over one's life

We can promote optimism in many ways within our classrooms and throughout the school community. All of the previous chapters' suggestions and strategies (as well as those in the chapters to follow) contribute to an optimistic outlook. We can share our passion and enthusiasm for our jobs and for our students. We can help students let go of past failures and think about what more they can do today and in the future. We can show them how to replace negative self-talk ("I can't," "This is too hard," "I give up," "I'm not good at this," or "I'll just mess up") with hopeful self-talk ("I couldn't last time but maybe this time," "I'll give it another try," "I'll practice more," or "Maybe today this will work"). We can help students plan a course of action to tackle a challenge or problem, and we can stick with them to help them stay focused on it. We can enlist our colleagues in consistently setting powerful examples of optimism both inside and outside the classroom. Most profoundly, we can **be** hopeful for each of our students.

Top 8 Ways to Spread Optimism

- Begin the daily all-school announcements with an optimistic statement.
- Look for and reinforce examples of positivity, tenacity, and hope.
- Create a place and process for students to leave positive notes for one another.
- Celebrate persistence and hope as often as you celebrate proficiency.
- Expose students to models of adults and youths in history who showed optimism.
- Invite students to suggest ways to turn pessimistic attitudes into optimistic attitudes.
- Refuse to repeat pessimistic statements or join in pessimistic conversations.

In the days that followed a national tragedy, I (Laurie) wanted to take some steps in our middle school to infuse some optimism that might be a small step toward lifting the atmosphere and spirits in our school. I showed a YouTube video to the staff, "Honk If You Love Someone," featuring a young man beside a street holding positive signs for people to see as they drove past. Some of the staff thought it was a bit "cheesy," and thanks to our long-time open relationship, they felt comfortable teasing me about it.

The following day, on my morning walk through the building, I heard a minor commotion in a team hallway. Two of the teachers were holding up signs—clearly an attempt to poke fun at my video idea. One read "SMILE," and the other read "IT'S A GREAT DAY TO BE A WILDCAT." But their snarky plan backfired. Their students got a kick out of the signs, so the next day, the teachers held a new sign: "WE BELIEVE IN YOU!" Each day after that, a new sign appeared. By the time state tests rolled around, the signs had daily themes. On the day of the science test, the sign read "MAY THE FORCE BE WITH YOU." On the day of the eighth-grade dance, it was "DON'T JUST STAND THERE. BUST A MOVE."

What began as an inside joke among teachers became something that students looked forward to. They had fun predicting what might be coming next. Simple signs such as "YOU'RE AMAZING" helped develop relationships and gave students an energizing, upbeat start to each day. Even the teachers were positively affected. One of the teachers who started it all said, "Quite simply, I think students feel we care about them. I can honestly say on a personal level that often their reactions are responsible for me having a better day." Almost five months after daily sign-holding began, I rounded the corner of the eighth-grade hall on the eighth graders' last day of middle school, and I saw those two teachers holding a large sign that read: "I SEE A COUGAR COMING." It was a nod to their graduating students' soon-to-be high school mascot, and they weren't making fun at all; they meant it with all their heart.

Sometimes teachers also need support to stay optimistic. For help recharging your own optimism, we highly recommend the book *Deliberate Optimism: STILL Reclaiming the Joy in Education* by Debbie Silver and Jack Berckemeyer.

PROVIDING INSTRUCTIONAL SUPPORT

When we hear a story about a teacher "who made a difference" in the life of a student, that story generally involves more than friendship or encouragement. In most cases, the teacher gave time and support that helped the student grow, strive, and achieve daunting personal or academic goals (or both). All the models of effective schools we've shared include this same component: They set high expectations and help students develop the self-belief, skills, and persistence to reach them. John Hattie's research on conditions and factors that influence student achievement finds the effect size of high teacher expectations to be 0.43, which is higher than normal on a scale of positive achievement results. In addition, the influence of teachers knowing their students well and thus giving appropriate, personalized instruction and believing that the students can achieve (i.e., teacher estimates of achievement) has an effect size of 1.29, which indicates that this relationship with students is likely to have a superior, positive effect on student achievement.[14] Research on developing caring and trusting relationships, showing belief in students and building a connected community also includes that same component (i.e., high expectations paired with the necessary resources and support to meet them) as a factor. This is one of the strongest proofs that a teacher believes in a student: that the teacher (or whole "village") will help **students** to take charge of their own actions to bring about the results they want.

According to psychologist and self-efficacy researcher Albert Bandura, the experience of mastery is the most critical influence on self-efficacy. Another strong influence is direct encouragement from a trusted person. Students concretely experience a teacher's belief when that teacher gives specific techniques that enable them to reach a goal.[15]

Richard Curwin—teacher, educational consultant, and author of *Discipline with Dignity*—suggests the following ways of showing your belief in students. Notably, they all relate to ways educators can adapt their instruction to enhance students' chances of achieving personal and academic goals. He says:

1. "Stop using rewards." Extrinsic rewards are the opposite of believing they can do it without being "paid."
2. "Encourage effort more than achievement." Doing one's best is one thing every student **can** do.
3. "Give second, third, and fourth chances." Mistakes help people learn. Help students practice to learn the skills they need.
4. "Don't say, 'You failed'—say, 'You haven't done it yet.'" Teach students that they **can** still do better.
5. "Increase opportunities to learn." The more chances they have to learn, the more they are likely to learn.[16]

Curwin also notes that children who need additional and more enriching learning opportunities (or even recess) are often those who lose those opportunities (e.g., due to behavior management issues or unfinished work).[17]

Gone are the days when we focused solely on the quality of a teacher's presentations; the focus now is on students' learning. If a student is not learning, the finely honed craft of teaching hardly matters. We've enjoyed a cartoon that shows two boys standing near a dog while one boy tells the other, "I taught Hairy to whistle." The other boy replies that he doesn't hear Hairy whistling. The first boy responds, "I said I taught him. I didn't say he learned it!" How many times have we as teachers been guilty of believing we taught something, regardless of whether the students learned it?

Just as middle level students are at varying stages physically, the same is true for their cognitive development (which affects self-regulation as well as academic skills). Teachers must be willing to adapt instructional strategies to fit the individual student's cognitive development. Giving students the appropriate instructional support tells them: "I believe in you. The way I taught the lesson the first time may not have worked for you, but that does not mean you cannot learn it. Let me try another way to help you understand." Teachers must become accomplished at scaffolding, teaming and co-teaching, using formative assessment to inform their instruction, designing cooperative learning experiences, re-teaching, adapting lessons to different modalities, incorporating technology, or doing whatever else it takes to help a student learn. Doing something one way, one time, is no longer enough. As students see teachers make repeated and varied attempts to help students learn, they will accept that the teacher believes in them. They'll begin to make progress and believe in themselves. (See more about instructional support in Chapter 6.)

Sadly, belief in oneself is often underrated in schools—or at least, nurturing self-belief is rarely a high priority. As we've come to understand that the mission of a middle school is entwined with helping students *belong* and *become*, we've become more zealous about the importance of students believing in themselves—because once students believe in themselves, the possibilities for what they can be or *become* are limitless. In giving our students the gift of belief, we find Goethe's maxim a good reminder: "Treat people as if they were what they ought to be and you help them *become* what they are capable of *becoming*."[18] This isn't meant to sound easy. It's hard work—harder than many people outside the educational setting realize (think politicians)—but ultimately, it is our mission to accomplish. We're up to it!

If a student is not learning, the finely honed craft of teaching hardly matters.

PUTTING IT INTO PRACTICE

As an individual, team, small group, or entire staff, use these activities to spark discussions, reflect on your current practices or situations, listen to others, or set goals.

1. Review the bulleted list at the end of the "Giving Students the Gift of Your Belief" section on pages 95-99. Which two or three items do you believe you practice on a regular basis? What evidence supports that? Which two or three items have you not thought about or not tried to implement? Create an action plan to put those into action. This would be a good exercise to discuss with a colleague or team; commit to holding one another accountable for building your repertoires of practices for "believing in students."

2. Ask each teacher to mentally review the first day of the school year, noting the activities and the amount of time spent on each task (e.g., rules? paperwork? class syllabus? instruction? active student participation?). Ask them to reflect upon the main purpose of the class and note how much time was spent on that purpose on the first day. After completing this task, move to small groups, and then to a large group, to discuss the primary purpose of classes and how that purpose is reflected in your school.

3. Survey students. Find ways to gather students' (anonymous) feedback about the school climate, community, and connectedness. Take their feedback seriously, and use it to inform your next steps.

4. Have a small group of teachers walk through the school to look and listen for specific examples of how the school promotes an optimistic outlook among both students and teachers. Share the results with the entire staff. Then discuss strengths and opportunities for improvement in this area.

5. Examine how your school provides instructional support for struggling students. How many different instructional strategies do you use on a regular basis? What opportunities are there for professional learning to help teachers build repertoires of methods for helping struggling students? If the data are available, examine how many failing grades or less-than-proficient marks were given during the last grading period. Discuss strengths and opportunities for improvement in this area.

In school, we have found a home and have been both accepted and scorned for our cultural backgrounds. Our three years have combined to one giant learning experience—an awakening to the vast world that lies ahead. From the moment we set foot on Bulldog territory, we gained a new sense of freedom. Over these past three years, we students have made rules and set standards that go beyond the classroom and the parent handbook. We have strived to earn respect and identity, and through this, our consciousness has been raised to yet another level. Many students begin to find themselves in middle school. However, we also come to have a better understanding of those around us.

— Calvin, Paty, Alexia, and America, Grade 8

Chapter 6

Support Academic Success and Personal Development

Education, particularly in a democracy, has to involve heart as well as head, attitude as well as information, spirit as well as scholarship, and conscience as well as competence.

— John H. Lounsbury

"Doing well in school" used to mean mastering content and skills—and getting good grades. In an age when we understand that we're teaching **students**, not just subject matter, we recognize that "doing well in school" is far more complex (and interesting)! Nowhere do *belonging* and *becoming* come together quite as powerfully for young adolescents as when they step into the world of academic learning. Our middle level students need to *belong* in order to *become* (in the sense of academic growth and accomplishment); in turn, their successes at *becoming* deepen the feelings and skills of *belonging.*

When we use the terms *academic success* and *personal development*, we're speaking of growth and learning that comprise the many aspects of both *belonging* and *becoming*. In a school setting, academic growth and personal growth are intricately intertwined with one another. It is nearly impossible (and not at all a good idea!)

to discuss the details of one without including those of the other. Personal growth (in such areas as positive relationships, self-awareness, social awareness, self-regulation, decision-making, autonomy, personal responsibility, personal satisfaction, and self-belief) are absolutely needed for and contribute to the academic learning process. And when students experience what it feels like to take on an academic challenge, work hard to master it, and learn something relevant and exciting—personal development skills get a boost.

Supporting young adolescents' academic and personal development jointly has **always** been a vital piece of the middle level concept. One of AMLE's 18 characteristics of successful middle schools is that "every student's academic and personal development is guided by an adult advocate"[1] (See Figure 3.1 on page 46). So it's imperative for all adults in middle schools to intentionally seek to support this joint development. Early in the middle school movement, William Alexander, who coined the term "middle school," called for the development of schools for young adolescents that promoted academic achievement **by being more responsive to the personal needs of the age group**.[2] In the shift to the middle level concept, schools put more focus on students' social and emotional development than had been the practice in junior high schools. As a result, middle schools gained a reputation of being "soft" on academic rigor. The fact is that, from the beginning, the middle level concept has advocated for high expectations **and** academic growth—to be accomplished in a supportive environment that employs beliefs, knowledge, and strategies appropriate for this age level.

Supporting young adolescents' academic and personal development jointly has always been a vital piece of the middle level concept.

The concept sounds so obvious: Of course we need to attend to the whole student! Of course personal development is inseparable from academic growth! But doing it is not so simple, particularly at the middle level. In her article "10 Things Middle Schoolers Should Know," author and speaker Kari Kampakis notes,

"It's rare to hear anyone say they ***loved*** middle school. Even people with positive memories don't tout the time as the best years of their lives. Simply put, it's an awkward season. It's a time of constant changes, social shake-ups, swinging emotions, and intense pressures." Kampakis goes on: "This age group is hungry for comfort and reassurance. I hear it in their voices and see it in their eyes whenever I speak to a group, a look of searching and longing to hear something—*anything*—to help them make sense of things."[3]

The change and awkwardness of this "season" make it all the more critical that middle level educators understand the varied characteristics of the age group, the extreme differences in development, and the need and ways to teach personal and academic matters together. As teachers, we help students learn to break difficult tasks down into doable chunks. We want to follow this same tactic for our readers. So we'll suggest manageable ways to accomplish the long-term goal of nurturing academic achievement in combination with personal growth. In this chapter, we'll summarize what we find are best practices and attitudes to help students grow and thrive in the many aspects of *becoming* as related to their academic-personal development. In addition, we'll focus a bit more closely on practices that help you capitalize on students' strengths and interests, offer students opportunities to explore, contribute to the development of growth mindsets (in yourself and in students), help to cultivate students' resilience, and give students second (or more) chances to succeed.

BUILDING AND BOLSTERING THE UNDERPINNINGS

Many elements of *becoming* fall into such categories as intrinsic motivation, engagement in learning, self-determination, self-efficacy, executive function, self-regulation, mindset, tenacity, personal responsibility, academic competence, and social and emotional competence. As is most likely true for you, we instinctively know that all of these are underpinnings of students' academic and personal growth. We've examined research, recalled our experiences, and listened to the experiences of many other educators—trying to understand what it is that helps students develop each of these elements in healthy, positive ways. **We're**

astounded (although not surprised) at the commonalities among the qualities, attitudes, and skills that constitute these elements—and at the practices that foster them. We can't help but notice how often growth (or lack of growth) in each of these areas demonstrably affects the others. We can't help but notice how often *belonging* or *relatedness* is found by researchers to be a major influence on positive development in elements one might ordinarily put into a *becoming* category.

We believe that these commonalities lead to practical guidelines for schools and teachers to do two things: (1) celebrate and continue what they are already doing to enhance academic and personal growth, and (2) learn, incorporate, and polish what they could do better.

To reduce repetition that would result from addressing different aspects of academic or personal development, we'll share practices that, when combined, strengthen the underpinnings and desired outcomes of both academic and personal education. Practices that we've described in the previous chapters (and in the chapters that follow) should certainly be added to these.

The Best Chances for Success

The list below identifies some of the most-often stated components or conditions found to increase young adolescent students' academic and personal development. Schools striving for the greatest possible effectiveness will do well to include them all in their vision and practice. (You'll see threads of the essential attributes that AMLE affirms as "musts" for an education of middle school students—with such descriptors as *responsive, challenging, empowering, equitable,* and *engaging.*)[4] Young adolescents are most likely to succeed in settings with:

- High expectations, stated clearly.
- Support to reach the expectations.
- Equity in treatment of all students—along with equity in the belief that all students are capable of learning.
- Emphasis on goals of learning over goals of grades or performance.
- Guidance for improving skills of executive functioning.

- Focus on students learning to set and attain goals.
- Expectations and support for students taking responsibility for their own learning.
- Highly effective, varied, and differentiated teaching and learning strategies.
- Teaching that is responsive to students' developmental characteristics and needs.
- Learning experiences that are personalized and relevant to students' interests and everyday lives.
- Learning experiences that engage students in active, participatory learning.
- Learning experiences that make use of student interests and strengths.
- Teaching of skills and behaviors for managing digital information and influences.
- Academic and personal challenge.
- Meaningful experiences of competence.
- Multiple opportunities for students to explore.
- Multiple opportunities for students to contribute positively to their classes, peers, neighborhoods, community, and the wider world.
- Plenty of collaborative learning experiences.
- Precise, frequent, prompt, and supportive feedback.
- Opportunities for re-teaching and re-doing.
- Encouragement of student autonomy and empowerment.
- Trusting, caring, respectful relationships.
- Programs and practices that foster school relatedness and *belonging*.
- A sense of student ownership of the school, class, and their learning.
- Many opportunities for choice.
- Many opportunities for students to have a say in decisions and processes.
- Serious attention to social and emotional skills along with social and emotional support.

- Value and respect for young adolescents.[5]
- Instruction that "fosters learning that is active, purposeful, and democratic."[6]
- Curriculum that is "challenging, exploratory, integrative, and diverse."[7]
- Access to "comprehensive counseling and support services" tailored to meet students' needs.[8]

Teaching Practices

The conditions that give our students the best chances for academic and personal growth lead to practices such as those that follow. Each of these practices includes skills and outcomes in many aspects of *belonging* and *becoming*.

Autonomy

Autonomy is a major component of building competence, self-determination, self-efficacy, motivation, academic engagement, and psychological well-being.[9] Students feel more connected to learning when they have control over some of its elements. Here, we'll define *autonomy* in the words of researchers Teresita Bernal-Romero, Miguel Melendro, Angel De-Juanas, and Martin Goyettee as "the capacities for self-organization, context analysis, critical thinking, forming relationships with others, and socio-political engagement."[10] These researchers have found that when students perceive their own autonomy to be allowed and even encouraged during the first few weeks of a class, their engagement is increased throughout the duration of the course or class (as opposed to the typical decline in engagement when no support for autonomy is perceived).[11]

Don't do for students what they can do for themselves.

Foster autonomy for young adolescent students in as many (appropriate) ways as possible. Give them plenty of chances to take initiative in classroom procedures and learning experiences. Ask them questions and give them guidance that will help them solve problems on their own. Increase their chances for exercising choice and having a voice in their learning. Don't do for students what they can do for themselves. Show that you believe they **can** successfully exercise control over aspects of their learning. Supporting autonomy for students includes relinquishing some teacher control and using non-controlling language.

Relevance

Learning experiences should be meaningful—related to students' daily lives; to the important questions, concerns, and experiences they have and witness; and to the issues and realities of their society and the wider world in which they live. This means that teachers must be acutely aware of the daily lives of students and the many sources of messages and influences that impact their thinking on a daily basis—including such things as their friends, families, cultures, peers of the same or opposite sex, the internet, social media, gaming, movies, music, and television.

Help students understand **why** any particular assignment, activity, or fact is important—that is, how it relates to the bigger picture. Always relate facts and ideas back to the main standard, concept, or skill being taught. Include topics and questions on their interests outside of school. Connect learning to their real lives and real-world situations: pop culture, current events, situations in their school and community, current fads, popular music, social media, video games, and relationships, as well as social, school, and global issues. Keep up on the technology and communications methods that are part of their young adolescent world; use these as tools for learning. But remember, this arena is changing so rapidly that what was "in" one week may have been discarded by the next.

Part of the impetus for getting to know students as a group and individuals (Chapters 2 and 4) is so that you can relate their academic experiences to them personally. As a part of any learning experience, continuously ask students the questions: "Why does this matter?" "So what?—what difference does this make?" and "How does this affect you?" Make a practice of having students stop in the middle and also at the end of a learning experience to reflect orally–or in writing–on how the skills or concepts relate to their lives.

Challenge

Humans learn best when they are challenged. Give students tasks and experiences slightly above their ability level—so they need to stretch. Things that are too easy bore them, and things that are too hard frustrate them. If they need help, provide the strategies, tools, and scaffolding to help them meet the challenge; meeting moderately difficult challenges increases a student's sense of competence and self-belief.[12] John Hattie, who has done in-depth research on influences affecting student achievement, found that boredom has a profound negative effect on student achievement. (The effect size for boredom is -0.46.)[13] The more a student realizes "I can do this—even if it was a stretch!" the more the student will be willing to take on the next challenge.

Clear Expectations

It isn't fair to hold students to high expectations if they don't know what those expectations are. Be clear about what you're looking for—in terms of behavior, relationships, following procedures, and outcomes for any learning activity. In his research, John Hattie (mentioned above) found teacher clarity to be high on the list of practices with the strongest positive effects on student achievement (with an effect size of 0.75).[14] "Teacher clarity" requires that teachers be explicit and clear about the reasons, importance, and expectations for learning activities as well as the criteria for success. The "clear" teacher does not assume that students know the goals or criteria: Ideally, teachers are clear in their own minds about where their own teaching is going, and students are clear about what is required of them.[15] Give students criteria for what mastery looks like. (Rubrics are one way to do this.) Share (in writing) the state standard(s) covered in a lesson or activity. Lay out expectations in language students can understand. Have them summarize, articulate, and discuss the expectations. They're more likely to meet expectations when there's no mystery about where they are going!

Instructional Support

Along with high expectations must come the instruction, support, encouragement, and time necessary for students to meet them. Excuses such as "I have high expectations, but my students just don't meet them" are not allowed! Offer a range of paths and a variety of tools that can help them reach goals. Provide plenty of opportunities for them to succeed. Help students see what they already know about a topic or what skills they already possess to follow a process. Differentiate assignments to accommodate needs of individual students. Scaffold tasks so that a student can meet a learning goal one step (or chunk) at a time. Consider pre-teaching a concept to students who may struggle with the initial instruction. Encourage students to keep a journal of their accomplishments along the way. Be there to push them to do a little better than last time. But don't step in too quickly to rescue students; honor their autonomy and competence by letting them try it themselves first. When students stumble, help them see failure or roadblocks as things they can do something about.

Engaging Experiences

Here we might also use the terms *active learning* or *student-centered learning*. However you label the experiences, use learning strategies that get young adolescents involved physically, cognitively, behaviorally, and emotionally—**doing** instead of sitting and listening. With attention to their interests and their developmental needs (such as needs to find meaning, move, socialize, argue, experience novelty, connect things to visual images), include such approaches as inquiry-based activities, interviews, demonstrations, cooperative learning, problem-solving, investigations, role-playing, brainstorming, peers teaching one another, frequent breaks to summarize or comment on what's been learned so far, debates, excursions, analyzing facts and concepts, or applying a process or concept to another situation. Include creative thinking, critical thinking, art, movement, media, technology, music, discussion, and humor. Allow them to demonstrate their mastery of a concept in a method of their choosing. Have students draw on their previous learning and personal experiences to connect to the topic. Above all, within all learning and curricular areas, students must have encouragement and specific experiences designed to let them explore, figure things out, exercise their creativity, and try new things.

Learning over Performance

When students take part in an activity with a goal of learning and understanding (*mastery orientation*) instead of with the goal of getting a good grade, pleasing teachers or families, looking smart, or doing better than other students (*performance orientation*), they are more likely to be deeply involved in the experience. They are more likely to relate to and enjoy the learning. Students are also more likely to want to follow through on the activity and achieve the goal. Students must experience mastery! Doing so heightens their feelings of competence and belief in themselves (both are aspects of *becoming*) and their senses of *belonging*.[16] Students with a performance orientation may avoid challenges, feel helpless when the going gets tough, and give up easily—believing they don't have the ability to do the work. In contrast, when the goal is to learn (*mastery orientation*), students are more likely to take on new challenges and feel motivated to figure things out. You can encourage students' mastery orientations by reducing competition and comparisons between student

Students must experience mastery! Doing so heightens their feelings of competence and belief in themselves (both are aspects of *becoming*) and their senses of *belonging*.

accomplishments and by emphasizing individual progress and effort (and perhaps making sure that grades and other assessments are kept private). When students meet a learning goal, provide lots of tools and ways to reflect on and demonstrate what they can **now do** or what they **now know**. You can also help students understand that there are tasks and goals that can be absolutely mastered (like learning some square roots) but that many things cannot be entirely mastered (like knowing every fact possible about ancient Chinese history). However, there are degrees of mastery in every subject.[17] There are chunks of topics or concepts that can be mastered. We can set goals to broaden understanding, improve performance to a particular level, or complete a task. In his book *Drive*, author Daniel Pink says that mastery is "the desire to get better and better at something that matters."[18]

Goal Setting and Attainment

Achievement, motivation, self-efficacy, and self-regulation increase when students set and pursue goals that are meaningful and appropriately challenging. Teach students strategies for setting and attaining academic and behavioral goals. Then see that they have plenty of practice doing it. They need to learn to identify and set realistic, relevant, and rigorous goals. They need to be able to articulate their goals in specific terms and discuss how they will know when they reach them. Then give tools and training for each step toward goal attainment: Make a realistic plan for reaching the goal by identifying specific actions that will be needed for success, diagramming or otherwise outlining the plan, setting a timeline, breaking the long-term goal into short-term goals, and laying out specific approaches to accomplish for each part of the goal pursuit. Offer strategies for monitoring their progress and making needed adjustments to the plan if needed. Discuss potential obstacles that may interfere with their success as well as ideas for eliminating or circumventing the obstacles. Review progress, make needed adjustments on a regular basis, and help students find ways to celebrate when the goal has been accomplished.

Collaborative Learning

Embrace collaborative learning as one of the most powerful forces for academic and personal development. Plan frequent partner and group experiences, and teach strategies for making decisions, planning and carrying out projects, solving problems, carrying out investigations, asking and answering questions, and researching. In addition to giving a boost to learning, understanding, and applying content, group work also fosters student connections, communication, individual responsibility, group accountability, independence, and many skills of self-management.[19] Plus, it meets young adolescents' need for socialization. (The brain learns best in connection to other brains!) Take care to organize groups heterogeneously so students encounter a mix of abilities, social groupings, genders, personalities, and ethnicities. In most cases, assign students to groups yourself; when students choose groups, some feel left out (negatively impacting their *belonging*), and students don't get the benefits of true heterogeneous experiences.

Embrace collaborative learning as one of the most powerful forces for academic and personal development.

Time

Students need time to absorb the meanings and implications of an activity. They need time to discuss concepts and see where they might lead. Too often we rush on to the next topic or activity. Plan ahead to include time for students to reflect, ask questions, voice opinions, hear ideas from others, write notes, and make connections.

Feedback

All students need (and deserve) feedback to get a sense of how they are doing in working toward a goal. In addition, meaningful and respectful feedback empowers students and builds their confidence as learners.[20] The purpose of feedback is to strengthen skills or learn something. Feedback that is specific, timely, and meaningful increases learning; avoid feedback that gives generalized praise ("Great job," "Nice work," or 'A') or generalized criticism ("Try again," "Unclear," "Needs more development," or 'C+'). Praise their **effort** (with descriptions of specific actions) and their progress toward goals—not their ability or intelligence. Provide targeted, precise feedback that identifies how the student is doing in relationship to the goals and helps students know what action to take next. Feedback should be given soon after the task is completed (or during the process)—in time for the student to make changes while the material is still fresh. Try to give feedback in private and in a positive spirit. Teach students how to give helpful, kind feedback to one another as well. Train students in ways to reflect on their work and to design steps they can take based on their self-assessment.

Specific Skills to Teach

Students need planned, specific instruction dedicated to skills for "doing school"—skills that apply across all content areas. We've presented these in a checklist form so that you can identify those you already teach and those you wish to add to your classroom. Incorporate mini-lessons, round-table discussions, video clips, or seminars to teach skills needed for learning in any subject area. See Figures 6-1 and 6-2 on pages 128 and 130.

Figure 6-1 Skills for Academic Success

Already Do This (Date)	Will Add This (Date)	Some Specific Skills to Teach and Practice
		Practice academic self-assessment and self-reflection.
		Take an active role in planning own learning.
		Set and attain goals.
		Give and receive feedback.
		Reason from credible evidence.
		Find and use strategies to solve problems.
		Make reasoned decisions.
		Explore; try new things.
		Manage time and assignments.
		Organize homework tasks.
		Get academic help when needed.
		Think about and describe thought or work processes (metacognition).
		Summarize.
		Report results.
		Ask good questions.
		Communicate effectively (in many different settings, situations, and formats).
		Listen actively and respectfully.
		Participate effectively in discussions.
		Work productively and cooperatively in groups.
		Keep up with a discussion or conversation.
		Take notes.
		Conduct an inquiry.
		Plan complicated projects.
		Complete complicated projects or abstract problems.
		Monitor and assess own progress (charts, checklists, journals).
		Learn from experiences.
		Learn from others who model skills.
		Bounce back from failure.
		Practice behaviors that cultivate a growth mindset.
		Use mistakes as learning opportunities.
		Celebrate success.

Students also need direct instruction to learn skills for social-emotional health and behavior. This category of skills covers an extensive list of factors—all related to our goals of helping young adolescents in their processes of *belonging* and *becoming*. CASEL, the Collaborative for Academic, Social, and Emotional Learning, has identified five broad social and emotional competencies with the following descriptions:

1. **Self-awareness:** The ability to accurately recognize one's own emotions, thoughts, and values and how they influence behavior. The ability to accurately assess one's strengths and limitations, with a well-grounded sense of confidence, optimism, and a growth mindset.
2. **Self-management:** The ability to successfully regulate one's emotions, thoughts and behaviors in different situations—effectively managing stress, controlling impulses, and motivating oneself. The ability to set and work toward personal and academic goals.
3. **Social awareness:** The ability to take the perspectives of—and empathize with—others, including those from diverse backgrounds and cultures. The ability to understand social and ethical norms for behavior and recognize family, school, and community resources and supports.
4. **Relationship skills:** The ability to establish and maintain healthy and rewarding relationships with diverse individuals and groups. The ability to communicate clearly, listen well, cooperate with others, resist inappropriate social pressure, negotiate conflict constructively, and seek and offer help when needed.
5. **Responsible decision-making:** The ability to make constructive choices about personal behavior and social interactions based on ethical standards, safety concerns, and social norms. The realistic evaluation of consequences of various actions and a consideration of the well-being of oneself and others.[21]

From this description of social and emotional competencies, teachers can extrapolate lessons to be taught and skills to be reinforced. We would suggest that you teach mini-lessons involving role-play, group discussion, brainstorming, and lots of student input and experience-sharing to teach and practice skills such as these.

Figure 6-2 Social-Emotional Skills

Already Do This (Date)	Will Add This (Date)	Some Specific Skills to Teach and Practice
		Recognize and celebrate one's own strengths and talents.
		Identify one's own challenges.
		Identify one's own needs, interests, goals, dreams, preferences, values, hopes.
		Identify (name) emotions.
		Identify things that trigger different emotions.
		Identify behaviors that flow from your emotions when they arise.
		Learn strategies for handling and appropriately expressing emotions.
		Build self-confidence.
		Set and attain personal (non-academic) goals.
		Appreciate diversity.
		Empathize with others.
		Treat others respectfully.
		Demonstrate—to others and to the school—behaviors that build a feeling of belonging and that help others belong.
		Build and sustain relationships.
		Work with a team.
		Take responsibility for one's own actions.
		Examine one's own motivations.
		Understand the motivations of others.
		Identify stressors, symptoms of stress, and ways to manage normal daily stress.
		Learn and use emotional coping skills (in response to disappointment, confusion, worry, fear, anger, insecurity, powerlessness, frustration, anxiety).
		Persevere.
		Bounce back from disappointment or failure.
		Identify and describe personal or social problems.
		Analyze situations. Observe facts and interpret their meaning.
		Identify and solve problems.
		Get help for problems or issues.
		Deal with social issues.
		Advocate for oneself.
		Deal with change.
		Screen out distractions.

Before we leave behind the topic of practices and skills that build and strengthen the underpinnings of academic success and personal development, let us not forget who it is that daily, consistently demonstrates to students how to **do** these things we want them to learn and develop: You. Yes, their peers are strong influences. But during young adolescence, adults (particularly trusted adults) still influence them most. Students are watching all your academic, ethical, social, and emotional behaviors. Model the attitudes, values, behaviors, passions, reactions, mindsets, and relationships that you hope students will develop.

CAPITALIZING ON STUDENTS' STRENGTHS AND INTERESTS

Anthony is passionate about robotics. Right now, in his seventh-grade social studies class, he's deep into researching to create a visual presentation that includes a history of robotics along with a step-by-step lesson on how to make your own simple robot. Up until now, Anthony has been enthralled with the building process. He's awed by what he's learned beyond the actual mechanics.

Natalia has *become* quite good at writing and performing rap music. She's using her sixth-grade language arts writing project as a way to teach others about the structure, themes, influences, and history of rap music. She plans to involve the class by pairing up other students and guiding them in a rap-writing session. She says her "mind is blown" by what she's learned about the beginnings, development, and impact of rap.

More than a century ago, John Dewey said, "Persons, children or adults, are interested in what they can do successfully, in what they approach with confidence and engage in with a sense of accomplishment."[22] What better way is there to engage students in meaningful, challenging learning than to start with a skill they already have or a pursuit that has already grabbed their interest? When you start with what students **already know and can do**, they have the advantage of beginning from a place of comfort—from a place where they already have some success. You can help them build from there, adding challenges and sending them in new directions to deepen understanding, to add more knowledge, to dig into aspects of their interests that they never thought to explore, to apply the knowledge or skills in new places, and even to teach what they know to other students.

Students must consider a learning experience personally meaningful and relevant—that is, worthy of their time and effort. They must be able to connect it to their experiences, their lives outside of school, the world they know, and things they know. When learning is built around their interests, areas of curiosity, areas of strength and confidence, or special areas of their knowledge or accomplishment, students do better in school. They are more motivated, pay closer attention, and care more about understanding the material. They are more likely to apply new concepts to their lives, to work harder, and to persist longer.[23]

We know that many student interests are fluid; young adolescents often hop from one passion to another. They try one sport after another, one club after another, or one instrument after another. That is normal. Frustrating as it may be for adults, this is just what we know is good for them—to explore many activities, skills, and interests. With each new interest or skill, there are more topics with which to engage them. But not all of their interests are fleeting. Specific personal talents and interests lead many people to success in school or life. As Mel Levine noted in an interview about nurturing children's strengths and affinities, some of the behaviors or affinities that teachers find troublesome in fourth grade can be traits that enable the student to *become* an effective CEO in adulthood.[24]

To connect learning to students' interests and strengths means, of course, that we must **know** what those interests and strengths are. This is why teachers work at thoroughly understanding the characteristics of young adolescents as a group and as individuals. It explains the emphasis on getting to know students as individuals and keeping that going all year long. (Remember Chapter 2?) All that information you collected about students and all the strategies you've learned for keeping up on their interests form a valuable base for making learning relevant to their lives and talents.

Capitalizing on students' interests and strengths also means continuing to notice (or finding out) what interests them and what strengths they're developing. Pay attention to their favorite trends, music, videos, use of social media and other internet platforms, games, out-of-school and in-school activities, cultural backgrounds, social concerns, questions about the world, problems, dilemmas, current events that affect them, hopes, and dreams. Notice what ignites, worries, and pressures them. Recognize their deep involvement in the world of digital connection, and understand that this is a way of life for them. They already are global networkers!

There are many ways to honor students' interests and strengths and many ways to make use of these to enhance their learning. This can take the form of an individual student's learning pursuits or lesson adaptations that teach to the interests of the whole group. The commitment to this should infuse all decisions about what and how to teach. When we see that young adolescents have a significant say and plenty of choice in their learning, we capitalize on both their interests and strengths. (See practices for this in Chapter 7.) When we know students love to explore—particularly outside—and we turn our Lewis and Clark history lesson into an outdoor expedition with canteens of water and tattered maps of clues for them to follow, we capitalize on their interests. When we pay attention to their love for socializing and adapt our choral music practice schedule to allow some time for this, we honor their interests. When we notice their increasing skills of autonomy and thus turn over planning of the next math unit to the students, we capitalize on their strengths. Our efforts to mix learning with their strengths and interests yields benefits beyond increased academic learning: deeper teacher–student relationships, clear demonstrations to students that we believe in them, greater self-efficacy for students, and increased experiences of *belonging*.

On the other hand, when students socialize too much or too vigorously, and we institute a silent lunch or shorten their break times, we ignore the benefits that come from embracing students' interests. (By the way, social skills they practice at school are critical aspects of *becoming* and *belonging*.) Whenever we disregard or minimize what students value—what they spend the rest of their time doing (when not in class), we set up a situation of *us* versus *them*, of it being *our* school instead of *their* school. (This, too, diminishes their opportunities to *belong* and impinges on opportunities to *become*.)

Unfortunately, we see many practices that limit some middle level students' access to, or participation in, the very learning experiences that engage them most. The United States' strong emphasis on reading and math has led to situations where schools heavily focus teaching time on what will be "on the test." This approach can decrease time and opportunities for students to explore, for teachers to plan lessons around students' interests and strengths, and for students to thrive in other subjects. Such practices affect all students, but struggling students appear to be most affected. We must find a way to pre-teach and re-teach difficult math concepts without removing students from their favorite vocational arts class or from their graphic design exploratory hour in order to do so. We must find ways to close students' academic gaps without offering a make-up reading class during the one period where the student can take band class.

Our friend and colleague Dr. Betty Crocker shared an experience about her middle school's proposed plan to replace science class for below-grade-level readers with extra reading instruction. On pages 271-272 in this book (See Appendix C), read her account of how she responded to this by changing her science instruction in a way that addressed the reading problems while keeping students in the science class they loved.

We see similar examples with students' participation in athletics, other extra-curricular activities, and exploratory classes. Most often, when a student is not performing well in class, it is due to a skills gap, a disability, a difficult home life, or poor work ethic. We tend to be a little more understanding of the first three but get really frustrated with the fourth. There are plenty of times when a student with poor work ethic is still able to survive academically while the hard-working student putting forth strong effort simply cannot master the required standards. Which of these students is more likely to be restricted from participating in extra-curricular activities or exploratory classes that allow them to use them greatest strengths or follow their greatest interests? The hard-working one who still cannot "make the grade."

Thomas R. Guskey, a researcher of grades and grading reform, claims that "No research supports the idea that low grades prompt students to try harder. More often, low grades prompt students to withdraw from learning."[25] In order to capitalize on students' strengths and enhance their learning by involving them with what they value, schools must find ways to avoid punishing students for skills gaps while rewarding students who do not have these gaps. Allowing students' skills gaps, disabilities, or difficult home lives to dictate their eligibility to participate in exploratory classes, athletics, clubs, musical groups, or other extracurricular activities deprives them of some of the most meaningful, engaging learning experiences the school can offer them.

Just as many schools and districts are developing graduate or learner profiles (requirements for what they want to see students learn and accomplish), and just as we've advised that you get to know students by creating individual development profiles for your students (see Chapter 2 and Appendix B), we suggest that you might try creating a type of learner profile that gives you an overview of individual students personally and academically. This general view identifies aspects of the individual that help you capitalize on the student's unique interests and gifts. Teachers can use learner profiles to build effective relationships, personalize learning, enhance engagement, develop an inclusive classroom, and identify what approaches or adaptations may be needed for a student. Students can contribute to the content of their own learner profiles. Such profiles are effectively used at all grade levels. With a little investigation of reputable online educational sources, you can find many ideas and even templates for these. Here are a few suggestions for the profile content:

- Skills, strengths, and interests
- Family, cultural, and community background
- Academic knowledge and skills
- Gifts and potentials
- Aspirations, goals, dreams, passions
- Struggles or potential barriers to learning
- Social and emotional characteristics and needs

- Character traits and strengths
- Likes and dislikes
- Life experiences
- How the student likes to learn
- Learning styles, best environment for learning

OFFERING STUDENTS OPPORTUNITIES TO EXPLORE

The Successful Middle School, This We Believe tells readers:

> The middle school is the **finding** place; for young adolescents, by nature, are adventuresome, curious explorers. Therefore, the general approach for the entire curriculum at this level should be exploratory. Exploration, in fact, is the aspect of a successful middle school curriculum that most directly and fully reflects the nature and needs of the majority of young adolescents, most of whom are ready for an exploratory process. Although some experiences may be labeled exploratory, it should not be assumed that they are, therefore, nonacademic. The reverse is equally true; a solid academic experience properly designed is exploratory. Exploration is an attitude and approach, not a classification of content.[26]

By the time they reach middle school, some students are developing into debaters, animators, dancers, volleyball stars, trumpet players, graphic artists, mechanics, cooks, writers, photographers, forensic scientists, fashion designers, naturalists, tech wizards, coding experts . . . and more! Some have been specializing since their parents or caregivers signed them up for Lego club or soccer when they were three years old. Others haven't had enough opportunities during or outside of school to know what they like and want to be able to do. For both of these groups, and for those in between, middle school is a time to explore, to take on a new hobby or skill, broaden their views of themselves, learn about capabilities they didn't know they had, and be exposed to possibilities they'd not previously considered—or possibilities they never dreamed they could touch.

Young adolescents should have chances to explore everything! (Well, not *everything.*) As we said earlier, exploration should be a part of many learning experiences in every classroom and in every part of the curriculum. In addition, a school's elective or exploratory classes offer great avenues for students to explore new possibilities or deepen skills and knowledge about interests they already have. There are dozens of topics and skills for exploratory classes at the middle level and numerous structures and schedules by which they can be included in the curriculum.

In the "middle," between elementary and high school, we must balance opportunities for students so that there are both required courses (for exposure) and choice courses (for honoring what students value and developing new interests). This structured choice can lead students who would never choose to pursue art on their own to begin to develop their talent after taking an art course, while allowing already budding artists to further develop their talents. Many middle schools require some exploratory courses (such as technology) while allowing students to choose from a selection of other courses. Others offer a rotation of required "elective" classes for the younger grade levels, giving students more choices as they progress through the grades. For times when a formal course cannot be offered due to scheduling conflicts or available resources, informal mini-classes, clubs, independent studies for individuals taught by "expert" volunteers, after-school programs, or participation in community programs can also help students find places to *belong* and develop skills of *becoming* something new.

Some Topics for Exploration

Agriculture
Animation
App design and creation
Archaeology
Architecture
Astronomy
Broadcasting
Business skills
Chess
Coding
Creative writing
Dance
Debate
Digital media production
Engineering
Entrepreneurship
Ethnic studies
Fashion design
Filmmaking
First aid
Flight and space
Forensic science
Food science
Gaming
Gardening
Geology
Global issues
Graphic design
Journalism
Languages
Life skills
Martial arts
Mechanics
Medicine
Meteorology
Microscopy
Music production
Mythology
Performing arts
Personal finance
Photography
Pop culture
Problem solving
Psychology
Researching
Robotics
Rocketry
Social media
Song writing
Stock market
Rocketry
Theater
Web design
Woodworking
Video production
Video game development
Virtual reality
Yoga

BUILDING SKILLS AND QUALITIES THAT DEAL WITH THE DIGITAL WORLD

Nothing influences and intersects with *belonging and becoming* for young adolescents quite like the realities of their digital connectivity: The smartphone is their constant companion. This reality affects most aspects of their lives and development at school and outside of school.

Regardless of whether students have access to their smartphones during class, their connectedness perpetually affects their school lives. The connections to friends, to internet information, to games, to social media, to texting, and to the multiple online influences is ever-present. Even when young adolescents are not able to use phones (as in classes where phones must be powered down or stored in lockers or at homes when family rules or controls shut them off), they are anxious or wondering what will meet them when they turn on their phones again—what likes or dislikes, friending or unfriending, texts, memes, or pictures await them (or have been distributed about them).

Most middle schools, if not all, have thoughtfully crafted policies and procedures for possession and use of phones and other digital devices at school; most other guidelines about devices are family matters. Whatever the rules, the reality is that the last few years have seen a marked increase in the numbers of smartphones in the hands of our 10- to 15-year-olds. It is a rare middle school where the percentage of students who have them isn't close to 100%. And the number of hours a day that the average young adolescent spends looking at a phone or other screen is astounding. Many teens look at their phones an average of 240 times a day in response to notifications.[27] In a recent survey of more than 200 tweens and teens across the United States, 97% of students used their phone during school hours, even with school phone policies in force.[28]

The difference from even three to five years ago is that the phones kids now have are not just for calls and texts. The smartphones that now proliferate the middle-schooler's life are web-connected at all times. This gives constant access not only to texts and group texts but also to all kinds of internet sites, social media platforms, and influencers—plus all the information in the world.

So what are we to do to support our young adolescents with these realities? In addition to consistently and equitably following school policies, educators can:

- Stay up to date on the latest information about young adolescent time online, use of particular sites, and online behaviors—as well as information about the effects on their health and well-being. Reputable sources such as the Centers for Disease Control, National Institutes of Health, U.S. Surgeon General, American Academy of Pediatrics, American Psychological Association, the World Health Organization, and the Pew Foundation conduct regular research and surveys and publish information for families and schools about the benefits and dangers, health effects, safe and wise online behaviors, and advice for those who live with and care for young people. Keep tabs on these resources; they update regularly. Share them with one another and with students.
- Harvard researchers Emily Weinstein and Carrie James, authors of *Behind their Screens: What Teens Are Facing (and Adults Are Missing),* surveyed more than 3,500 teens across the United States. They say that the teens' responses clearly show that "they want and need more support around so many issues they're facing behind their screens." The researchers caution that many adults are "not leaning into today's challenges, and as a result we're not meeting them. But this doesn't have to be the case. When we better understand what our students are facing in their connected lives, we're better positioned to meet their actual needs."[29]
- Adults must move beyond blaming screens and instead empathize with what it means to be a young adolescent today. Often adults don't understand what kids are up against in this connected world. Try to understand (and believe) what they face. It is not as simple as telling them to stay off their phones or to avoid social media.[30]
- Our students and our children need adult help and support in building skills for coping with and managing real situations. Keep an ongoing discussion with students about their connected lives. Learn what they're learning, reading, watching, playing, thinking, and wondering. Talk with them about the hard stuff: the benefits, the risks, the dangers, the cautions, the

long-term effects to their physical, social, and mental health. Give them strategies for setting boundaries. They can be encouraged to use platforms and behaviors that create opportunities for exploring healthy interests and for friendship, social support, and healthy socialization.[31]

- Make *social media literacy* a part of their education. Teach students skills for determining what sources, influencers, and information are reliable, appropriate, and safe. When you use technology in class, teach them how to evaluate sites and find credible information. Strengthen those critical thinking skills! Teach students to question accuracy of content and to be alert to misinformation, bias, discrimination, bullying, and manipulation. (Advisory classes are key places for this; but it should be part of any class that uses technology.)
- Make *general digital behavior literacy* a part of their education. Teach skills for appropriate and safe digital behavior and communication. Find some good videos that spark discussion of real issues. Alert them to the dangers of content that encourages young people to take part in risky (and downright stupid) behaviors. Teach healthy practices regarding content, contacts, safety, and privacy. Encourage students to seek help, to build healthy relationships online, and to refrain from constant social comparisons. (Again, include this in advisory class topics, but it should also be part of any class that uses technology.)

"When we better understand what our students are facing in their connected lives, we're better positioned to meet their actual needs."

- Young adolescents are often anxious or worried about their over-use of their connections. Yet, the majority of teens surveyed claim that social media is a positive factor that helps them feel confident, authentic, outgoing, and included (a sense of *belonging*). Learn the benefits of connection and build on those with your students. As well, encourage students to challenge themselves and their friends to cut back on obsessive digital connection.

- Consult AMLE's companion texts *Successful Middle School Instructional Technology* and *The Successful Middle School Advisory* for suggestions about guidelines, places, topics, and strategies for using and discussing technology with young adolescents.
- Share tips and resources with parents and caregivers—they are hungry for assistance in this digital world. Share the importance of adult monitoring and counseling—or better yet, banning—of early adolescents' social media use. In particular, encourage parents and caregivers to set time limits on device use in the evening and nighttime, particularly before bed and after they are in bed. Many young adolescents are deprived of sleep and physical activity because of digital connection. They need at least eight hours of sleep without disruption; insufficient sleep disrupts their brain development and mental health functions.[32]

DEVELOPING A GROWTH MINDSET

Often a student says, "I can't do that." And too often, a teacher thinks of a student, "They can't do that." All students need a mentality shift that allows them to say, instead, "I can't do that **yet**." And all students deserve teachers with the same mentality shift: teachers who think, "They can't do that **yet**."

Stanford psychologist Carol Dweck spent three decades researching why some students achieve their potential while others with just as much intellectual ability do not. She concluded that students' motivation and achievement were affected by their mindsets—their underlying beliefs about whether their abilities were fixed at birth or could be developed.[33]

Dweck shared the discoveries and insights of her research in her book *Mindset: The New Psychology of Success*. She coined the term *growth mindset* to describe the belief that intelligence and abilities can improve and develop over time and the term *fixed mindset* to describe the often-held belief that people (including themselves) are simply born with certain intelligence and abilities that they can't do much to change. Furthermore—and very encouragingly—Dweck found that mindset could be changed through specific teaching and learning efforts and that changing to a growth mindset could significantly boost students' achievement. Her research also found that teachers' mindsets affect the beliefs that students have about their abilities and thus also affect students' mindsets.[34]

In the last few decades, improved understanding of mindsets has had a major impact on education. Thousands of educators have applied the principles to promote dramatic changes for students. When students believe that their current performances can be improved, they adopt a mindset that says, "Although I can't do it right now, with hard work, I can improve." With this belief, they are more motivated to work toward growth and improvement. And, when teachers have the same growth mindset—believing that students can improve through hard work and perseverance—they are likely to expect more from their students. Instead of thinking, "This student can't do this," the teacher thinks, "There are many possibilities for what this student can learn; let's see what they are!"

A body of research shows that a growth mindset can improve performance and help students retain learning long-term. A growth mindset also supports self-efficacy—that is, people's belief in their ability to succeed or accomplish a task.[35] Not only can we encourage students to believe in themselves and their abilities to take on challenging tasks—we can also share what's been learned about the brain! We can teach students that it is possible to "grow their brains" and achieve more.[36] In tandem with self-efficacy, a growth mindset contributes in dynamic ways to a young adolescent's *becoming* successful now and in the future. "Smart is not something you just are; smart is something you can get!"[37] (As an interesting aside, Carol Dweck took up piano as an adult and learned to speak Italian in her fifties.)[38]

Long before the concept of mindsets was a hot topic in education and the term *growth mindset* had come into vogue, I (Patti) learned an important lesson from one of my sixth-grade students. Mark was a bright kid who received services articulated in an IEP, having been diagnosed with a learning disability in reading that had caused him to be reading several years below grade level. Whenever a task involved a considerable amount of reading, Mark would become frustrated and upset by his inability to read and comprehend as easily as other students. Often, he dissolved into tears and usually just gave up. When I talked with him about this, it was clear that he thought of himself as "dumb," regardless of the fact that he was doing fairly well in other subjects, especially in ecological science—an area of special interest to him.

Despite numerous discussions, nothing seemed to persuade him that he wasn't "dumb." One day, I tried a slightly different approach based on something I had read about brain research. I explained to him that it wasn't that he was dumb; it was just that his brain was wired differently from many other students' brains, and so it took a longer time for him to understand what he was reading. I told him that, for example, many brains translated reading by going from point A to point B to point C, and so forth. His brain might need to process the ideas by going from point A to point C, back to point A, jump ahead to point D, and then return to point B. (Please remember, this was back in the 80s—less was known about how the brain operated, and this explanation was not based on deep brain research; it was more a case of a desperate teacher trying to help a student understand why he wasn't reading as well as his peers and that it was important to keep trying!)

"Smart is not something you just are; smart is something you can get!"

It's likely that Mark had heard other explanations of why he struggled in reading. But for some reason, at this particular point, that explanation clicked with him. He seemed to take it as an assurance that maybe, if he kept at it, he would get better at reading. When I saw how Mark responded to this new understanding about his brain, I was inspired to try some new strategies. I started by helping him set short-term, achievable reading goals. Then I paired him with another student and showed them a tactic called "say something" for increasing comprehension. They stopped at the end of each short section and said something—asking a question about the text, connecting something from the text to a personal experience, making a prediction about what might come next, or making an inference about what something meant.

Mark started to put more effort into trying to read, and his ability to read did improve. It didn't happen overnight or without struggles. But shifting his thinking from "I'm dumb and can't read" to "Maybe I can learn to read better if I try harder" made a difference. And, by the way, today he is a contributing member of his community and owns his own business (and yes, it has to do with the outdoors—his middle grades interest). Now I understand that I had helped Mark begin to develop a growth mindset. In addition, I had instinctively tried some different strategies to support the spark of understanding about his brain.

I (Laurie) also learned something several years ago that I now realize had to do with fixed mindsets (though I didn't use that terminology at the time) and the ability to change them. I remember a student, Luis, in the middle school where I was principal. Like the boy in Patti's story, Luis had an IEP based on his documented disability. Unlike Mark however, Luis struggled in all of his classes. Also unlike Mark, Luis had a pretty upbeat attitude about his classwork and didn't seem to let the challenges he faced get him down. His teachers, however, were not as confident in Luis's ability to make progress toward his learning goals. In addition to overcoming the barrier of concerns they had about his ability to learn, they had to grapple with questions about their own skills to help him. They were stuck in a place of little hope for him and for themselves.

But together, Luis's teachers gathered the courage to face their insecurities and try something different. Teachers who were using a co-teaching model began by welcoming Luis into their general education classrooms. With the assistance of Luis's paraprofessional, they were able to make specific plans for Luis's daily instruction (differentiation at its best) while still attending to the needs of other students. In addition, they moved away from judging Luis's success solely in terms of his proficiency with the content standards. Instead, they began to view his growth as the greatest measure of his success. Although Luis did not always show proficiency on standards, he did meet his own growth goals, which gave a boost to everyone involved. Luis's teachers adopted the motto "fair does not mean equal." It took time, collaboration, risks (and failures), lots of differentiation, and patience—but their beliefs about Luis's abilities changed. And instead of seeing (and worrying about) what Luis **couldn't** do, they looked for—and found—what Luis **could** do.

One of the things we both learned from these students and that we see more clearly now that we know about mindsets, is that a growth mindset is not just about a student or teacher trying harder. In her article "Carol Dweck Revisits the 'Growth Mindset'," Dweck says:

> . . . a growth mindset isn't just about effort. Certainly, effort is key for students' achievement, but it's not the only thing. Students need to try new strategies and seek input from others when they're stuck. They need a repertoire of approaches—not just sheer effort—to learn and improve.[39]

Dweck is speaking here about students, but the same holds true for teachers and all other persons who move toward a growth mindset. In one of the stories told from our past, Mark not only tried harder but also took advantage of some specific strategies offered by the teacher and assisted by a peer. In the other story, the teachers put in more effort for Luis. But that was not all they did; they also took different actions. They took a risk, stepped out of their comfort zones, and changed the way they operated.

The Teacher's Mindset

While the education world is abuzz with ways to help students develop growth mindsets, we often forget about the teacher's mindset. As is true with teachers' self-efficacy and belief in students, teachers' mindsets also influence their students' mindsets.[40] When a teacher has a growth mindset, students are more likely to change mindsets and believe they can learn if they work hard and use specific strategies and assistance from others. But this must be a genuine mindset—not mere lip service to the concept. Many teachers say they have a growth mindset, but their classroom behaviors and practices don't reflect that. Students can sense their teachers' beliefs: They know when teachers have their minds made up about a student's abilities. It is very difficult to help students feel as though they *belong* in a class and that they can *become* (meet class goals) when they sense that the teacher doubts—for whatever reasons—that they *belong* there or can reach the goals.

Researchers Aneeta Rattan, Catherine Good, and Carol Dweck contend that when students are struggling, teachers show a growth mindset not by comforting the students ("Oh, I see you're having a hard time with this. Lots of students struggle with writing") but instead by giving them specific strategies they can use to make progress.[41] In her book *Fall Down 7 Times, Get Up 8,* author Debbie Silver explains it this way:

> Rather than just admonishing students to work hard at something, we need to model the effective preparation we want them to use. Whether we are talking about a study skill, an athletic performance, or some other area we need to guide students in specific techniques for practicing effectively and efficiently.[42]

In other words, "just try harder" doesn't cut it! Here are some ways teachers can work toward having a growth mindset more often and about more students.

Reflect on your own mindset. Pay attention to beliefs you have about students—to your thoughts, assumptions, explanations, and statements. Notice if you place blame when frustrated and where you place it. Do you catch yourself saying any of the following?

"I have high expectations. Students just aren't meeting them."

"I've taught the material, but students just didn't pay attention."

"I've reviewed this a thousand times; students need to do their homework."

"These students are doing the best they can, considering their lives at home; they can't do any better than this."

Think of yourself as a learner. You are capable of getting smarter, too! Do you believe that you have capabilities to learn new things, teach better, develop your brain, succeed with new programs and strategies? (You can! You, too, are *becoming*, and you're a wonderful example of this for your students.)

Learn from your peers. One of the best ways to learn a growth mindset is to watch it at work in others—particularly people close to you, people who have similar jobs and challenges as you, and people you admire. In turn, try to model a growth mindset for others.

Support professional development in growth mindset. Everyone in a middle school will benefit from increases in growth mindset. Encourage your school to dedicate time and resources to providing training for staff **(all staff)** in this quality. Just as we need to help students with specific practices to change their mindsets and make academic and personal progress—so, too, do teachers need concrete actions to have growth mindsets more often. Remember, it doesn't come just from trying harder!

Support one another. Ask for and give feedback to colleagues. Commit to reflecting on your own mindset and the manifestations of others'. Commit to helping one another grow.

Don't expect perfection. Don't assume that you or anyone else will have a 100% growth mindset. In an interview with Christine Gross-Loh of *The Atlantic*, Carol Dweck said, "Nobody has a growth mindset in everything all the time."[43] Working toward a growth mindset is a lifelong process. As with many other positive and healthy behaviors, you must keep practicing it in all areas of your life.

The Student's Mindset

The good news about mindsets is that they **can** change. Help students believe that ability is not fixed and that it can grow, and make sure all students understand that this means them **and** all the other kids in school. Think of what this can do for students' sense of *belonging*—to know that the other students believe they **can** do better! And think of the boost this gives to their trust in their possibilities for *becoming* as a learner! We'll share some practices to help students develop or increase growth mindsets. We guarantee that some of these will sound familiar; they're the same practices that affect so many other facets of academic and personal growth (of *belonging* and *becoming*).

- Consistently reflect on your own mindset.
- Model a growth mindset.

- Build camaraderie with students in the pursuit of a growth mindset; let them know that most people question their own capabilities or fear they can't do better at something (even you).
- Focus on learning rather than performance.
- Give students opportunities to redo and fix their work.
- Encourage students to seek and tackle challenges.
- Praise students for effort, persistence, working toward goals, or taking on challenges—but not for ability alone.
- Give feedback that is specific and leaves the student knowing what to do next.
- Foster autonomy; let students have control over some of their own learning.
- Give students time and ways to examine and explain their mistakes.
- Watch how you react to mistakes. (Do you see them as "bad" or harmful?)
- Always show students how one can learn from correcting mistakes (not from **making** mistakes—but from **correcting** mistakes).
- When students struggle, don't attribute this to their intelligence (or ability).
- Teach students that struggling is not a bad thing; instead, it means you're working hard at something that is important!
- Teach students about neuroplasticity—about how brains can change and grow smarter.
- Reinforce positive classroom relationships as well as students' self-efficacy and sense of *belonging*.
- Design the kinds of learning experiences students deserve: relevant, honoring their interests and talents, and full of action, collaboration, and engagement.
- Teach growth mindset hand in hand with study skills, skills of self-regulation, specific skills of content areas, and other specific academic and personal skills. (See skills listed in Figures 6-1 and 6-2 on pages 128 and 130)

When answering questions about what teachers can do to foster growth mindsets for students, Carol Dweck said, "Focus on the learning process and show how hard work, good strategies, and good use of resources lead to better learning."[44]

Attribution Theory

Along the lines of mindsets, teachers should take into consideration the impact that *attribution theory* can have on students. This concept is based on human tendencies to seek out the causes of our successes and failures. In other words, to what do we attribute what happens to us?

Common attribution factors in our culture are (1) native ability, (2) difficulty of the task, (3) luck, and (4) effort. The only factor that is perceived to have no potential for change is native or genetic ability. Face it—no matter how hard I (Patti) try, I'll never be a coloratura soprano. As educators, we do need to help students have a realistic view of their native abilities to help them avoid frustration in certain areas. A student with a short, stocky build may not be successful as a long-distance runner, but can that student be guided into a sport (perhaps wrestling) that is better matched to body type?

But if a student incorrectly attributes a failure to native ability, when in reality there was another reason (perhaps it hadn't been learned yet, or not enough effort was put in), it becomes troublesome. How many times have we heard a student say something along the lines of "My dad told me he wasn't good in math, so neither am I"? Too many times, this line of attribution has led students to actually believe that they can never be good in math.

We're all familiar with (and have probably invoked them ourselves in the past) the factors of luck and difficulty of the task. "I passed but couldn't believe how easy that test was!" "It was just luck I got the math problem right—I guessed the answer." "Running the mile in P.E. class was too hard for me. I just couldn't finish and took the lower grade." "It was so lucky—I was in the right place at the right time, so I got the job."

And that leads us to the only factor we have control over: **effort**. We can choose how much or little effort to put into a task. "I failed the test, because I didn't make the effort to study for it." "I nailed my solo for the choir. I was worried, but I practiced it a lot!"

All of this has implications for us as educators. First of all, we must attend to our own attributions of student performance, because teacher viewpoints and subtle messages influence students. Teachers' belief in students, as well as their explanations to students of success and failure attributed to controllable factors, have a major positive effect on students' hope and motivation to work toward success.[45] We need to listen and be aware of the conditions or factors to which our students are attributing their successes and failures. Misguided perceptions of the cause versus the reality of the cause can impact students' self-concept, motivation, and expectations of future success. And if students are making the effort and still having trouble, they may shut down and stop trying. We must help them understand that "ability often actually changes incrementally over the long term."[46] Knowing this helps students keep up the effort and belief. It's up to us to provide them with the support and help they need to be successful.

CULTIVATING RESILIENCE

Resilience is the ability to recover from difficulties, serious hardship, or adversity—all the attributes, attitudes, resources, and skills a person has to cope and take care of themselves in hard times. There are times when resilience must be defined as the capacity and capability (through a set of skills) to adapt to circumstances that threaten our very lives, development, or function—and to adapt in ways that lead to positive functioning. Harvard Medical School psychologist Robert Brooks has studied resilience for decades and has authored many books on the subject, including *Raising Resilient Children.* He explains:

> The main way I look at resilience is the capacity for people who have faced adversity to bounce back and to cope much more effectively with life. I see it as people who really have very good coping strategies. And they also have an optimistic attitude. They feel that even though they have faced difficult times, that there are ways they can overcome them.[47]

All of us experience adversity—it's a part of human life. It's inevitable that our students will encounter stress, disappointment, failure, illnesses, accidents, and setbacks. Some of this happens in school, but much of it comes from their lives outside school. Some of our students experience acute stress, chronic difficulties, terrible tragedies, or trauma. Whatever adversity they meet, they come into our classrooms and our care, and we must do everything possible to help them recover and move forward with life to experience hope and joy.

As teachers, we can each be an adult from whom our students gather strength.

We would love to protect our students and our own children from setbacks, devastating changes, and probably all adversities of any kind. We can't do that. But the good news is that resilience can be developed. According to Brooks, his research on resilience has consistently identified one essential factor in helping children cope with adversity and *become* resilient: having at least one of what he calls "a charismatic adult" in the child's life—"an adult from whom a child gathers strength."[48]. He goes on to say, "So the person feels that, okay, I'm having some difficult times, but there can be better times ahead. Also, what the charismatic adult does is help the person see that they have the resources within themselves to start to make these changes."[49]

As teachers, we can each be an adult from whom our students gather strength. We can model resilience, but we can't do it for them. We **can** be there for them. We **can** communicate unconditional acceptance. We **can** help them acquire the attributes that enable them to find the resources within themselves to increase resilience. And we **can** help students develop a resilient mindset—a "relative" of the growth mindset. For persons of any age or situation to bounce back from difficulty, they must believe that it's possible to do better, to get better, to survive and thrive. With a *growth* mindset, students believe that their brain can develop to learn and accomplish things; with a *resilient* mindset, students believe that there are things they can do to recover from hardship and to thrive.

A working paper from the National Scientific Council on the Developing Child at Harvard University summarized the other conditions (besides having a significant adult relationship) that counterbalance the negative effects of significant adversity for children. These are all conditions that involve one or more adults in an assisting role:

- Help identifying their strengths (often called "islands of competence") and building belief in their personal control—belief that they have the resources to solve problems and influence what happens in their lives
- Help learning and practicing skills for adapting to the difficult situation—skills of self-regulation, decision-making, planning, coping, and controlling emotions
- Help and encouragement in finding ways to enrich the lives of others[50]

A guidebook on resilience from the Parenting for Life program, sponsored by the Psychology Foundation of Canada, adds these conditions:

- A sense of *belonging* and knowing how to reach out to people who are there for them
- Developing optimism and hope[51]

We want our students to thrive. Encouraging persistence, grit, and resilience takes a set of skills that is sometimes overlooked. Students need to learn how to deal with struggle—believing in themselves, managing their emotions, and finding healthy responses. As educators, we are **right there** in position to help students gain tools to help themselves overcome stress, mistakes, failures, unexpected changes, setbacks, and other adversities without sinking into depression or hopelessness, giving up, or blaming their struggles on what they think is their own innate inability to make things better. We (the authors) are not big fans of the catchphrase "Failure is not an option." Failure, like disappointment and many other adversities, is always an option—failure is an inevitable part of life. We would rather students learn a different catchphrase: "Giving up is not an option."

During this time of rapid changes, young adolescent students are developing habits and traits that they will carry into adulthood. Although it is never too late to develop resilience, it is far easier for young people to learn now, rather than later, how to accept and cope with adversity. And developing the skills and mindset of resilience gives them much greater chances for having fulfilling, balanced lives. It's heartening to know that teachers and schools have a key role in building resilience—and that what we do can make substantial differences for our students. The Parenting for Life program referenced above asserts that, "Experts have different theories and terms for talking about resiliency, but one point is unanimous among them: *the single most important factor in child resiliency is relationships.*"[52]

Top 13 Ways to Cultivate Resilience

- Model resilience and optimism.
- Let students gather strength from you.
- Help students name and express their emotions.
- Show students how to turn negative thoughts and statements into positive ones.
- Encourage appropriate assertiveness.
- Help students *belong* in the school setting.
- Help students identify their own inner resources that they can use to overcome their problems.
- Increase students' self-belief.
- Boost students' sense of autonomy and competence.
- Share real-life and literary examples of people who recovered from adversities.
- Remind students that you believe in them.
- Teach students coping skills.
- Help students find ways to help others.

GIVING SECOND (AND THIRD AND FOURTH) CHANCES

If we believe that challenge, self-belief, mastery, goal attainment, autonomy, learning from correcting one's mistakes, competence-building, perseverance, resilience, and a growth mindset all contribute to academic success and personal development, then why would we give students just one chance to reach a goal, such as completing a project, doing well on an assignment, writing a paper, or passing a test? How dare we say, "You can't keep trying," "You can't show that you can do better," or "Sorry, even if you worked hard, that was your only chance to get this right"?

All students deserve "whatever it takes" to help them *become* the most successful student possible.

Many students need more than one chance to learn a concept and demonstrate their knowledge of it. In the same vein, some students need far more than basic content knowledge and must be given opportunities to go beyond the basic requirements of school. No two students are alike, but all students deserve "whatever it takes" to help them *become* the most successful student possible. Thus, it is a teacher's responsibility to do everything possible to ensure that all students meet not only the required learning goals but also the goals appropriate for each student. Just as we encourage students to make revisions to an essay, so, too, should we allow them to rework other assignments—and, yes, even some assessments.

When students have a chance to learn from their mistakes and redo or rewrite, not only do they often perform better in terms of scores or academic accomplishment—they also experience increases in hope, motivation, and growth mindset. And, additional opportunities help ensure students actually learn content instead of simply performing poorly, earning a low grade, and then moving on without having mastered the content—which certainly doesn't benefit the student. These second (and third and fourth) chances teach students that failure sometimes happens, that failure isn't the end (but instead is the first step toward growth), and that failure doesn't define them.

Author Rick Wormeli addresses this topic in the article "Redos and Retakes Done Right: Allowing Students to Redo Assignments and Assessments Is the Best

Way to Prepare Them for Adult Life." He reminds teachers, "The goal is that all students learn the content, not just the ones who can learn on the uniform timeline. Curriculum goals don't require that every individual reaches the same level of proficiency on the same day, only that every student achieves the goal."[53]

If you don't already do so, start the practice of allowing (and even encouraging) second chances on assignments and assessments (for full credit). Before you start, however, lay out your criteria for redos and retakes—in what cases this can happen, how they will be assessed, how much time a student has, how many do-overs a student can have, and what kind of agreement you'll have ahead of time with the student (and in some cases, with parents or caregivers as well). Make it clear that any redo or retake is at your discretion—but be careful to exercise that discretion equitably. Be sure that you and the student compare the final "do" with the original "try" to see the student's progress.

Also, do more research about this topic and how to do it well (and how not to do it). We recommend that you read Wormeli's entire article (mentioned above) and another article, "The Right Way to Do Redos," which includes practical tips on managing redos.[54] Wormeli also gives advice on this topic in two *YouTube* videos titled *Rick Wormeli: Redos, Retakes, and Do-Overs, Part One* (and *Part Two*).[55]

When we look back at the many attitudes and practices suggested in this chapter—along with the long lists of skills to teach—we're reminded again of the complexity of the process of *becoming* capable at both academic and personal skills. We're also reminded again of how incredible and harmonious this partnership is between *becoming* and *belonging*. Even with all that educators know about the interrelatedness of our students' personal, social, emotional, ethical, and cognitive development and needs—the priority is still often placed on academic achievement (generally measured by test scores or grades). This choice ignores the awesome network of qualities and assets that contribute to academic achievement and to a whole, well-functioning person. An exclusive emphasis on academics or personal development alone doesn't work, because there is no real separation between them. All the positive, productive, healthy attributes students need to develop are embedded in both!

PUTTING IT INTO PRACTICE

As an individual, team, small group, or entire staff, use these activities to spark discussions, reflect on your current practices or situations, listen to others, or set goals.

1. Examine how your school's master schedule affects students' opportunities to take exploratory classes. How many elective classes does your school offer? Do students have choice of classes? Does the schedule force students to lose time in non-academic classes if additional assistance or catch-up work in academic classes is needed? Are there opportunities for students to explore areas of interest outside of formal classes (e.g., mini-courses, brown-bag lunch groups, clubs, online groups)? How can the schedule and other exploration opportunities be improved to allow students access to all classes, particularly areas of interest that are most meaningful to them?

2. Examine school practices and policies regarding student participation in activities based on academic performance. Are students restricted or prevented from participating in a course or activity if they are not passing in a required content area course? Do coaches or club leaders work together with teachers to encourage students to do better in academic classes? Is there consistency across the staff in how these practices are implemented? Is any consideration given to a student's work ethic, or what the student **did** learn, over final academic performance?

3. Group discussion: Review your school's procedures for allowing re-teaching and redos. Is this a common practice in your school? Do all teachers participate? Is it mandatory or voluntary? Is there consistency? If there are no established procedures, discuss the need for developing procedures and what they might look like if created.

4. Use the "Log of Teachable Skills and Practices that Increase Belonging" from our ASCD book *We Belong: 50 Strategies to Create Community and Revolutionize Classroom Management* available as Appendix I included on pages 286-287 in this book. Discuss how you can intentionally integrate these practices in your lessons to help support students' academic success and personal development.

GROW

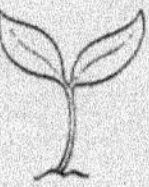

Growth screams at me from across
the room.
My mind spirals as I doubt myself
and where I am.
It grows twice in size while I stay
on the ground.
I look it in the eyes as it stares back
at me.
It grows smaller, or do I grow
Bigger?
I turn around so I can't see it.
It breathes down my neck as I shut
my eyes.
I feel a shiver down my spine as
I open my eyes to see myself growing.
I can't breathe. I don't want to see it.
I can't bring myself to trust it.
I don't know if I don't want to grow
Or if I can't.
What if I can't grow at all?
My heart quickens.
My stomach flips.
My mind spirals
I don't want to be alone.
I can't be stuck here, can I?
I want to grow—
No, strike that!
I need to grow.
I am not letting myself be left behind.
I'm following my own path
Made by
My Self-Growth.

– Diego, Grade 6

Chapter 7

Honor and Foster Student Voice and Choice

Teachers who find their kids' ideas fascinating are just better teachers than teachers who find the subject matter fascinating.

— Philip Sadler

At the 1989 Convention on the Rights of the Child, the United Nations General Assembly passed a resolution internationally affirming that each child has "the right to express his or her views freely in all matters affecting the child, the views of the child being given due weight in accordance with the age and maturity of the child."[1]

What is more fundamental to *belonging* in any setting and *becoming* in any pursuit than the right to express one's views freely in matters affecting oneself? And what is more essential to the foundations of our mission as educators than the beliefs and values that lead us to honor and attend to this right? For beneath any actions to welcome and nurture the voices of our students lies a belief that **all** of them have not only the right, but also the capabilities and wisdom, to identify their interests and their needs to express their opinions and perspectives and to take part in important decisions that affect their lives at school.

Student voice: In the school context, the idea of *voice* for students refers to the extent to which students are able and free to express their viewpoints, values, opinions, suggestions, preferences, perspectives, beliefs, and values—all of which draw from their personal experiences and backgrounds. But *voice* goes beyond simple expression: If we acknowledge that students are people with rights, then we must respect what they say. In a school, voice includes the degree to which students' expressions are listened to, valued, taken seriously, considered, and acted upon when making decisions about their instruction and other aspects of their school lives. Student voice is about the level of their involvement and investment in the life of the school—as individuals and as a group. The concept encompasses many facets of voice—in informal contacts and discussions, in instructional matters, in representing cultural perspectives, in formal systems (such as governing bodies), and in contributions to evaluative feedback and meaningful decisions.[2]

Student choice is inherent in the definition of student voice. Voice truly exists only where there is choice.

Student choice: The concept of *choice* in the school involves a setting wherein students have options in the practices of the classroom and school, including in their learning experiences. But the concept of *choice* transcends mere options. Student choice at its best means that students have meaningful, relevant choice—choices that are not just selections from a list of options, but choices that involve a student's action and participation and that support development of the student's autonomy and competence.

Voice and choice: Student choice is inherent in the definition of student voice. Voice truly exists only where there is choice. And offering authentic choices entails honoring and strengthening voice. An environment where students have many opportunities for choice communicates to students that their voices matter. Together, these concepts affirm that students **do** have insights into and interest in their own learning—and that they **can** make meaningful decisions about the design of their own learning and school environment. Fostering both *voice* and *choice* is a smart way to draw students into active participation in their own *belonging* and *becoming*.

HONORING AND FOSTERING VOICE

Why?

We start from the truth that each student deserves to be heard: This is the foremost reason for honoring and fostering student voice. In addition, benefits abound when we offer students authentic and constructive ways to express themselves and take an active role in making decisions; these are benefits for students and all those who work with them. In its 2016 School Voice Report, the Quaglia Institute for School Voice and Aspirations asserts:

> In order for schools to be successful, they must **listen** to, **learn** from, and **lead** with the students and teachers who comprise the very life of the school itself. Students who believe they have a voice in school are seven times more likely to be academically motivated than students who do not believe they have a voice.[3]

This report and multiple other research studies have positively linked student voice to a number of the very aspects of *belonging* and *becoming* that are so critical to students' personal development, well-being, and success in school—as well as to school improvement.[4] When schools focus on developing and acting on student voice, they report the same outcomes and changes found in the research.

Here are some of the outcomes and changes that have been found in the presence of meaningful practices to elevate student voice:

- **Students learn better. Achievement increases.**

  Motivation and engagement increase.

  School attendance improves.

Students shift into active roles as shapers of their education.

Students get involved in learning processes in ways they may not have before.

Students value their education more.

Students are more committed to what they're learning.

Students are more willing to take on academic challenges.

Students' levels of effort and persistence increase.

Exploration and curiosity increase.

Students feel increased self-worth and believe in themselves more.

Students take more initiative and grow in autonomy.

Students perceive themselves as increasing in competence.

Students gain confidence and a sense that their ideas make a difference.

Students perceive learning as more relevant.

Students take on more responsibility for their learning.

Students gain a sense of themselves as learners.

Students' leadership abilities increase.

Students' sense of being worthwhile and doing something worthwhile grows.

Learning becomes more diverse as diverse voices are heard.

- **Students feel a greater sense of *belonging* to their school and classes.**

  Students identify more with school programs and events.

  Students are more likely to get involved in classroom and school activities.

  Students' attitudes about school improve.

  Students develop a sense of purpose.

  As students hear one another's voices, they learn more about one another.

  By listening to peers, opportunities to value and respect one another increase.

Relationships with peers improve.

Students feel more valued by teachers.

Student attendance improves.

- **Teachers teach better.**

  Learning is redefined as a joint venture between students and teachers.

  Teachers see more positive attitudes in their students (and often, in themselves).

  Teachers learn more about their students.

  Teachers learn more from their students.

  Teachers find that their relationships with students deepen.

  Teachers gain insights into students' ideas and capabilities.

  Teachers learn more about how individual students think and learn.

  Teachers are better able to plan effective learning for and with students.

  Teachers learn more about how their teaching is working.

  Teachers learn about students' understanding or misconceptions of concepts.

  Teachers are more excited about learning.

  Teacher attendance and job satisfaction improves.

How?

Much has been discussed about how to give voice to students. But in reality, we educators cannot **give** voice to our students, for each human being already has a voice. Instead, we give honor to their voices. We give messages about the value of their voices. We give priority to listening to—and learning from—their voices. We create and give opportunities for their voices to be heard. We give students structures and supports that help them strengthen their own voices. And we give ourselves the ability to act upon what we learn from them. Instead of asking how to give voice to students, we should ask, "What do we do with the voices that our students bring to us?"

Researchers Barbara McCombs and Jo Sue Whisler are advocates of the learner-centered classroom and its success at increasing student motivation and achievement. We can't help but notice that every part of their description of a learner-centered classroom (or school) connects to the concept of **how** to enhance student voice. They have defined *learner-centered* as beliefs, characteristics, dispositions, and practices of teachers that:

1. Include learners in decisions about how and what they learn and how that learning is assessed;
2. Take each learner's unique perspectives seriously and consider these perspectives part of the learning process;
3. Respect and accommodate individual differences in learners' backgrounds, interests, abilities, and experiences; and
4. Treat learners as co-creators in the teaching and learning process.[5]

When we consider the kinds of actions and strategies to recommend to our readers, we are first inspired to share the words of Benjamin Levin, who researches the role of student voice in school improvement (and ardently believes that students **must** be at the center of school improvement efforts). Levin said that we must "make it normal, even expected, that students would have reasoned, informed, and respected voice in school decisions."[6] One of AMLE's 18 characteristics of a successful middle school reminds us that successful middle schools exist when "a shared vision developed by all stakeholders guides every decision."[7] We must not forget that students are critical stakeholders and as such deserve a voice in school improvement efforts.

Instead of asking how to give voice to students, we should ask, "What do we do with the voices that our students bring to us?"

In its beginning, or minimal form, fostering student voice means that students give ideas or opinions when they are asked to do so (without a promise that anyone will act on their ideas). At its best and most complex, fostering student voice "calls for a cultural shift that opens up spaces and minds not only to the sound but also to the presence and power of students."[8] In every aspect, from simplest to most complex, student voice is an important part of school culture.

What schools and teachers believe about students' wisdom and abilities to take active roles in their own education will be reflected in the level of voice in a school or classroom. But it is not just the belief that makes the difference. In fact, it could be argued that the belief isn't real if there is no action to improve the level of student voice that is invited and incorporated. There are limitless strategies for taking action that fosters student voice. Here are some practices to explore and expand as you work to increase the level and positive impact of student voice:[9]

Doable steps: Start from where you are and plan to take one step at a time toward increasing the level of student voice. But wherever you are, and whatever your goals, always keep these truths as a part of your belief system and let the beliefs show in your attitudes and actions: Students have the right to be heard. They deserve respect for their ideas, interests, and opinions. They have ideas worthy of inclusion in decisions and plans. You can and will learn from your students. Middle level students are full of new cognitive powers, hunger for autonomy, boundless curiosity, and questions—non-stop questions. We can let it drive us crazy, or we can corral these developmental characteristics into meaningful expressions of voice that include students in making important decisions and contributions. And we must "make it normal" that they do so.

Interactive teaching: Plan to include some expression of student voice in every lesson: lots of discussion (in pairs or in groups, on many topics—academic and otherwise), frequent student response as the lesson is developed, questions and answers (with students and teacher both doing the questioning and answering), periodic feedback, and intermittent review of what they've learned and understood.

Voice-friendly instructional methods: Plan to involve students in such endeavors as exploration, inquiry, experimentation, activity-based learning, solving real-world problems, creating strategies and solutions, student-led conferences, peer mentoring, and argumentative writing and speaking (and formal or informal debate). Be sure to include instructional approaches and techniques on students' interests, choices, passions, and goals. Try student blogs, which are a way for students to express their ideas and perspectives in writing and with images (including videos). Blogging is a nonthreatening way to practice self-expression because the audience is invisible!

Interactive management: Make sure student ideas and experiences are a part of classroom protocols. Give students as much responsibility as possible for designing and managing procedures in the classroom.

Discussion: Make space for discussions on many topics—interesting intellectual ideas (students can initiate by sharing something they heard, learned, or wonder), questions, social issues, classroom learning, or classroom life. First let students solve problems and discuss opinions in pairs as they prepare for a wider classroom discussion; this helps to ensure that more students will share.

Connections: Before, during, and after learning activities, have students make connections—to their experiences, to things they already know, to what is important in their lives, to how the new skill or information can be applied to other contexts. You can give them a few minutes to complete such statements as "This connects to . . . ," "I could see this working with . . . ," or "This is relevant to my life because . . .".

Feedback: Find a variety of ways for students to give and receive feedback. Ask for frequent questions or comments on classroom procedures and lessons. Take pauses during lessons and ask students what they're wondering about, what they're hearing, what they understand, or what they see as important. Have them summarize what they've learned by telling one another, demonstrating it, writing it in a journal, on a sticky note, or in a post or text message.

Collaborative learning: Make collaborative pairs or groups a standard part of learning in your classroom. When students work together (having been taught appropriate ways to do so), their voices are heard and used. They grow in understanding and appreciation of their peers as they learn about the subject and about one another.

Research: Provide chances for students to gather information and viewpoints on important topics (classroom or school procedures, for example), summarize what they learn, draw conclusions and consider implications, present their findings, and use their findings to make suggestions related to school concerns.

Reflection: Include daily reflections on such things as their goal attainment, learning outcomes, thinking processes, questions, confusions, work progress, specific learning experiences, or conditions and experiences in the classroom. Students can do so orally, on reflection forms, or in journals.

Goal setting and attainment: Student voice is elevated when they set their own goals, articulate their goals, design and carry out plans to meet the goals, and evaluate their outcomes and processes.

Inclusion on school governing bodies: Commit to the idea that students are valuable contributors to decision-making groups in the school. Realize that, in fact, students offer perspectives, information, and ideas that can't be gained from any other source—and that it would be a loss to make decisions without that input. Bring students into team meetings, faculty meetings, staff leadership team meetings, and even school board meetings. See that there is student representation on school councils, task forces, and information-gathering committees.

Choice: Offer middle level students an ongoing selection of choices in all aspects of their school lives. (See more on this later in the chapter.)

Students in charge: Shift some of the power. Nurture students' autonomy and responsibility. Let students take charge of classroom procedures, decisions, tasks, and teaching wherever it is possible, workable, and appropriate for their developmental level. (Don't underestimate what they are capable of doing responsibly.)

Teaching the teacher: Student voice researchers Julia Flutter and Jean Ruddick heartily recommend using students as "expert witnesses" of teaching and learning, because students are keen observers of school life and have valuable insights to offer.[10] Ask students to describe the content, concept, skill, or process they've learned. Ask them to describe and evaluate how and what you've taught. Ask them to redesign a lesson you are planning to teach or have taught. Ask them to tell you how they learn best. Ask them to share observations about what works and doesn't work in the classroom.

Student-led conferences: One of the most meaningful experiences students can have in exercising voice occurs when students plan and lead a conference with a parent or caregiver. We've mentioned this before, but the process is so voice-centered that we needed to mention it again. With some teacher guidance or an agreed-upon list of contents, students choose which evidence of their progress, performance, and passions in their school lives to show their families. They also choose how to present it and what to say. In short, they are the designers and implementers of their own conferences.

TOP 8 WAYS TO FOSTER VOICE

- Ask students for their perceptions, opinions, feedback, and ideas. Listen. Take them seriously.
- Plan for students to interact with you and one another during lessons.
- Include students on school governing bodies.
- Use student surveys and focus groups that enable them to share reflections, opinions, evaluations, and suggestions anonymously.
- Give students ways to reflect frequently on what and how they have learned.
- Put students in charge whenever and wherever possible. They are capable of this—probably more than you think.
- Use them as "expert witnesses" of teaching and learning. They know things you don't!
- When you invite student voice, act on what you learn from students.

Seeking and Listening to Students' Perceptions and Opinions

When I (Patti) was a middle school principal, our district passed a bond levy that provided for a budget that included money for new playground structures at the elementary schools. Perhaps unsurprisingly, I came up against some stiff district-level skepticism when I began lobbying hard to have a playground structure built for the middle school, too. Many treated it as a foregone conclusion that young adolescents would disparage the playground equipment as "babyish" and that it would go unused. But I persevered, and in the end I got the go-ahead. Realizing that the older students might be the hardest to sell on the idea, I set up a mixed group task force of students. I gave them catalogs of playground equipment and asked them to design a structure that students would use. They came up with a plan, worked with the contractor to incorporate their ideas, and watched as the structure was built. The first day it opened for use, students swarmed over the new structure, as the counselor remarked, "like ants on Terro [a liquid ant bait]." The students' plan was a hit with every grade level; all it took for a successful outcome was asking students for input.

"Whose voice is heard in this school?" This is a question for all educators to ask. What happens in schools and classrooms is most often the result of adult decision-making: decisions handed down from the district office, from administrators, or from teachers or other staff. The nature of organizing and planning in a school (master schedules, programs, supervision duty, school-improvement processes) lends itself to school being a world dominated by adult decisions. Our earlier discussion gave many reasons why it is critical to bring students into these processes. We know that when students believe they matter, and that their perspectives and suggestions matter, they are much more likely to engage in learning processes. And we know that, as the level of student voice rises, so, too, does the level of teaching, learning, and personal development in a school and its classrooms.

The most basic actions resulting from our commitment to student voice are asking to hear it and listening to what we hear. We can't assume that students will automatically say what they need to say or what we need to hear. Because many young adolescents believe that school is about adults and not about them, or perhaps because they have not been taught to advocate for themselves, they may not be comfortable speaking their thoughts. Even for those students who do speak up, it's not enough to wait for them to bring ideas or share concerns of their own volition.

As the authors, we in no way wish to minimize all the efforts already underway in schools to support and develop student voice or power. We know that schools have student councils and student leadership groups that do great work coordinating food drives, spirit weeks, school dances, and other (very important) school events. However, often these traditional student organizations don't provide enough opportunities for students to give consistent and meaningful input to decision-making in their school—and they don't always include **all** students. Teachers and administrators must actively seek out **all** students' opinions and insights to learn their perceptions about their classrooms and about the school outside the classroom doors.

Researchers Mari-Ana Jones and Sara Bubb have found that student voice contributes well to school improvement **but** only when alternative structures—such as those task forces, idea-generating groups, and information-gathering committees—provide for a wider democracy in the schools with a **much** greater number of students contributing. Unlike most student councils, such alternative group members can be chosen at random rather than being appointed or elected—making for broader representation.[11]

To offer the best chances of elevating voice for all students, educators must create specific strategies, initiatives, and tools to elicit ideas, information, and evaluations from students. These may include the following approaches:

- Task forces
- Interviews (Student-student, student-teacher, teacher-student with results shared)
- Periodic student evaluations of learning experiences
- Periodic student evaluations of classes
- Daily or weekly journal entries with reflections on the week's learning

- Questionnaires (created by students or teachers)
- Student surveys (created by students or teachers)
- Ongoing processes for students to give feedback
- Student committees to research and address school issues
- Long-term or short-term student decision-making groups
- Student presentations to school governing bodies
- Student membership in school governing bodies

Below are other strategies we've found to give powerful representation to—and action influenced by—student voice:

Student involvement in the process of selecting new staff members: We did this in a middle school where I (Patti) was principal, and it worked very well. We invited students to give a tour of the building to candidates who had come to interview for staff positions. The students then shared their perceptions of the candidates with the selection committee.

Students working with the board of trustees: When I (Laurie) moved into the role of district superintendent and my daily interaction with students diminished, I was challenged to find meaningful ways to directly gain input from students. Inspired by a strategy modeled by a colleague, I began (and have continued) a practice of hosting student-led district board work sessions. In each session, 10 students chosen by their peers have an opportunity to "make a pitch" for their ideas for school and district improvement. Their audience consists of school board members, administrators, teachers, staff, and students' families. The results have been astounding. Students have learned valuable skills, their voices have been heard, and their sense of *belonging* to their school and district has soared. Equally important, the adults have learned from the students in ways they never imagined. An article I wrote for *AMLE Magazine* explains this process and tells the story more fully. See the entire article, "Students Take the Lead," (Appendix E) on pages 276-279 in this book.

Student leadership councils: The staff in the middle school where I (Laurie) was principal found another exciting way to elicit student wisdom. We drew on a group of students specifically for the purpose of hearing student voice in ways that would make students a force in school improvement. This Student Leadership Council gave 30 diverse students responsibilities for listening to their peers and then forming plans for addressing students' concerns. Through research, good communication, taking the pulse of the school, and designing creative solutions and actions, students on the council took part in serious decision-making and effected important changes. Because the students on the council drew opinions from the entire student body, all students' voices were strengthened. As an additional benefit, all of the students on the council showed many gains in personal autonomy, competence, and leadership skills. Some students made amazing turn-arounds from negative to positive directions in their attitudes and behaviors. For the full story and description of the council, see the article "Student Leadership Council" (Appendix D) on pages 273-275 in this book.

Student surveys: Student surveys are highly effective tools for gathering student perspectives and advice. (Students generally enjoy doing these, especially when their responses are anonymous.) Teachers or schools can create surveys to gather ideas or feedback on one or several topics. A survey can be specific to one classroom, a grade level, a team, or an entire school. Any survey that asks for students to reflect on their school experience is an opportunity to honor and learn from student voice. With easy-to-access survey tools such as Google Forms and Survey Monkey, teachers can develop many kinds of surveys. A middle level classroom teacher might design a survey with categories and prompts (to which students answer *strongly agree, somewhat agree, somewhat disagree*, or *strongly disagree*) such as the following:

- Relationships
  - My teacher knows and cares about me as a student and a person.
  - My teacher values and respects me as an individual.

- Relevance
  - I can apply what I learn in this class to the real world.
  - I understand how I can apply what I learn in this class to something in my life either now or in my future.
- Rigor
  - My classwork is challenging.
  - Most of my assigned classwork requires me to apply what I have learned, solve problems, and really think about what I have learned.

There are dozens of categories and purposes for student surveys. Teachers can design questions or statements to discover students' perceptions about how time is used in a class, whether the teacher explains concepts in multiple ways to give lots of chances for understanding, whether students find the class engaging, whether students' ideas and suggestions are valued, whether students are treated fairly, or whether students have easy ways to get help when they need it. Surveys can provide information about students' sense of *belonging*, whether they perceive the class is increasing their competence, whether they are encouraged (and trusted) to learn independently, what instructional methods fit them best, how the school (or class) reflects and encourages diversity, whether they feel they are gaining what they need to *become* successful in high school (and beyond school), and any number of other topics. Student voice is elevated even more, by the way, when students help create the surveys!

The ultimate goal of using surveys is for teachers and other staff members to obtain meaningful feedback that will lead them to examine and reflect upon their effectiveness in the classroom or school.

The ultimate goal of using surveys is for teachers and other staff members to obtain meaningful feedback that will lead them to examine and reflect upon their effectiveness in the classroom or school. Knowing how students feel about each of these areas can help classroom teachers and schools set improvement goals for areas that will increase students' success at *belonging* and *becoming*.

Student surveys can also be accessed online. AMLE offers student and family companion surveys to its Successful Middle School Assessment that helps schools to both better understand how it is meeting the needs of its young adolescents and compare student, family, and staff perceptions of key school structures. The Quaglia Institute for School Voice & Aspirations also has surveys that target student voice, teacher voice, and parent or caregiver voice. The Student Voice Survey[12] measures eight conditions in a school that affect student voice. It is based on Quaglia's *Our Framework: The 8 Conditions that Make a Difference®* that "help educators ensure that the work they are already doing fosters an environment characterized by positive relationships, engaged learning, and sense of purpose." These eight conditions are:

1. Belonging
2. Heroes
3. Sense of Accomplishment
4. Fun & Excitement
5. Curiosity & Creativity
6. Spirit of Adventure
7. Leadership & Responsibility
8. Confidence to Take Action[13]

Students rate their level of agreement (from *strongly disagree* to *strongly agree*) with a series of statements related to each of the above eight conditions in their school. Other organizations, such as the Search Institute or Cognia, offer a range of surveys with which teachers can listen to student voices. Knowing students' perceptions about each of these conditions identified in surveys can help guide us as we work to nurture these conditions in our schools.

Student input on classes and teaching style can give us information we can't get from test scores. It may even help us predict what that test score will be before students take the test, as students' perceptions tend to mirror their achievement results. If students are telling you that something's not right, they are probably correct, and their achievement results will likely reflect that same perception.

With both school and classroom level surveys, it's helpful to get feedback while you can still use it. Issuing student perception surveys on the first day students return to school after winter break provides enough time for school leaders and teachers to gather and then actually use the feedback they get to benefit students. This midpoint of the year is an ideal time to get feedback (especially when students are fresh from a school break, had no homework due that morning, and are still thinking about holiday fun—and not how their teacher may have made them angry before the break).

Student input on classes and teaching style can give us information we can't get from test scores.

For more ideas about questions to ask and topics to discuss with students, we suggest Kathleen Cushman's book *Fires in the Middle School Bathroom: Advice for Teachers from Middle Schoolers*. Cushman traveled around the country to record the voices of middle school students, asking questions and engaging them in discussions about their lives and learning in middle school—and asking them for advice they want teachers to hear. Her aim, she said, was "first and foremost to attune the teacher to the rewards of listening closely to students themselves."[14] Use Cushman's insights and findings to do more listening to your students.

Making It Safe for Students to Share Their Opinions

If we are to encourage students to openly share their input, then it must be done in a safe environment, particularly if their perceptions contain ideas they find difficult to share. Taking any risk, whether as a student or an adult, always opens up the possibility of failure or embarrassment. If a student shares an opinion and is met with ridicule by the adult (or other students), the student will likely avoid sharing opinions in the future. Thus, when we invite student voice, we must be sure that it happens in a positive school culture that permeates all classrooms, supporting risk-taking and free (appropriate) expression of their viewpoints.

- Give students ways to offer opinions in private (anonymous surveys or questionnaires provide a safety net for students to share perceptions with "those who are in charge," particularly if the questions are about "those who are in charge"). Honor this privacy. Ask permission for sharing any student comments that are not anonymous.
- Establish guidelines within the class and school about how opinions are to be received and welcomed.
- Work to ensure that the adults in the school set a strong precedent for responding to opinions (students' and other adults') with respect.
- Teach students how to share and listen to one another's opinions respectfully—without ridicule or negative comments. Practice this in the classroom often.
- Consistently remind students that, even if others disagree with them, they still have value as people and their opinions still have value.
- Honor the value of student voice by responding when they take the risk of speaking or writing their opinions. Thank them for their reflections, information, and ideas. Tell them specifically what you learned from them and how they were helpful.

Acting on Students' Perceptions and Opinions

Student perception data is equally important as the academic data typically collected by schools and teachers. Yes, we also dislike the four-letter 'D' word at times. However, with all of the data out there to help guide continuous improvement, many schools still don't gather their most easily accessible data (which, by the way, is also the least expensive to analyze): students' perceptions and opinions. As educators, we are always looking at data. We talk constantly about data-driven or data-informed decisions. Yet, are we reviewing students' perceptions even half as much as we review their test scores? (We would guess that the answer in most schools is "no.")

There is a difference between being listened to and being listened to with respect and taken seriously. There is a difference between taking students' voices seriously and taking authentic, concrete actions to use the knowledge we get from listening to students. This is true about all situations in which you seek students' thoughts and experiences or in which students initiate sharing their voice. This is true for a student's brief statement analyzing which learning strategies best help that student learn to solve equations. It is true for the presentation a group of students gives before the school board to argue in favor of a change in detention policies. For any instance of students expressing their voices, the greatest value comes from what happens next.

Be aware that **what you do** with the results of a student survey has a greater effect on students' *belonging* and *becoming* and on raising the level of student voice (or not raising it—or even lowering it) than does the students' satisfaction at getting to express their opinions in the first place. If a student takes the risk of sharing an idea, opinion, or experience and there is no response—or if there is some affirming verbal response but nothing further happens—that student will get the message that the expression was not worth the risk. Unfortunately, this happens all too often: We ask for students' opinions, we get them, but they go nowhere. And students don't ever learn why nothing seemed to happen. Before we ask to hear from students, we should have a plan for what we'll do with the information they give.

Take students' reasonable suggestions about procedures and learning in the classroom and find ways to integrate them into or replace current practices. Bring student ideas relating to wider school topics to teams, committees, administrators, or boards that make decisions on relevant matters. (Better yet, arrange for students to present their honed ideas themselves.) We should never ask for student suggestions or opinions without taking action, letting students know what was done with the information they gave, and making sure that at least a lot of the time, their voices made a difference, changed something, made something better. They must see some of their ideas put into action. They must get feedback on what we learned from them. This is the best way to affirm student voice and to raise the level of its expression.

Teaching Students to Appropriately Share Opinions and Respond to Feedback

When we seek students' opinions, we must not assume that they know how to give them. Expressing one's voice—one's closely held beliefs, creative ideas, opinions, and evaluations—involves a host of personal, academic, and social skills. Teachers must teach students how to share opinions clearly, appropriately, respectfully, and in ways that make them likely to be heard and to make a difference. We must help students see that yelling across the room that a test "is stupid" is neither an appropriate nor productive way to share input (even if they do, in fact, think that the test is stupid). They need to know that an opinion shared in that manner is likely to be disregarded. However, students blurting out unpolished opinions, such as the example above, most often should be viewed by adults just as that: unpolished but not necessarily "bad" or wrong. As adults, we want to help them polish their input, not squash it altogether. When students have opportunities to be heard, it's pretty impressive how appropriate, mature, and thoughtful they can be (all aspects we want to see in a student who is growing toward *becoming* a young adult). We owe it to students to teach them skills that will enable their voices to be heard in the most satisfying and effective ways possible.

To elevate student voice in positive, compelling ways, we must help students learn and polish skills of speaking, writing, and listening. They need to learn and practice argumentation, skills of researching (to find evidence to support opinions, where necessary), organizing, reasoning, collaborating, reflecting, and discussing. They need to learn and practice such personal and social skills as respect, politeness, kindness, tolerance, suspension of judgment, authenticity, patience, open-mindedness, self-regulation, and impulse control (aspects that content standards alone cannot teach). Most of these skills and behaviors we already incorporate into our classes and other school activities. They can be honed and reinforced through mini-lessons, role-playing, and class discussions. All of these skills and processes mentioned in this section, by the way, strongly contribute to students' *becoming*—both academically and personally.

Back before Oregon had statewide laws prohibiting smoking on school grounds and at school activities, students who had been studying the impact of secondhand smoke in their health classes came to me, the principal (Patti), with an idea. Although no smoking was allowed in the school building, they explained that spectators coming to outdoor events like football and soccer would smoke, often while standing behind the players on sidelines. The students didn't like others smoking on campus and wanted it banned. With the guidance of their teachers, who mentored them on the steps, skills, and behaviors needed, students created a presentation to take to the school board, requested time on the agenda, and went before the board to plead their case. (Imagine the research, writing, speaking, respect, anxiety control, argumentation, and other skills needed to prepare and execute this plan!)

The school board listened and agreed to discuss and consider their request. After doing so over the course of a few months, the board implemented a policy that prohibited smoking on all school grounds and at all school-sponsored activities. The students had a good reason to celebrate and had learned how to address a concern and request changes in an appropriate manner.

At one of our (Laurie's) recent student-led board work sessions (as previously discussed), one of the proposals to the board from a student with a hearing impairment was to implement an American Sign Language club. This student and her friends wanted to be able to better communicate with one another. After hearing from the student and working through some logistics, the student's interpreter began offering an informal American Sign Language club during the students' lunch period. Once implemented, there were often so many students who wanted to attend that rotations had to be set up. This student and her peers felt listened to, heard, and validated by the board and the school, and they felt an increased sense of *belonging* when so many other peers wanted to be included so that they could better communicate with one another. And, we began to see many students working to use their newfound skills.

It is equally important to help students understand that when their suggestions are not implemented, it does not mean that they were not heard or that their opinions were not valued. For example, a common concern of middle school students is that the lunch period is too short. (Most of the time, teachers feel the same way!) Students are not usually aware of scheduling complexities, class-time requirements, and other regulations that make it impossible to extend a lunch period even by a few minutes. But they need to know about these kinds of complications. Explain the behind-the-scenes details that affect the issues they bring up. Don't underestimate their ability to understand such complexities, which are the stuff of real life and good information for them to have.

Help students understand that when their suggestions are not implemented, it does not mean that they were not heard or that their opinions were not valued.

Acknowledge students' arguments regardless of their validity, paraphrase their concerns, and explain the constraints that may preclude satisfying their wishes. These actions will go much farther toward helping students feel they were heard than if they get a terse "no, we can't do that" for an answer. Often, we owe students far more of an explanation than we are initially inclined to give. When we take the time to explain, we honor student voice, as well as students' maturity and capabilities.

In summary, when we listen to and act on their preferences, interests, and perspectives, students feel invested in their own learning, their passions flare, and their persistence in learning activities is strengthened. And when we listen to students' voices and use what we learn from them, our classrooms and schools are better for our students and for ourselves. Let us find ways to honor and listen to what every student can teach us! Adam Fletcher, researcher and avid advocate of student voice, emphasizes that student voice is only as strong as the least engaged student.[15]

HONORING AND FOSTERING CHOICE

Why?

We honor and foster student choice for the same reasons we honor student voice. As humans, students deserve to have a say in their lives both in and outside of school, and choice is a primary component of voice. It's a vehicle through which students can be agents of their own learning and of many other processes of their *belonging* and *becoming*. A student will not have any sense that personal contributions actually make a difference in learning or classroom life when everything that student does in school happens at the direction of the teacher (the teacher chooses the topics, sets the goals, makes the rules, prescribes the exact path to reach the goal, decides all the outcomes, decides the consequences, designs the assessments, and grades the assessments). Even as adults, we tend to be more accepting of ideas, more eager to finish a project, and more willing to take on additional workloads if we are given some form of choice in how those tasks are completed. Thus, just as we must take seriously students' perceptions and opinions, we must also take seriously the importance of allowing students some (appropriate) self-direction over work they are asked to do. Daniel Pink, author of *Drive: The Surprising Truth About What Motivates Us*, identifies autonomy (think of this in terms of individuals making choices) as a fundamental human need or drive.[16] It is no exaggeration to say that denying students meaningful choice impedes their ability to learn and *become*.

As with other efforts to elevate student voice, a school environment that offers meaningful choices for students boosts many aspects of *belonging* and *becoming*. Increases are found in such qualities and characteristics as autonomy, intrinsic motivation, engagement, self-efficacy, self-determination, self-regulation, self-esteem, task effort, perceived competence, achievement, cognitive flexibility, curiosity, creativity, interest in school, trust of teachers, feelings of respect and worth, comfortable relationships with peers, sense of *belonging*, and general well-being at school. In general, the environment of choice establishes a context for meeting the developmental needs of young adolescents. Students who have choices take more initiative in school processes and learning opportunities. When they can pursue their own interests and questions, students find learning to be more relevant, and they make better use of their own talents and strengths. When we give students choices, they get the message that we believe in their competence to make decisions and succeed. This respect inspires them to take more responsibility for their own learning and *become* even more competent. When they have choices in what they learn and how to learn it, students are more willing to take on challenges and to persist and finish tasks. When students have choices regarding classroom rules and procedures, they are more likely to follow them.[17]

What?

To enhance voice, autonomy, and other aspects of *becoming*, students should have appropriate, meaningful choices in the following:[18]

- What they learn
- How they learn
- How they will work (alone or with others)
- Where they learn
- With whom they learn
- Specific learning tasks
- Driving questions to ask
- Tools for learning (resources, technology, etc.)
- Homework assignments
- Ways to gain new information and skills
- Ways to practice and expand skills
- Ways to expand and deepen knowledge
- Ways to explain their thinking and learning processes
- How they show what they learn
- How they show mastery of a concept or skill
- Criteria for success
- How they are evaluated on what they learn
- What goals they set
- Making plans for attaining a goal

- Timelines for their goals
- Classroom (or team) rules, processes, and procedures
- Implementation of classroom rules and procedures
- Evaluation of classroom rules and procedures
- Some school rules or procedures
- Options for choices

How?

Here are some suggestions and ideas to consider as you embrace and expand the commitment to integrating student choice into classroom and school life. As you work with these suggestions, stay alert to the many ways that the practices and skills described will contribute to growth in students' academic and personal *becoming.* Upon close inspection, you'll realize that many also enhance aspects of *belonging.*

Believe in students' ability to choose. Believe that your middle level students are capable of self-determined, autonomous learning as well as of the cognitive and self-regulation skills that will enable them to take an active part in their own learning and classroom life. Show your belief by giving them real choices. They are more likely to use these capabilities when they feel some control over their learning.

Model making wise choices. The best way to teach students how to make wise choices is to show them. Talk through the processes of gathering (or examining) options, weighing options, looking for options that relate to your own interests or skills (or that answer your questions), deciding which options are reasonable or doable, and discarding those that are too easy or beyond moderately challenging. Let them watch and listen as you make and follow through on choices. Talk about figures from history, literature, or current events who have made wise (or unwise) choices.

Teach the skills needed for choice. Along with showing your belief that they are capable of making choices, teach students how to do it. Teach them the skills that support autonomy, decision-making, and self-determination. Be sure to plan ongoing mini- lessons that help them learn to break down learning tasks into manageable steps; define, set, and articulate attainable goals; make plans to attain their goals; identify their own interests and capabilities; make reasonable choices; organize tasks to meet their goals; monitor their progress as they work; collaborate with others to solve problems and make decisions; ask for help when they need it; and learn other skills they'll need to be successful with the choices they make.

Offer meaningful choices. When choices meet students' needs for autonomy, competence, and relatedness (in harmony with their personal and cultural values), students are motivated and engaged. Having options that are tied to their individual questions, curiosities, interests, strengths, abilities, and real lives inspires students to work hard. This supports their intrinsic motivation and shows that you know them, understand them, and respect their preferences. It invites students to invest themselves in quality work that matters. To reap the benefits that are possible with student choice, the choices offered must be relevant and, thus, meaningful.[19]

When an assignment says, "Solve ten of the twenty practice problems on the worksheet" or "Answer every other question at the end of the chapter," there is no boost given to students' autonomy or competence.

Offer real choices. Researchers Patal, Cooper, and Wynn refer to the importance of **"action choices."** These are choices in **how to do** something, rather than choices of which items to complete from a list the teacher provides. The positive effects of choice are stronger when students are not just choosing from among various teacher-generated versions of the same task.[20] For example, when an assignment says, "Solve ten of the twenty practice problems on the worksheet" or

"Answer every other question at the end of the chapter," there is no boost given to students' autonomy or competence.

Don't overcomplicate the choices. We've listed many areas for different kinds of choices, but students don't have to be making all those choices at once. Your students may progress to a project for which they choose what, how, where, when, with whom, and on what timeline they learn—and also go on to choose how the learning will be assessed. But each one of these choices is valuable in itself. These kinds of choices can (and should) be practiced one at a time.

Don't discount small choices. Choices can be big or small. Not every choice in life will be a major one, so students need lots of experience making small choices as well. Sometimes the choice involves a small assignment in which a student pursues a personal interest or explores something that has sparked curiosity. As long as the choice is meaningful, it is worthwhile. These can be worked into every facet of classroom life and learning. There are many situations and decisions in a school day when teachers can offer students clear, simple options for choice.

Keep choices challenging. To be effective for learning and growth, a choice must be complex—but not too hard. Offer choices that are challenging enough to build competence but not so difficult or complex that they are beyond the possibility of students reaching them. When you're preparing options for a class assignment, you'll need to include a range of difficulty, but help each student choose an option that will be moderately challenging to the individual student. If the options are relevant to a student's interests, the student will be willing to take on the challenge.

Make the requirements clear. With any choice—whether it be about academics, policies, procedures, behaviors, or planning events—students must know what is expected. There may be a variety of ways to reach the goal, but we can't expect students to get there if they don't know what the goal is. Be sure that students can state the requirement—for example: "Demonstrate that you can solve a multi-step equation with two variables when one variable is known" or "Introduce a claim and support it with logical reasoning and relevant evidence from credible sources" or "Choose a way and time to do your classroom job. Just be sure that the end result of doing it fulfills the job description."

Connect academic choices to clear standards. As teachers, it's our responsibility to ensure that curriculum, instruction, and assessment practices lead students to mastery of the standards. When another goal is to increase student voice and choice, plan your instruction to offer choices in some aspects of working toward a standard. Be sure that the complexity of the choices matches the complexity of the curriculum standard.

For example, there are multiple ways a student can show mastery of a reading standard, such as "cite evidence from a text that analyzes what the text says explicitly and implicitly." (There is a standard similar to this for middle level students in every state.) For choices, students may choose to work on the standard through two of the following: describing development of the main character, identifying the theme, showing the author's purpose, exposing author bias, summarizing the key conflict or claim of the text, analyzing literary devices used, or showing relevance of the information to real life. Students can also choose **how** they will show mastery; they may select from such options as writing an essay or song lyrics, drawing cartoons or diagrams, giving a speech, acting out a scene (with citations from the text), giving a TV-style news report, joining with another student to hold a debate, or creating and showing a media presentation using any number of presentation tools found online or through computer software.

The important point here is that, regardless of the choices for ways to work on the standard and demonstrate mastery, **all students are working toward the same standard.** That is the clear goal. But in taking some control over the process, students will be more engaged with the material, work harder to complete it, and find more enjoyment and meaning in their work. As a result, students with choice are far more likely to master the standard than if they had no ownership in the assignment.

Limit options. There is such a thing as choice overload. In a key study on student choice, researchers Sheena Iyengar and Mark Lepper offered college students a short-essay assignment for extra credit. They gave one group a choice of six essay topics from which to choose; the second group was offered 30 choices. From the group with fewer choices, more of the students turned in the assignment, and they also wrote better essays than those in the group with 30 choices. From this and other studies about student choice, Iyengar and Lepper concluded that although an excess of choices initially excited the choosers, it ultimately "undermined choosers' subsequent satisfaction and motivation" and left them "dissatisfied and having more regret about the choices they had made."[21] The takeaway from this is: Offer students a moderate number of choices, because too many choices can demotivate them!

Give choice about choices. In so many cases, students are capable of creating or helping to create the options for how to learn, how to show what they learn, how to evaluate their progress or performance, or how to set procedures for the classroom. Include students in brainstorming and deciding the options as often as possible.

Give feedback on choices. Provide feedback on students' choices both during and after the assignment or other situation in which they are acting on their choices. Give precise information and advice about what you see happening, how they've progressed, what you see them learning, what they might need to re-think, what they can improve, and what's working.

Teach students to monitor their progress. Before students start working on assignments they've chosen, give them ways to evaluate their progress toward chosen goals. This can be in the form of rubrics, checklists, timelines, journals, or brief notes. They can pause at intervals and self-assess what they have learned or accomplished, asking themselves whether there is anything they need to adjust or do differently or whether there are any areas in which they need guidance. Even when the teacher offers the choices, look for situations in which the student can create a personal (appropriate) option.

Don't consider choice an "add-on." Student choice is not something you add on to learning. It is not "supplemental" or "enrichment." It is something that should be an integral, required, normal part of everyday learning and classroom life. The benefits of student choice are not realized by a single experience of choice: The benefits accrue as students have ongoing experiences making and following through on meaningful choices.

Beware of "Grecian urns." Be careful not to sacrifice educational value in the name of giving students a choice. Often, students choose a "project" that turns out to be a choice with a "wow" factor—but one that doesn't really meet the educational goal. In her article "Is Your Lesson a Grecian Urn?" teacher and education blogger Jennifer Gonzalez argued that there are "far too many 'Grecian Urns': projects that look creative, that the teacher might describe as hands-on learning, interdisciplinary teaching, project-based instruction, or the integration of arts or technology—but that nonetheless lack any substantial learning for students."[22] She observed students making papier-mâché Grecian urns to meet a standard about understanding the complexity of a culture by exploring cultural elements. But when she talked to the students, it was clear that they had gained little or no understanding of the complexity of the ancient Greek culture. True, the students could choose how to design their urns—but that choice didn't lead them to the indicated goal. (If the goal or standard had been in the field of visual arts, this may have been a different story.)

Student choice is not something you add on to learning. It is not "supplemental" or "enrichment."

Gonzalez encouraged teachers to consider each project: "Does it consume far more of a student's time than is reasonable in relation to its academic impact? If students spend more time on work that will not move them forward in the skill or concept you think you are teaching, then it may be a Grecian Urn. And it may need to go."[23] She suggested that teachers can spot "Grecian Urns" by watching out for excessive coloring or crafting, an overload of cool tech, low-level thinking, or a significant part of the grade being based on attractiveness or creativity. Read her full article for advice on how to revise assignments that may be "Grecian Urns" or "Grecian Urn-ish." And remember the caution stated above: Match the complexity of the choices to the complexity of the standard.

Examining a "Choice" Assignment

Here's how a teacher in Montana put student choice into practice. Her primary goal was to teach her sixth graders to *become* critical readers able to analyze and evaluate a text's purpose and ideas and the author's presentation of them. In this assignment, she also hoped to inspire students to appreciate literary texts and fall in love with reading by finding texts that connected to their lives and experiences. She said, "It's not just the content; it's the process. A student needs to be able to apply the process (and passion) to other works so that, with any text chosen, the student can *become* a critical reader of that work."

To help her students reach the goals (which included numerous English language arts standards), the teacher developed a reading model involving a good deal of choice. Early in the school year, students were given a list of different literary genres from which to choose their reading selections. The requirement was to choose eight different literary works over the year from among nine different genres: traditional fiction, realistic fiction, historical fiction, science fiction, fantasy, mystery, biography, informational, and poetry. As the year progressed, students chose works that matched their personal interests and curiosities. The teacher worked with students to ensure that their choices matched the chosen genre (i.e., *The Devil's Arithmetic* is not science fiction) and that they chose books appropriate for their individual reading abilities (high-level readers shouldn't be choosing *The Three Little Pigs*, and readers struggling with sixth-grade-level materials probably shouldn't be reading all seven novels in the *Harry Potter* series). Each student had the responsibilities of choosing wisely and completing the chosen books (and accompanying assignments).

Because the key academic goal centered on critical reading skills, the teacher had prepared reading guides and assignments for each genre that students followed and completed as they read. In addition, she made of list of critical reading skills and compiled some questions that would lead students to develop abilities to understand each text and how the author wrote it. The list included such skills as previewing, identifying and interpreting key purposes and messages of the text, describing tone, recognizing bias, making inferences, finding meaning, analyzing the author's story-telling and writing techniques, analyzing author techniques for developing characters, analyzing how a plot or main idea developed, analyzing parts of the text and how they relate to each other, and evaluating how (and how well) the author accomplished the intended purpose. Students used these lists to guide their reading; in addition, students conferred once a week with an adult. (Adults available for this included the teacher, a classroom aide, a family volunteer, and another school staff member.) In such conferences, the adult and student used the skills list and questions to work together toward mastering standards related to critical reading.

The teacher also offered students choices for **how** to demonstrate their progress toward *becoming* critical readers. They were required to choose a different option for each of the eight books they read. Options included comparing the work to lyrics in multiple songs, writing and sharing a poem using similar techniques found in the poem they read, creating a comic strip to show development of a main idea, making a poster diagram to show relationships between ideas or events in the text, designing a "bias detector" slide show to share text evidence (illustrated) that revealed author bias, and writing a letter to the author critiquing the way they accomplished (or failed to accomplish) the intended purpose.

Nothing increases the sense of *belonging* or *becoming* (in many different ways) more than having the power, the say, the importance, the responsibility, the brain-stretching, the maturity, and the accomplishment that comes from sharing your voice—knowing your voice is wanted and respected—and having, exercising, and being accountable for your choices. Students want to know, "Do I see myself on the walls of the school?" "Am I in the eyes and hearts of the people who work with me at the school?" "Am I embraced as me—both the me I am now and the me I can *become*?" Giving students plenty of appropriate and meaningful choices and other opportunities to elevate their voices allows each one to answer "Yes!" to all these questions.

TOP 8 WAYS TO FOSTER CHOICE

- Believe that students are capable of making choices about their learning and school lives.
- Teach students skills they need for making appropriate choices.
- Offer real (not manufactured) choices—choices that involve students' action.
- Give students choices in what to learn, how they learn, and how they show what they learn.
- Make choice a normal, frequent part of classroom life.
- Let students create the choices.
- Offer choices that are meaningful and relevant to students' lives and interests.
- Offer choices that are challenging—but not out of reach.

Putting It into Practice

As an individual, team, small group, or entire staff, use these activities to spark discussions, reflect on your current practices or situations, listen to others, or set goals.

1. Review the data your school collects to reflect on improvement. Does it include students' perceptions? If so, are these perceptions gathered informally from staff or from surveys of students? Are the perceptions from a school-wide or classroom perspective? Discuss how your school uses these data to help with continuous improvement. Do you report back to students about steps taken for improvement based on their perceptions? If you don't seek out students' perceptions, what can you do to change that?

2. Ask teachers to bring at least one example of the best instructional strategy used to give students choice in their classrooms. Create sharing groups by mixing teachers across subject areas, teams, and grade levels. Have each group choose a recorder to list ideas and the name of the teacher who shared it. Collect the lists from all groups, compile the ideas, and share them with everyone.

3. Ask staff members to respond to questions like the following: "What would your students say if asked . . ."
    - How often do classroom assignments allow for choice for students?
    - What opportunities do students have to share their ideas and concerns?
    - Are student concerns listened to and acted upon? Why or why not?
    - What kinds of choices can students make in how they learn something, how they show what they learn, and how that learning is assessed?
    - Do you have assignments that resemble "Grecian Urns"? If so, how can you improve the educational value of these assignments?

Then convene a group of students and ask them the same questions. Share student answers with the staff, and then compare and contrast answers. Were there surprises? Based on the answers, identify areas that need work.

4. Review National Student Council's Raising Student Voice & Participation (RSVP) Executive Overview available at natstuco.org. Consider the possibility of using this school-wide process to gather suggestions, ideas, and opinions from your students, and create an action plan to effect change in the school and/or community.

Dear Middle Schooler,

Of the years, 2020 to 2023, I have been in middle school. These three years of your life will be different, confusing, and impacting, but despite all of that, they hold the most memories. Therefore, I challenge you to make these years the best, and with this I provide a list of advice to you.

- Following what everyone else does to fit in only causes you to lose yourself.
- Nothing lasts forever, even friends. The ones that hurt the most to let go of teach the most important lessons, but the ones that remain are the ones you never forget.
- When things seem challenging, look both ways—how far you have come, and how far you will go.
- Never let anyone get inside your head, even yourself.
- No matter the problem, there was always a solution (except math).
- Overthinking wastes time, and time is something no one can get back.

I wish you the best of luck. Remember, it's your life, and your story, so be careful how you write it.

— Kami, Grade 8

Chapter 8

Develop Student Leadership

Education is too important to be left solely to educators.

— Francis Keppel

Middle school students! They want to be active. They want to participate in real life situations. Some want to serve. Some want to be in charge. Some are curious about the world around them and want to make it a better place; these students can be very compassionate toward those less fortunate than themselves. Many are eager and willing to advocate for others. They want educators to "respect and value young adolescents" (the first of AMLE's 18 characteristics for successful middle schools).[1] Our young adolescent students possess the intelligence and skill potential to *become* powerful forces for change and improvement. They all have a strong need to *belong*. And we can help them *become* more caring and compassionate preteens and teens (and eventually, adults) who can help others and who can help make their schools and world better places.

Those of us who work with young adolescents recognize their desire to contribute their energies and ideas toward making a difference. In today's world that is highly focused on social media, we hear the term "influencer" used frequently, and young adolescents can be very susceptible to the behavior and decisions that influencers promote (which are not always in the best interests of young adolescents). But do students realize that there is a difference between someone who declares themselves to be an "influencer" and someone who is truly a leader?

As middle level educators, we must help our students move beyond the simple idea of influencing others and help them develop the skills it takes to *become* an authentic leader. By teaching them to recognize the qualities that demonstrate good leadership, and through providing them with opportunities for leadership, we help them begin to develop the skills needed to *become* leaders themselves.

But we sometimes struggle with exactly how to help them do that. When students take on leadership roles, even small ones, they *belong* to their schools and communities in new and meaningful ways. Leadership experiences also move students along paths toward *becoming* in many of the ways we've already discussed in this book. Authentic leadership experiences draw on and accelerate growth in such qualities as self-motivation, self-efficacy, confidence, self-determination, self-discipline, responsibility, perseverance, growth mindset, social awareness, empathy, values exploration, motivation, grit, healthy relationships, ethical development, confidence, autonomy, competence, creativity, communication, decision-making, and expression of voice.[2] Leadership researchers also find that successful development of student leadership promotes greater improvement to school culture and increases academic engagement, both for the student leaders and for those other students they influence.[3] Furthermore, teacher educator Peggi Zelinko explains that "leadership training is a powerful instructional strategy to engage students in authentic and experiential activities where they can both learn and apply SEL skills of all kinds."[4]

Development of leadership skills and traits also has a direct impact on students' engagement and academic success in the classroom. Students tend to apply leadership skills—such as organization, communication, time management, problem solving, courage to take risks, and collaborating effectively with others—to complete tasks and improve their academic performances. These students often *become* role models for their peers and play an important part in helping create a positive school and classroom environment.[5]

All of these benefits mentioned above are compelling examples of *becoming*—both academically and personally! They demonstrate that leadership experiences of any kind are powerful forces for *belonging* and *becoming*.

CEMENTING THE FOUNDATIONS OF LEADERSHIP DEVELOPMENT

A six-year-old neighbor of mine (Patti) told me she loves being the line leader in her kindergarten class. I asked her why (in truth, expecting that her reason would have to do with the good feeling of being first). Her answer: "I like being the one who gets to help everyone else get to where they want to go." When a middle school orchestra performs its spring concert, my friend's son conducts one of the pieces. (Five other orchestra members each conduct a piece as well). His self-esteem and confidence, along with his musical skills, have soared. A niece, who is a high school sophomore, mentors a group of sixth graders in an exploratory coding class. At the same time that she is developing teaching and relationship skills, she is also stretching her own understanding of coding processes as she works to restate them in ways the younger students can understand.

The benefits of student leadership experiences—short- or long-term, simple or sophisticated—are countless. When schools provide opportunities for all students to gain and practice leadership skills, they offer exciting ways for all students to grow personally and academically. In the Center for Creative Leadership's 2019 white paper, "Transforming K-12 Schools by Investing in Leadership Development," researchers posited that investment in high-quality leadership development in schools "can directly impact student success in the classroom—and beyond."[6] Another extremely important finding was that student leadership is integral to the development of a positive, connected school community: **All members of the community benefit** when many students take on leadership roles.[7] Overall, schools do a better job of accomplishing their missions and nurturing their students (and staff) when students learn to lead. Moreover, colleges, businesses, governments, and other organizations in our society and world will need capable leaders in the generations to come. Where will these leaders come from? They must come from our schools! "Leadership training for our students is an investment in our present and future."[8]

The Center for Creative Leadership surveys leaders in business, government, nonprofit organizations, and education, asking a series of questions about leadership needs and qualities. Their *Leadership Insights Survey* included questions about the age at which students should begin leadership experiences, whether leadership development should be part of the regular school curriculum, and how widely leadership training should be offered. Of the 462 respondents from all sectors, 97% believed that leadership development should begin by age 21, with 90% saying before age 18 and 50% believing it should begin in elementary school. In addition, the report showed that "the vast majority of respondents (84%) believe leadership development opportunities should be offered to **all youth**, and an even higher number (90%) feel it should be a part of **every** student's educational experience."[9]

As we discussed in Chapter 1, schools across the country are developing lists of competencies students should have when they graduate from high school; some are even developing such lists for students in grades K–8 as well. Many of these lists include leadership competencies and skill sets—which are expected of **all** students.

Adam Fletcher, creator of the Meaningful Student Involvement (MSI) model for school improvement, argues that students should be equal partners in **all** phases of the operation of a school. The MSI model "promotes student engagement by securing roles for students in every facet of the educational system and recognizes the unique knowledge, experience, and perspective of each individual student."[10] Fletcher also states:

> Every day more educators are showing that they value students by involving them in meaningful ways in school. These teachers and administrators say that it is not about "making students happy" or allowing students to run the school. Their experience shows that when educators partner with students to improve learning, teaching and leadership in schools, school change is positive and effective.[11]

The foundations for all student leadership efforts in our schools will come from what we believe about students and leadership. Just as with other programs that elevate development of crucial aspects of *belonging* and *becoming* for students, leadership development programs must begin with an examination and clarification of our beliefs and philosophies. Fortunately, beliefs related to this topic should flow naturally from the commitments we have already made to create connected, inclusive, equitable, caring communities; to believe in students; to promote their self-efficacy and autonomy; and to champion student voice and choice.

Authors of *The Handbook for Student Leadership Development* include the following among the beliefs they see as foundational to student leadership development:[12]

- Leadership can be learned.
- Leadership is developmental.
- All students can develop leadership.
- All schools must find ways to develop leadership capabilities and skills for all students.

The staff in each school—ideally in collaboration with students and families—can take a fresh look at the practices and programs for student leadership. We educators can ask what these practices show about our beliefs. Do our actions reflect a belief that young adolescents are capable and responsible enough to be given authentic leadership opportunities within the school? Do they show that we believe **every student** has the potential to *become* a leader and that the school should nurture every student equitably to *become* an engaged citizen and a contributing leader? When we examine our current beliefs and practices, we should look at all the facets of our school and all existing leadership-development efforts. This must include the leadership development that occurs naturally for many students in classrooms, on sports teams, and in all the organized clubs and groups on our campuses. We should take the time to clarify the goals for any programs (formal or informal) we have and for any we wish to add. Our examination must include a close look at how we chose the goals, how we chose the activities and programs, and how the facets of our overall program are monitored and evaluated.

If we share the beliefs above, we certainly cannot continue to view leadership-development experiences primarily as the domain of exclusive clubs or representative committees that include only certain students. We can't rely solely on sports teams or other extracurricular programs to provide the only leadership experiences students need. Doing so is an impediment to *becoming* for too many of our students (probably the majority of them). We must expand the definition to encompass new, creative, and diverse options that offer possibilities for **all** students to gain the benefits of leadership—leadership they experience for themselves and that they see in other students.[13]

RETHINKING STUDENT LEADERSHIP TRAINING

Schools are at different places in their efforts to address leadership development. The programs they design must fit the unique needs of their students, but when the belief and commitment are to include **all** students in **meaningful** ways, schools must strive to raise the levels of:

1. Leadership skills and qualities for all students, and
2. Student participation in leadership by giving students multiple authentic opportunities with enough possibilities that allow them **all** to actually **be** leaders (and *become* even better leaders).

Developing Leadership Skills and Qualities

When we considered and researched the skills and qualities of leadership, we ended up with a long list. (When you consider this topic, you'll likely come up with ideas to make it even longer!) Also, we quickly became aware of how much the composition of the list reminded us of the skills and qualities we've discussed throughout this book. But they take on new meaning and new urgency in the context of the leadership development that is so necessary—and so achievable—for our middle level students.

At first, we were overwhelmed by the all-inclusiveness of the skills and attributes that our students need to be leaders and can develop and grow, if given leadership experiences. This is true regardless of whether we think of student leadership in roles that seem large (ongoing or public, with lots of extensive contributions) or small (short-term, part of everyday school experiences). We thought, "How do we fit in a whole new repertoire of skills to teach?" We quickly realized that schools and teachers already take seriously these skills and qualities and that attention to them is already a part of school classrooms, programs, and practices—across content areas and activities. What we educators must do now is think about how these skills and qualities relate to leadership roles and give students opportunities to develop them **within** leadership roles.

We can't rely solely on sports teams or other extracurricular programs to provide the only leadership experiences students need.

A good leader:

- Shows kindness and respect to **all** others.
- Speaks and acts responsibly.
- Inspires others to be better tomorrow and make some part of the world better.
- Examines personal values and viewpoints.
- Is assertive but tactfully so.
- Is confident but not overbearing.
- Understands individual strengths, challenges, and motivations.
- Values and welcomes all members of the community without any discrimination.
- Is eager to hear and embrace other viewpoints.
- Shares decision-making.
- Helps others feel confident.
- Makes other people better.
- Is humble.
- Is persistent.
- Keeps an open mind.
- Is creative: tries new approaches and ideas.

- Gives credit to others.
- Does not assume to be the only person who knows the best way to do everything.
- Does not blame others but instead takes steps to help correct a situation.
- Focuses energy where it will do the most good.
- Expresses gratitude to others.
- Asks for and welcomes help.
- Communicates before acting.
- Consults with others.
- Takes initiative.
- Takes responsibility.
- Accepts and demonstrates accountability.
- Keeps a cool head.
- Works hard.
- Delegates: doesn't try to do everything alone.
- Models ethical behavior.
- Learns to deal with and respond to mistakes.
- Is willing to correct mistakes and learn from them.
- Shows passion about personal beliefs.
- Has a sense of humor.
- Doesn't hog the spotlight but instead shines it on other people.
- Is truthful.
- Is trustworthy.
- Does not gossip.
- Invites evaluation of personal leadership.
- Seeks to learn from others.
- Seeks to keep on learning.
- Uses personal power responsibly and caringly.
- Is real: shares personal beliefs and does not try to be somebody else.

Some leadership skills and qualities to develop, expand, and practice:

- Kindness
- Compassion
- Respect
- Effective speaking
- Respectful listening
- Self-expression
- Self-awareness
- Self-direction
- Making decisions

- Shared decision-making
- Discussion
- Collaboration
- Conflict resolution
- Conflict response
- Goal setting
- Analyzing options and situations
- Reflection
- Giving and receiving feedback
- Flexibility
- Cultural awareness
- Caution and discretion in online presence and communications
- Building healthy relationships
- Emotional stability
- Emotional intelligence
- Responsibility
- Empathy
- Honesty
- Humility
- Courage
- Integrity
- Reasoning
- Reasoned, compassionate evaluation
- Self-esteem
- Self-belief
- Self-confidence
- Ethical behavior
- Organization and planning
- Problem solving
- Creating and making presentations
- Public speaking
- Project management
- Team building
- Working with a team

Wow! What a list of components for our young adolescents' processes of *belonging* and *becoming*—all of which can be enhanced with leadership experience. Development of these qualities and skills can be a part of every classroom and school activity. If they do not already, teachers can plan specific, targeted situations for students to make and defend decisions, identify and take on different roles in classroom activities, practice giving and receiving feedback, analyze what they've learned, evaluate results of learning activities, discuss concerns in the classroom, learn from mistakes, solve conflicts, adapt plans due to changing circumstances, listen respectfully to one another, work in collaborative groups, write mission statements for a class or team, set goals and work to achieve them, design and carry out service projects, reflect on personal responses to classroom situations or group work, or further any other quality or skill listed above.

Offering Plenty of Authentic Leadership Opportunities

To make strides toward leadership development for all students, educators must think creatively—beyond formal leadership programs. Yes, a fair number of students in a middle school can develop leadership skills in traditional clubs, sports teams, student councils, and leadership electives. But in most schools, these will not cover the majority of students. Moreover, schools often do not purposefully specify, track, or evaluate what leadership skills are actually being developed within those programs, nor for which students. (A student can be on a sports team for years without developing or practicing leadership skills; that student may see a good leadership example in the coach but might not have opportunities to lead.)

The concept of offering leadership development for all students goes far beyond the idea of teaching all students a number of leadership skills—that is, teaching in a way that has students listening, watching, reading about, or discussing qualities and skills (but not doing any actual leading themselves). It even goes beyond practicing those skills in real-life situations. Although such learning is a necessary component, leadership lessons are more valuable—and more likely to be internalized—in experiential settings where the learner is **actually practicing leadership**.[14]

Schools must purposefully design situations in which each student has the experience of being the leader. This must be a school-wide approach based on school-wide goals. To meet the goal of reaching all students, most schools will need to add opportunities for experiences that hand over leadership to students—within the regular curriculum, in their classrooms, in specialized leadership classes, in all school organizations, in partnerships outside the school, in service learning, and in community engagement. Furthermore, because students are diverse, the school's plan must also include diverse strategies and approaches.[15]

Researcher Adam Fletcher describes conditions for "meaningful student involvement" (MSI, as his school improvement model calls it):

- Students develop complex learning skills.
- Students are equal partners in education.
- There is no discrimination regarding who can participate.
- Students are integrated into organizational and attitudinal change.
- Students gain validation through action and involvement that empowers them.
- Student participation in experiences is measurable and effective.[16]

If students are to be equal partners, if they are to gain validation through powerful action and involvement, if all students can lead and should have chances to do so—and if we believe in student voice and choice—then we must surely include students in planning leadership opportunities. And if we believe that there should be no discrimination regarding who can be a leader, and that a diverse student body (and all student bodies are diverse) means we must offer diverse approaches, then it's even more certain that students must take part in planning the goals and details of a leadership development program that will interest them. That's the best way to ensure student enthusiasm, ownership, and engagement—and it's the best way to ensure program success, too.

COMBINING POSSIBILITIES INTO PROGRAMS

An overall school design for student leadership development will likely be unique to the school itself. Cookie-cutter programs are not as effective as those tailored to fit the needs of the students and the vision of the school. The specific program structure is not what matters; what matters is that it meets the conditions for meaningful student involvement and reaches the school's leadership development goals for all students. Each school must ask how to increase authentic leadership experiences through which all of its students have many chances to **be** leaders.[17]

As middle level leaders ourselves, we are enthusiastic about re-thinking student leadership development. We're thrilled to witness what happens in the lives and enthusiasm of students (as well as their teachers and schools) when we expand the boundaries to offer all kinds of new leadership experiences for students. We encourage you, too, to push the boundaries, to mix all kinds of options, and to shape an overall student leadership development program that works for you—even if its shape is like none you've ever seen!

Top 6 Suggestions for Student Leadership Development

- Include all students in your plan to develop leadership skills.
- See that every student has several leadership experiences each week.
- Involve all students in leadership that serves others.
- Make relationships and ethics central to leadership training.
- Give students tools and time to reflect on leaders (including themselves).
- Purposefully plan ways to evaluate all components of your leadership development program.

Formalized Programs

Most schools have some formalized "leadership" experiences designed to build and promote leadership. Even these experiences must be personalized to the needs of the specific school. Traditionally, only leadership classes include leadership training. Other formalized programs, such as student councils—elected or appointed—tend to include discussion and decision-making related to student concerns. But actual, comprehensive leadership training may not be part of the experience. Students taking part in formalized experiences—whether they are elected, teacher-chosen, or volunteers—must understand how their involvement and leadership impacts others (both positively and, if used inappropriately, perhaps negatively). In a world where people tend to be very self-centered (particularly at this age), all students need to see how they, as individuals, can make a meaningful difference in someone else's life.

In the process of creating an overall plan for student leadership development, school staff (again, hopefully with student participation) need to consider the following for each formalized experience (whether it is already in place or currently being considered): how it fits into the overall school goals and plan for leadership development, what leadership skills will be taught (and how and by whom), what responsibilities and activities the organization or experience will take on, how to involve as many students as possible, when and where it will take place, who will oversee it, and how it will be evaluated. The following are a few models being used in successful middle school programs around the country:

Elective or exploratory classes: Many schools run effective leadership development programs as part of their elective or exploratory course offerings. In some cases, students choose a leadership class or are assigned to it as a part of the schools' rotating cycle of electives. These classes may last a trimester or a quarter in order to include as many students as possible in the experience. Depending on the school, a leadership class may be taught by an administrator, teacher, or counselor. (Schools might consider using a student as a co-leader, one who has completed the class and also gained real leadership experience.)

Voluntary training: In some situations, schools run successful leadership programs simply by admitting however many students want to attend (or can be handled by the leaders). For example, in one school we visited, three leaders host a leadership class every Wednesday morning before school at 7:30. The only requirement is to be there on time. The classes have an average attendance of 90 students a week, with about 200 different students attending over the course of a year (and most of the 500 students at this school are bus riders).

Elected leadership groups: Many middle level schools use an elected student council model; others have adapted this model to involve more students in leadership, whereby small groups of students—instead of an individual—may run for an office or position. Another variation on this model is to have each team choose two or three representatives to attend a weekly leadership meeting at the school. Each quarter, different students may be selected to attend.

Teacher-selected leadership groups: In another model for student leadership organizations, staff members choose student leaders (students who obviously function as leaders—although their leadership ability may range from positive to not-so-positive). The goal is to nurture students' leadership potential from wherever they are starting! This method also helps to curtail the "popularity contest" effect on elections. Because this type of leadership group would limit those who participate, it is important that it not be the only leadership group on campus. (See the article titled "Student Leadership Council" (Appendix D) on pages 273-275 for more on this idea.)

Possibilities Beyond a "Program"

There are dozens of possibilities for experiential leadership learning opportunities—both in the classroom and around the school—that can occur frequently and for many students, beyond what we usually think of as a "program." These include such opportunities as:

- Student-led decision-making groups within regular curriculum areas
- Student-led cooperative learning groups

- Student-planned and student-led lessons within the classroom
- Student-planned and student-led classroom procedures
- Peer tutoring or mentoring
- Peer counseling (with training)
- Student-created and broadcast podcasts
- Student safety patrols in hallways
- Mentoring or tutoring of students from younger grades
- Student-led classroom or team meetings
- Student-led conferences with school personnel
- Student-led conferences with parents or caregivers
- Student-led committees to make recommendations on a specific issue
- Student-led task forces to research topics of concern

In addition, a school may establish any number of leadership groups for a particular length of time or purpose. These can exist alongside the experiential lessons in classrooms and established long-term leadership groups such as student councils and after-school programs. Below, we describe some activities we have seen planned and implemented successfully by middle school student leadership groups. With any experiences such as these, make sure that students take the lead in planning, implementing, and evaluating.

Service in the Wider Community

- Host a back-to-school night for senior citizens. Have a school bus pick up residents from local retirement homes. Plan activities like bingo, digital communication skills (tablets, computers, internet use), dancing (it warms the heart to see a middle schooler jitterbugging with a senior citizen), a cakewalk, and crafts.
- Hold a "scavenger hunt" food drive for those in need. Students (and staff) form teams of eight, give themselves a team name, and collect items on a list. Each item brought from the list (generally food or money) is worth a set number of points. Teams compete to see who can accumulate the most

points. The winning team is awarded a "night on the town" (pizza, movie coupons, bowling, etc.). Leadership kids plan and host a breakfast or lunch for the winning staff team.

- Adopt a local senior citizen's residence or nursing home. Go Christmas caroling, plan a Valentine's Day party for them, organize an old-fashioned sing-along, bring them cookies, or just go visit to get better acquainted.
- Participate in community events. Help out with Special Olympics or a Down Syndrome Buddy Walk. Sponsor a booth at a local festival. Build a float for a holiday parade. Help put together food baskets at the local food bank. Ring the bell at holiday time for the Salvation Army.
- Partner with a local community service organization such as Rotary or the Lions Club to work together to meet the needs of the community (where oftentimes students and their families are the recipients of this community service).

School Climate Builders

- Leadership students can plan and host fun assemblies based on game shows (try "Family Feud" or "Who Wants to be a Millionaire?"), talent shows (variations of "America's Got Talent" or "The Voice,") or athletic competitions (staff and students competing on tiny tricycles, running an obstacle course, etc.). Assemblies can also serve to introduce staff to students at the beginning of the year or to teach students the rules in a fun way (a dress code demonstration with teachers breaking the rules is always a big hit with students!).
- Recognize and celebrate staff. Students create a silly costume from the costume closet and visit staff members on their birthday; a song is sung, and birthday treats are served on a fancy tray. Give ornaments at holiday time. Bring treats for Teacher Appreciation Day. Host a brunch for Secretary's Week. Plan a special day to honor the custodial staff, office staff, food services staff, maintenance staff, etc.
- Organize spirit days (everyone wears school colors), theme days (the 50s), holiday events (decorate doors for holidays), or contests (guess how many candy hearts are in the glass display case).

- Produce a video to encourage proper behavior. Act out harassment situations. Have the narrator ask the viewers to pause the video for a discussion. Finish by acting out several solutions.
- Invite members of the community to attend an assembly to take part in the "Hands are Not for Hurting" program. Visitors cut out purple hands and take the pledge in front of the school. All students are then encouraged to make the pledge during the following days.
- Honor a Student of the Day. Each morning, draw a student's name from a jar containing all student body names, and announce the name drawn as the Student of the Day. The winner comes to the office to receive a treat and other affirmations planned by the student leadership group.

Service in the School

- Form a greeter's group to welcome new students, help them find their way around the school and learn school routines, sit with them at lunch (an important need for students), and help them navigate school life.
- Lobby to change school procedures. (One group successfully lobbied the entire staff to change a long-standing "no gum" rule.)
- Organize an activity night. Think beyond just a dance: Show videos, have carnival-type booths (face painting, bean bag toss), play games in the gym, compete at bingo, hold a karaoke contest, etc.
- Be responsible for changing the school reader board, running the school recycling program, or reading the morning announcements over the intercom.
- Help with fifth grade orientation and fall registration. Act as tour guides for school visitors.
- Organize a skate night for students and families from the entire school district or your feeder elementary schools.
- Host a "transition to high school" event for eighth graders. Bring in high school students and staff to share experiences and information.

- Plan a way to honor teachers during Teacher Appreciation Week or support staff during Support Staff Week. One leadership group sponsored "Doug Day" to recognize the work their custodian, Doug, did to keep the school clean.

Fundraisers

- Hold a penny war. Create containers for each grade level as well as one for the staff. A penny placed in a container gives that group one point. Silver or paper money counts for negative points (a dime is –10, a dollar bill –100). Students try to put pennies in their team's jar and silver or paper money in the other teams' jars.
- Sell hat passes. If your school has a "no hats" rule, on a given day let students purchase a "hat pass" to wear on a special "Hats On" Day. Students who purchase a button with an anti-drug message (or for some other cause) may wear a hat as long as the button is showing.
- Students donate money to get a staff member (or a group of staff members) to do something mildly embarrassing (like kissing a pig or getting a pie in the face) in front of the entire school.
- Hold a car wash. Take pledges for a Bowl-a-thon or Jog-a-thon. Have a bottle drive.

Earlier in the book, we emphasized the role that teacher–student relationships play in helping students to *belong* to their classrooms and school and to *become* in a multiplicity of areas of growth. Leadership development is yet another area of *belonging* and *becoming* where relationships play a key role. Middle school students often erect smokescreens that make it hard to identify their potential or interests. But a teacher, advisor, or other adult advocate who has gotten to know the individual student and who has built a trusting relationship with the student knows the student's talents and interests. This is the very person who can steer the student toward suitable leadership opportunities and support the student in leadership development. In the presence of a strong adult–student relationship, there is a valuable resource to identify student potential—and to connect that student with other students who share similar interests and potential. This can help to increase the sense of *belonging* at the same time the student is *becoming* a leader and developing many other aspects of *becoming*—socially, cognitively, emotionally, and psychologically!

I (Patti) remember a time at my middle school in southern Oregon when such a relationship paid off to help a student who otherwise may never have found her way into any positive leadership situation. The school established a peer mediation program—a form of conflict resolution that trained students to help their peers work together to resolve everyday disputes. For such a program to work effectively, it's important to select peer mediators who reflect the population of the school. A teacher recommended a student for the program who, at first glance, appeared to be a poor choice. Julia was a bully known for disruptive behavior, yet she was "popular" with a large number of students—possibly because they admired her "power." But the teacher knew more about Julia than the rest of us, and he had faith in her potential. Trusting the teacher's advice and relationship with Julia, we took a chance and selected Julia for the program. She participated fully and attended all the training (which involved mentoring in skills of leadership, collaboration, and conflict resolution as well as skills of self-regulation, interpersonal relationships, and respect). Julia became one of the most effective mediators we ever had in the program. By the next year, she had turned herself around to *become* a positive force in the school. She continued with the program into high school and eventually became a speaker and representative for the organization that provided the initial training. This all happened because a teacher who had built a relationship with her recognized Julia's potential, even when most of the remainder of us saw her as troublesome.

Other Thoughts and Advice on Leadership Development

- Every quarter, when you review assessments and progress for all other areas of *belonging* and *becoming*, create a category for examining each student's participation in leadership development training and experiences. Create a checklist or table where you can keep track of all the opportunities each individual has been given for authentic leadership.

- Every student leadership group needs an adult guide who has a heart for kids and for the mission of the group. This is a must!
- Communicate leadership events regularly and clearly with the staff and students who are not in the leadership group.
- During and after leadership activities, review and emphasize leadership concepts and qualities.
- Emphasize responsibility and accountability throughout all leadership experiences for students.
- Use lots of hand-on and team-building activities, but don't forget to add a reflective component.
- Have a focal point for your fundraising activities. Adopt a pet project. For example, in Oregon, many student leadership groups joined the effort to raise money to build a new addition to the state children's hospital. The end result? The young people raised more than a million dollars!
- Think beyond using just teachers or administrators as advisors to student leadership groups. At one of our schools, two classified employees and one teacher started an outstanding leadership program.
- Just because students are in a leadership group does not mean they will be actual leaders. You must create opportunities for this to happen. When such a group plans events, the adult supervisor should not be the leader with a student as an assistant—rather, the students must be the leaders or co-leaders for events. Rotate student leadership to let many students gain experience in leadership roles.
- Students need to explore traits of effective leaders. Students can shadow the mayor of their town, attend a school board meeting, or design and administer a survey for local leaders to answer (including high school student leaders and sports team captains).
- Students need experiences reflecting on leaders and leadership. Once students learn some qualities of good leaders, they should reflect on what they see in leaders around them—in their school, community, states, nation,

and in the world. Ask them to think about their role models and celebrities as leaders and to evaluate them as leaders.

- One of the most important duties of leaders and leadership groups is to serve others. See that all students have experiences in using their leadership skills to help someone else.

To conclude this chapter on developing student leadership, we will share a story from Meridian Middle School in Lynden, Washington, where the school's student leadership group has been helping their school return to a sense of normalcy and revitalization after several years of COVID-19 restrictions. "After coming out of a few years of limited social activities, it has been really great to see students experience the joys of spirit weeks, dances, and assemblies again," said Assistant Principal Robert Kratzig.

The leadership class includes students in sixth, seventh, and eighth grades; last year when they hosted just one outdoor social at the end of the school year, it was a great success. "I had staff tell me that kids enjoyed the outdoor social so much that they said they would want to come to school more if we had more activities like that," said art teacher and leadership advisor Alison Yeager. "Last year, we really focused more on just being a good leader. This year we are actually able to work in groups, and we are able to plan more events."

Students say the increase in social activities not only makes school more fun, but it also gives them a chance to make their school a more welcoming place. And the school staff agrees that building positive school culture leads to more engagement in the classroom. "I have seen first-hand just how important student leadership is to creating a culture of belonging at a school," Kratzig said. "We want to create a school where students want to be each day. When students feel connected to their school and that the people here—both staff and classmates—appreciate who they are as a whole person, it increases academic achievement and buy-in in the classroom."[18]

PUTTING IT INTO PRACTICE

As an individual, team, small group, or entire staff, use these activities to spark discussions, reflect on your current practices or situations, listen to others, or set goals.

1. Make a list of leadership opportunities available to students at your school. Review the list, and determine how many of the activities involve organizing activities (school dance, canned food drive, etc.) versus leading (principal advisory group, making changes to school procedures, peer mediation, mentoring, etc.). Is the balance between organizing versus leading appropriate? Are you too heavy on one side? What types of opportunities are missing?

2. Examine your school's data on student leadership. How many students are given the opportunity to participate in leadership development—both formalized and "casual" programs? Do the formalized programs involve groups that are heterogeneously mixed (in gender, social group, age, socioeconomic status, ethnicity, etc.)? How can you use these data to improve opportunities for more students?

3. Work with students to create a survey on student leadership in your school. Let students tell you about their perceptions of leadership development, whether they are actually having leadership experiences, what student leadership contributes to their school lives, and what changes they would suggest. Make sure that students are involved in reviewing, analyzing, and reporting the results as well as that the school's governing and decision-making bodies listen to what the students have to say on the matter.

Middle school is a great time to learn new things and grow as a person. Middle school can also be a challenging time, but it's important to remember that everyone is going through the same thing. With the support of friends, family, and teachers, middle school can be a positive and rewarding experience.

— Dionne, Grade 6

"You wear braces!" Bob exclaimed, "Me too!"
I watched in amazement as he opened his mouth, revealing the same rubber bands and braces that I had.
I smiled.
Maybe I was wrong.
Maybe it was OK to be different.

— Alan, Grade 6

Chapter 9

Celebrate Belonging and Becoming

Celebrate what you want to see more of.

— Tom Peters

Acknowledging what students do right can never be wrong! Too often in education, there is a focus on what needs to be fixed. So much energy is poured into addressing problems that there's little energy left to pay attention to what's working, growing, or going well. In this book, we've framed the mission and goals of middle level education in terms of students' *belonging* and *becoming*. If these processes (and the dozens of qualities, behaviors, and skills that they entail) are what our work with middle level students is all about, then *belonging* and *becoming* are what all students and educators need to celebrate!

When we use the phrase "what students do right," we mean to expand the "do right" idea far beyond the boundaries of playing by all the rules, diligently achieving, or being a model student. There are hundreds of ways for students to do something right or well (something that shows their growth in *belonging* or *becoming*). Within each student there are many actions, insights, behaviors, and accomplishments to recognize and celebrate—if we educators are there to notice, if we enlist students in looking for them, and if we widen our search. The more we expand the actions, situations, and people we celebrate, the more inclusive we are in ensuring that students know they are valued and that they matter.

The very process of learning to celebrate enhances students' *belonging* and *becoming*. When they recognize what they have contributed, their *belonging* increases. When they recognize what they have accomplished, and receive positive feedback for what they have done, their *becoming* increases. When they celebrate with a group of fellow students, all of them gain affirmation that intensifies their *belonging* and *becoming*. As students examine and acknowledge their own growth, they make strides toward *becoming* as learners and thinkers. Research affirms a wonderful array of positive academic, social, and emotional outcomes from celebrating in schools—with such benefits as:[1]

- Boosted self-esteem and self-determination
- Increased student motivation and engagement
- Greater personal joy and satisfaction with schoolwork and events
- More effective goal setting and greater responsibility for own learning
- Enhanced emotional safety and more positive classroom culture
- Improvement in memory and other cognitive functions
- Expanded growth mindset and the will to try harder
- Healthier relationships and group solidarity
- Heightened creativity and optimism
- Stronger sense of *belonging* and value to the group
- Reinforced expectations for supporting one another
- Intensified excitement for learning
- Diminished apathy
- Strengthened resilience
- More overall enjoyment of school
- Greater sensitivity to the needs, gifts, and rights of others

When there is an intentional plan to look for, notice, appreciate, and celebrate students' growth in positive directions—it's good for everyone in the school. We all know that teachers and administrators can't ignore the chaos of changing classes, pretend that lunch with 300 adolescents isn't happening, or act as if the bus loading zone doesn't exist. A parent or caregiver isn't likely to call the school and complain, "You didn't brag on my child today." Yet that same parent or caregiver will most certainly call if their child felt unsafe in the halls because there isn't enough adult supervision during class changes, didn't get to eat lunch, or missed the bus home.

When there is an intentional plan to look for, notice, appreciate, and celebrate students' growth in positive directions—it's good for everyone in the school.

Charles E. Hummell, author of the best-selling pamphlet *Tyranny of the Urgent,* coined that title phrase to characterize an ongoing conflict in many organizations and groups (including families) between things that are *urgent* and things that are *important*.[2] In schools, we often address this struggle by attending to the things we **have** to do while ignoring the things that are not urgent or required, even though they may be important. But when we change our thinking and view celebrating students as no less urgent and necessary than class transitions, lunch duty, and bus dismissal, we honor our students. And adults benefit, too: Teachers find more joy and meaning in teaching and enjoy their students more, while parents and caregivers experience greater school connection, pride, and joy.[3] You'll be amazed at the positive impact on the entire school culture and the attitudes of teachers, administrators, and all staff members when students' growth is celebrated and when the work of the adults who helped them *belong* and *become* is celebrated as well.

DECIDING WHAT TO CELEBRATE

Think of celebrating as noticing, appreciating, enhancing, and continuing positive experiences, occasions, behaviors, accomplishments, contributions, and values.

Back in Chapter 1, we described many characteristics to form a definition and picture of both *belonging* and *becoming*. At the end of the chapter, we encouraged you to create your own lists of what is included in *belonging* and *becoming* in your school and classrooms.

In the Conclusion (see pages 249-262), you'll find middle level students' reflections on manifestations of *belonging* and actions that help students *belong*. Let these lists and reflections be guidelines when you consider what to celebrate! For example, if you see that your students *belong* to their school when they . . .

- Feel a sense of identification with their school or groups in it
- Feel safe at school—physically, socially, emotionally, and psychologically
- Feel that they have a voice in school
- Feel respected throughout the school
- Believe in their own indispensability to the group
- Trust their teachers and their peers
- Believe that they have as much value as anyone else
- Are confident that others see them as valuable
- Feel securely connected with others in their school and classes
- See themselves as being part of a supportive community
- Not only feel support but are also able to accept it
- Feel wanted and needed
- Feel like individuals—not stereotypes
- Perceive and trust that the *belongingness* they feel is likely to continue

. . . then these are the things to look for and celebrate when you see them! When students show visible signs of *belonging*, when they reflect on their sense of *belonging* and can tell how and why it is there or has grown, when they can describe their personal *belonging* in positive terms—**celebrate!** When you, or students, or anyone else in the school see a student **do** something to help another student *belong*—recognize and affirm this.

Likewise, if you believe that your students are *becoming* when they . . .

- Learn academic skills and show their learning proficiently
- Hone various processes for continued learning
- Build a necessary base of knowledge
- Think critically
- Learn to find, process, evaluate, and use information
- Take on challenges, reaching beyond what they thought they could do
- Strive for mastery
- Work productively within groups
- Engage effectively in discussions
- Reflect on and process their own learning and behaviors
- Make reasoned evaluations about real-life situations and influences
- Contribute to the well-being of the school community
- Explore new ideas and interests
- Make responsible choices and decisions
- Grow in autonomy
- Take risks and try new ideas
- Express their voices
- Interact with others in healthy ways
- Show curiosity and inventiveness
- Demonstrate persistence
- Rebound from failure or disappointment
- Learn by correcting mistakes
- Develop a growth mindset
- Expand learning beyond their community
- Develop skills to learn and interact with others

- Use technology proficiently, ethically, and safely
- Set and work to achieve goals
- Participate productively in their society
- Dream big and seek to discover what their futures may hold
- Demonstrate respect for, and acceptance of, all people around them
- Show compassion
- Resolve conflicts
- Develop hopeful, optimistic attitudes toward learning and life
- Solve problems of all kinds independently and with others
- Regulate their behaviors
- Cope with peer pressure
- Channel emotions in positive ways
- Deal positively with stress
- Believe in themselves
- Persist to finish a task or reach a goal
- Develop resilience
- Take on leadership roles
- Show any number of other behaviors or qualities on your *becoming* list

. . . then these are the things to look for and **celebrate** when you see them! It's an occasion to **celebrate whenever** we see students actively trying, not giving up on, making progress at, or mastering any of the many academic or personal qualities, skills, or behaviors of *becoming*.

Watch for these indications of *belonging* and *becoming* in students, and have students watch for them in one another. Model them yourself. Recognize and affirm them as often as possible. Celebrate the fact that the entire processes and aftermaths of celebrations build an awesome treasure chest of long-lasting memories for students and adults in your school. And be aware that you dignify all students when you include them in identifying what to celebrate and how to celebrate themselves and one another and in planning and managing those celebrations.

In addition, let's celebrate one another. Teachers, administrators, nonteaching staff, volunteers, and students and their families can notice examples of adult efforts to:

- Develop trusting, caring teacher–student, student–student, and adult–adult relationships.
- Deepen *belonging* and *becoming* for ourselves and one another.
- Offer learning experiences that are engaging and relevant.
- Give students second (and third and fourth) chances to succeed.
- Work together to move everyone toward a growth mindset.
- Do a better school-wide job of enhancing student voice and choice.
- Build a connected, equitable school community.

CONSIDERING HOW TO RECOGNIZE AND REWARD

Teachers and other adults in the school recognize and affirm students dozens of times in many ways every day. There are frequent verbal encouragements: Adults constantly seek to boost self-confidence, acknowledge hard work, and affirm learning of new skills and reaching new goals. The process of encouraging academic and personal growth and acknowledging it when we see it happen often includes rewards and incentives. Many schools have school-wide programs to encourage and reward positive behavior.

Rethinking Recognitions and Rewards

A growing swell of research in the field of motivation has taken a hard look at how rewards—particularly extrinsic awards and incentives—affect students' behavior. A major conclusion of such research is that outside rewards often undermine students' intrinsic motivation. This has given us pause to reconsider many of the ideas we had about "motivating" students. There's no question that young children have self-motivation—just watch a preschooler try to climb a ladder or get dressed without help. Children start out curious, constantly exploring and discovering, trying to do things for themselves. But often, somewhere along the way, many young people learn that they can "get something" for doing what they are already supposed to do. Often that "something" is a tangible reward; often that "something" is approval from an adult.

Albert Bandura found self-efficacy to be foundational to motivation. He posited that the roots of self-motivation lie in our belief that we have power over our own lives and can effect changes in our lives—in essence, that we are able to create satisfaction or success for ourselves. Bandura's research found that the higher a person's sense of self-efficacy, the higher that person's intrinsic motivation will be, the harder someone will work toward a goal, and the longer that person will persist. He also found that people with higher self-efficacy were able to recover more quickly from failure.[4]

> **The roots of self-motivation lie in our belief that we have power over our own lives and can effect changes in our lives.**

Other researchers have explored the conditions for fostering self-motivation and found that students learn best when they go after challenges of their own volition. Their intrinsic motivation leads to greater learning and greater satisfaction with learning, whereas extrinsic rewards dampen self-motivation, particularly the motivation to perform tasks that individuals choose or tasks that are highly interesting to them. The results of a meta-analyses of well-controlled experiments exploring the effects of extrinsic rewards on intrinsic motivation showed that "all tangible rewards, all expected rewards, engagement-contingent rewards, completion-contingent rewards, task-contingent rewards, and performance-contingent rewards significantly undermined intrinsic motivation."[5]

Extrinsic rewards can lead to behaviors that are the exact opposite of what we would hope to encourage. In an often-cited study on rewards, researchers gave children tangible rewards for drawing more often. But when the reward was removed, the students drew less often than they had before and were less likely to draw later for pleasure.[6] Other studies produced similar conclusions: A reward may initially motivate the student, but after a while it can cause a loss of interest, diminish intrinsic motivation, and sometimes extinguish the behavior altogether.[7]

In his book *Drive: The Surprising Truth About What Motivates Us,* Daniel Pink summarizes the flaws of "carrots and sticks" (a system of extrinsic rewards and punishments):

1. They can extinguish intrinsic motivation.
2. They can diminish performance.
3. They can crush creativity.
4. They can crowd out good behavior.
5. They can encourage cheating, shortcuts, and unethical behavior.
6. They can become addictive.
7. They can foster short-term thinking.[8]

Most educators praise students for hard work, meeting goals, or behaving appropriately (these are verbal rewards). We'd wager that the words "good job!" come out of the mouths of teachers and coaches more often than any other expression of affirmation. But even praise can be less effective—or perhaps even more harmful—than we've thought. Praise can become so generalized, repetitive, and automatic that it loses its authenticity. The phrases "good job!" "well done!" or "I'm so proud of you!" lose their meaning to excessive familiarity.

As with other forms of extrinsic rewards, praise can undermine intrinsic motivation. Students can become dependent on adult approval rather than finding pride in themselves. Alfie Kohn, author and speaker on rewards, parenting, and teaching, says that many adults have created "praise junkies" whose self-efficacy and self-motivation are harmed when the child works to accomplish something because it will please an adult. He identifies some problems with praise, saying that it can do the following:

- It can be manipulative—reinforcing something that is dependent on the adult's convenience or feelings.

- It can create "praise junkies," making children dependent on our evaluations about what is appropriate behavior.
- It can steal the child's pleasure. Children deserve to feel their own pride in their accomplishments and decide when they feel that way. Adults doing it for them takes that power and right away from them—making it instead about what the adult sees and thinks.
- It can cause children to lose interest in sustaining the behavior once the reward is over.
- It can actually reduce achievement, because praise puts pressure on the student—so the student takes fewer risks and performs more poorly than the students who weren't praised.[9]

In an interview for OneDublin.org, Carol Dweck cautions us to take particular care **not to praise students for their intelligence or ability** (as we discussed in Chapter 6). Praising students for being smart, she claims, backfires. "It puts them in a fixed mindset and not wanting challenges. They don't want to risk looking stupid or making mistakes. Kids praised for intelligence curtail their learning in order to never make a mistake, in order to preserve the label that you gave to them."[10]

Learning about how outside rewards (including verbal rewards) may affect students' own motivation does not suggest that we should quit encouraging, complimenting, or celebrating their behaviors, efforts, and accomplishments. Instead, it means that we must do so thoughtfully—that we must learn to do it in ways that are non-manipulative and that boost students' sense of control and their own joy in what they've done.

Intrinsic motivation flourishes in settings that encourage autonomy, competence, and relatedness (that is, connection to the student's interests, personal goals, other schoolwork, and their lives outside school).[11] Like self-motivation, self-efficacy is heightened when a student masters something challenging and experiences a new sense of competency. In addition, tangible rewards do not have the same dampening effect on self-motivation if "they are not expected or not contingent on task behavior." In other words, when students don't feel controlled by the rewards, the use of the rewards doesn't do the same damage to their self-efficacy and self-motivation.[12]

In her research on how rewards affect creativity and motivation, Harvard psychology professor Teresa Amabile also found that an extrinsic reward can have a positive effect if it is given unexpectedly, as a congratulation. She recommends, as do others, that we not use extrinsic rewards as carrots—but that we instead give the reward when effort is obvious or a task is completed.[13] In a report summarizing findings from studies on student motivation, the Center for Education Policy explains that rewarding specific actions that students can control—completing homework, mastering a specific task or skill, reading a book, or solving a tricky math problem—works better to motivate them than rewarding accomplishments that may seem out of their reach or beyond their control.[14]

Intrinsic motivation flourishes in settings that encourage autonomy, competence, and relatedness.

Alfie Kohn suggests some alternatives to praise—actions that support students' self-motivation rather than leading them to lean on adult approval. He encourages adults to consider saying nothing (let children make their own decisions about how an accomplishment makes them feel), stating what you saw (without evaluation, letting them know you noticed), and asking questions (get them talking about their experience with and feelings about the accomplishment).[15] Other research finds that verbal feedback does enhance intrinsic motivation when it is sincere, gives feedback on specific tasks, promotes autonomy, boosts self-efficacy, and helps to increase competence.[16]

TOP 9 TIPS FOR CELEBRATING BELONGING AND BECOMING

- See that every student is authentically celebrated many times.
- Broaden the criteria for recognition to include many qualities and actions of *belonging* and *becoming*.
- Recognize input more often than outcome.
- Celebrate effort, not ability.
- Avoid awards that make students dependent on adult approval.
- Use rewards in ways that boost student autonomy, competency, and relatedness.
- Teach students to celebrate with self-rewards.
- Celebrate the intangible rewards of *belonging* and *becoming*.
- Involve students in designing recognition programs and in choosing rewards.

Recognizing and Rewarding Thoughtfully

Of course, we want to avoid recognition and rewards that diminish students' self-belief and self-motivation. We want to preserve their natural curiosity and interest—not dampen it. We want them to celebrate their accomplishments as coming from themselves. We want them to be proud of themselves. And we certainly don't want them to think that they complete schoolwork, earn good grades, treat each other kindly, or make responsible choices just to please an adult or to get a slice of pizza. We don't want them to become addicted to getting prizes for something they should be doing anyway. Intrinsic motivation is part of *becoming* the best we can be—and isn't this what we want for our students?

Most schools wrestle with the question of how to celebrate students' successes—and even how to define success itself. Already in this chapter, we've given you some suggestions about relating success to aspects of *belonging* and *becoming*. We honor the power of intrinsic motivation and believe that, ultimately, students must find the will within themselves to achieve and prosper. At the same time, realistically, we see that extrinsic motivation plays a role in what humans do. Think about the adults you know. Does Hans run because he loves running, or because his doctor told him to lose weight? Does Maria drive at the speed limit because it's the safe thing to do, or because she's afraid of getting a speeding ticket? Does Roberto clean his house because he loves to do housework, because he doesn't want to live in a dirty house, or because his wife will nag him if he doesn't help with house cleaning? Does Sue go to work because she thoroughly enjoys her job or because it pays a good salary? In many cases, our motivations are likely some combination of internal and external.

A meta-analysis of research on the influences of rewards finds that the two are not mutually exclusive—that extrinsic motivation may undermine the intrinsic or deter self-determination. But if rewards do not undermine feelings of autonomy and competence, and if the extrinsic rewards are unexpected (i.e., not offered beforehand as an enticement to good performance), they can complement the intrinsic rewards. Researchers conclude that students learn best in an environment of high intrinsic motivation and moderate extrinsic motivation (grades being part of the extrinsic factor).[17]

So what do we do?

- We remember that what we want for our students is for them to *belong* and *become.*
- We remember that the goals for students are to *become* competent in skills of both processes and to experience overall satisfaction with themselves, their performance and learning, and their school lives.
- We work at habits of thinking about what messages our words and acts of recognition send to students: Do they contribute to an increased sense of being valuable, wanted, and respected (*belonging*)? Do they state specific things that you've seen students trying, changing, or working hard to complete (*becoming*)? Do they help the student feel more competent (*becoming*)? Do they encourage students to rely on their belief in themselves (*becoming*)? Do they help the student feel more powerful (*becoming*)? Are they tailored to the task and the student, rather than clichéd (*becoming*)? Above all, are they sincere?
- We do not plan for rewards and recognition (celebrations) without coming to terms with what we believe about them. When we do use praise and other extrinsic rewards, we do so with a better understanding of how to be sure they work. We plan to celebrate students in ways that bolster their internal motivation, develop their autonomy, increase their competence, build their self-esteem, and relate to their lives.
- We must ensure that we know how individual students will respond to praise and rewards. (There are students who will vow never to repeat the work, behavior, or action for which they were just publicly praised or acknowledged.)
- We pay close attention—all day, every day—to what we say and do, to be sure it sends the messages about rewards that we truly want to send.

Here are some guidelines to keep in mind as you use rewards (including verbal rewards), recognition, and rewards systems that let you delight in—and celebrate with—students as they seek to *belong* and *become*:

- Try to avoid using rewards as incentives—as something students know for sure they will "get" if they accomplish something specified. Give rewards at the end of a task without mentioning the reward at the beginning.
- When you use extrinsic rewards, start with a reward as a motivational nudge, but reduce their frequency so as to allow students to experience internal satisfaction from the behavior rather than depending on the reward.
- Use tangible rewards—trophies, certificates, prizes—judiciously and occasionally.
- Give recognition more often than tangible rewards.
- Recognize or reward such behaviors as competence, persistence, resilience, creativity, and kindness.
- Recognize and reward things students can control—many small things in a day.
- Follow Carol Dweck's advice to differentiate **acknowledgement** (recognizing or thanking students who do what's expected of them) from **praise** (which puts a value judgment that sets the action apart as exceptional). She notes that "acknowledgement is best to use when students meet expectations and praise is best saved for when they exceed them," **but** the praise must not consist of "canned phrases," and it must be completely sincere and generally given in private.[18]
- Praise the process—efforts, trying strategies, exploring, working to solve problems and answer questions.[19]
- Prize mastery of skills over final, absolute performance.
- Praise input more than output.
- Identify behaviors, rather than outcomes, to encourage.
- Recognize or reward progress toward goals or reaching a specific goal.
- Recognize or reward success that is within students' grasp.
- Adapt rewards to individuals. The same reward doesn't work for every student.
- When giving recognition, describe what the student did or is doing ("You defended a claim with relevant, powerful information. Your argument

convinced the entire audience!" "You stood up to the kids who were bullying Simone. That took courage, and it helped Simone feel safer.")

- Instead of statements about yourself ("Your attitude makes me feel good" or "This makes me proud of you"), help them make statements that describe their own satisfaction or pride: "You must be proud of yourself. How does it feel to have solved that problem?"
- Rewards work better and are more meaningful when students can choose something. Let them identify special privileges or activities that are appropriate rewards.
- Include rewards other than tangible prizes—things students enjoy, such as extra recess or technology time, time to collaborate with a group, time to read or write, time to listen to music, a dance-off, etc. (Try to include rewards that increase relationships and connections.)
- Help students understand the reasons for these desired behaviors—that they make school a healthy place where everyone can grow.
- Help students understand the meanings and value of their behaviors—how they connect to their well-being and their lives both in and out of school.
- Ask students questions that help them reflect on their successful experiences.
- Teach students how they can monitor and celebrate their own success.
- Teach students to self-reward—to find ways of congratulating themselves for meeting goals.
- Find ways for students to (genuinely) affirm one another.
- Discuss the concept of rewards with students. Explain the differences between *intrinsic* and *extrinsic*. Start conversations about how rewards affect them.
- As with celebrations, make sure students take part in identifying rewards and choosing how, where, and for what they are given.

In some cases, the extrinsic rewards seem to be our best tool to motivate behavior that resists change or development by any other means. Knowing that the end goal is to foster self-motivation, sometimes we must begin with the small steps of what may seem like flagrant bribery. There were times when I (Patti), as a teacher or principal, used extrinsic rewards in small, measured steps to help a student gain the experience of a healthy, safe, or productive behavior. But I recall one situation that challenged me profoundly to juggle the belief in intrinsic motivation with the usefulness of an extrinsic reward.

One late October day, a student was abruptly transferred into my sixth-grade classroom from another room in the school. I was never told the reason for the transfer; I learned only that the student was challenging and hadn't been doing well with the previous teacher. As it turned out, "challenging" was putting it mildly. Andrew was new to the school. He was taller and more physically developed than the other sixth graders. He could see shapes and shadows but was legally blind. He was a diabetic who needed insulin on a regular basis. He was bi-racial in a primarily white community. He spoke in a loud, deep voice. Other students were intimidated by his appearance, as well as his verbal and physical actions. They were leery of becoming friends with him, and his overall behavior was disruptive to learning.

Andrew's mother tried to be cooperative as I worked to help him improve his social skills and focus better on his learning—but she, too, was at her wit's end and didn't understand the issues. She claimed he was a "model" child at home. In her eagerness to help, she offered to come and sit in the back of the classroom every day so she could watch his actions. I discouraged that idea, explaining that her presence would likely cause Andrew to behave differently. A few days later, she arrived at the classroom door before students were admitted to the building. She was very excited about a plan she had devised, which would allow her to sit in the back without Andrew knowing she was there. Her plan? She had already started on it—she was wearing a gorilla suit and carrying the head under her arm. (She intended to put it on when the students entered.) Needless to say, we did not use her plan.

I continued to work with the mother and the school psychologist to design a traditional behavioral plan. It identified five basic behaviors (e.g., speak more softly, stay on task, keep hands to self) for Andrew to focus on controlling. On a chart, we divided the day into seven time periods. Andrew was to receive a "yes" or "no" for each of the five behaviors during each of the seven time slots. For a day to be considered "successful," he had to accumulate 30 "yes" notations out of a possible 35, and a successful day granted privileges at home each evening.

The plan hadn't been in place for very long (it was semi-successful, and behaviors were improving somewhat) when the mother came into the classroom to announce that we were changing the plan. She had bought Andrew the stereo set of his dreams and put the box in his bedroom closet where he could see it every day. When he had gone 30 consecutive days with at least 32 "yes" notations per day, he'd get the stereo. The psychologist and I agreed to try it but were both concerned about the message this would give Andrew about getting something for doing what he just needed to do. We also wondered about the precedent: what might she buy him next? It took quite a while for him to manage himself for 30 consecutive days, but eventually he "won" the stereo set.

What happened next was most interesting. By this time, it had become a matter of pride for him to get as many "yes" notations per day as possible. During the time he was aiming for the stereo set reward, he had experienced enough success in controlling his behavior that he had come to enjoy that sense of accomplishment. He also saw that when he had his actions under control, other students responded more positively toward him—friendships began to develop. He had started out with strictly extrinsic motivation: He wanted that stereo set! But somewhere along the way, that intrinsic motivation began to develop. He was compelled to do the right things because doing them, he said, "felt good inside me." And isn't that what we hope for all our students to experience and continue to experience through their lives?

CREATING WAYS TO CELEBRATE

Schools grapple with decisions about how to inspire students to *become* respectful, responsible, and self-regulated in their academic and personal behavior and how to celebrate when their actions show these qualities. We've noted that there are unlimited ways teachers, students, and all adults in the school can celebrate progress and success in *belonging* and *becoming* every day.

A School-Wide Plan for Celebrating Student Successes

In addition to these practices—which become a normal part of the daily routine—many schools establish school-wide systems for motivating and celebrating student successes (academic, behavioral, or both). Task forces or committees put their heads together to create (or adapt) all sorts of plans to fit their unique school communities. There is no one "best" way to do this. Your school needs a plan that meets the needs of your students and works to further your own goals.

If we want our students to feel that their school and classrooms are places where they can *belong* and have a say, and if we truly value their voices and leadership abilities (skills of *becoming*), then it is critical to bring them into the process of designing such a program. This seems especially fitting when the decisions concern practices that affect virtually every aspect of the students' school lives. So design or re-examine your school-wide practices, hand in hand with your young adolescent students.

In a summary report on student motivation, the Center for Educational Policy urged educators to "think carefully about the pros and cons of instituting a reward program to spur students' motivation."[20] The report shared some characteristics to consider if the school does institute such a program. Among them are:

- Reward students for mastering specific skills or increasing understanding rather than for reaching a level of performance.
- Reward behaviors or tasks that are clear and that students believe are within their control and achievable.
- Reward tasks that are challenging enough to hold interest but not so challenging that they lead students to feel incompetent.
- If possible, offer rewards linked to academics (such as books).
- Allow students to opt out of pursuing a reward.
- Give rewards promptly so that they are clearly connected to the student's action.
- Identify individuals who are socially important to students, and have them give out the rewards.
- Avoid conditioning students to depend on a reward.

- Target behaviors or tasks that students feel are achievable, clearly articulated, and within their control.
- See that teachers receive professional development on student motivation.[21]

We would add one more:

- Develop tools and processes to monitor and evaluate the program. Include students in the evaluation and decisions that are made from the results of the evaluations.

Celebration for Self-Regulation

Consider recognizing students who have no discipline referrals and who are proficient in or passing all classes for a grading period (every mid-quarter, every quarter, or every semester). Reserve some time for these students to be celebrated with an opportunity to socialize with peers in a structured and supervised environment or some other simple show of recognition. A key to this type of recognition is that grades or proficiencies and discipline start over each assessment period and are not held against a student for a future assessment period. It's also important that students who are not eligible for this recognition do not feel that they are being punished with extra work or tasks. We find that what usually works for them is a simple study-hall time to catch up on work. What we want to do is teach students to monitor themselves and to work toward improvement—and that includes giving students second chances (redos, retakes, or fresh starts) when appropriate.

More Celebrations

Here are some less formal ideas for celebrating student behavioral and academic accomplishments that we have used and collected these over the years:

Positive mail: Design and print off a variety of simple postcards so staff can easily mail a positive note to families. To expand on this idea, print a set of mailing labels, and leave them in the staff room along with enough postcards for all students. Challenge the staff to write and send a positive note to the families of every child during the next two-week period.

Purple tickets (or any color you choose): Each week, all staff members find a ticket and a postcard in their mailbox. These are used to recognize students (more postcards and tickets are available upon request). The teacher writes a positive note to mail home about the student (with specifics about accomplishments). The student is given the ticket to bring to the office for a drawing. On Thursday, two names are chosen from the jar. Those students get to invite any staff member of their choice to a special lunch on Friday. Arrange for local restaurants to donate lunches!

Shout out the news: Publicize news about school and non-school achievements in your bulletin, school newspaper, school display cases or bulletin boards, website, school social media page, or family newsletter. Make sure this bragging includes a wide variety of accomplishments in many areas of *belonging* and *becoming*.

Lunch with the Principal, Donuts with the Dean, Cookies with the Counselor (you get the idea): Ask teachers to watch for instances when students use their voices to make positive contributions to the school community or to speak up for other students. Select three to five of these students each week to meet with a school "official" and discuss their reflections and suggestions about what's working well at the school and what needs improvement.

Lunchtime recognition: Playground and cafeteria supervisors hold tickets to give to students who are seen cleaning up after themselves or performing another helpful or respectful deed. Tickets are put into a drawing for a small prize at the end of the week.

Be creative: Don't limit formal recognition to academics or highly visible accomplishments. Give recognition for being a good friend, showing responsibility, bouncing back from difficulty, making improvement, helping someone *belong*, helping to make the school a safe place, and so on. Enlist students in expanding the list. Also, make this a task for a professional development session for your entire staff, leaders included.

When a school builds a culture of positive recognition—recognition for multiple indications of *belonging* and *becoming*—all students (many of whom might not be recognized otherwise) can have many chances to feel validated and affirmed within their school. When we add the school-wide program to all the possibilities described at the beginning of this chapter for celebration in classrooms and other activities, all students can feel themselves living in a community of validation. For an all-school program to be successful, the standards for specific recognitions should be well considered and clearly stated. So, here are a few words of caution: Do not lower standards in an effort to include more students. The recognition must be authentic—because false praise is worse than no praise at all. Students will rise to meet the expectations you set when they know that you believe they can do it. If there are enough qualities and categories that you're noticing, there will be chances for **all** students to be "caught" meeting the criteria for success.

If there are enough qualities and categories that you're noticing, there will be chances for all students to be "caught" meeting the criteria for success.

Out-of-School Accomplishments

Although it is admittedly easier to celebrate students' accomplishments that happen at school, you will build bridges of goodwill with families and the community when you recognize accomplishments that occur outside of school as well. Many students participate in non-school clubs and events such as 4H, scouting, arts, dance and other athletics, volunteer activities, and community service events. Some of the most astounding advances in *belonging* and *becoming* occur in experiences that happen outside the school walls.

Find a way to encourage students and families to share good news from the "outside world." This can include such ideas as having a hallway bulletin board designated to post news articles and pictures about students' accomplishments, using a display cabinet for short-term displays of trophies, ribbons, and other displays, or inserting out-of-school accomplishments into the reading of the daily bulletin or morning announcements. Not only do such methods recognize students for their efforts beyond school, but they also help staff members and students learn more about individual students and thereby deepen student–teacher and school–family relationships. The "accomplishments" celebrated in this way don't have to be all about winning competitions or getting awards. Show off anything students are doing that demonstrates efforts to *belong* or *become*. Note: Show your students that their school community can keep celebrating them after they move on from middle school. Your current students will enjoy learning about and being inspired by the accomplishments of former students from the school who are now in high school, college, or the working world. (When I (Patti) served as a middle school principal, our students loved the hallway bulletin board we dedicated to this.)

COMMUNICATING SUCCESSES

Sadly, today's young adolescents tend to get a bad rap. Too often they are portrayed in the media as rude, self-centered, and uncaring. Descriptors such as *immature*, *moody*, or *hormones on wheels* are often used to describe this age group. Although these generalizations may contain some elements of truth, if taken as gospel, they discount the complexity of the age group. Young adolescents are experiencing rapid physical and emotional changes as they struggle along the road to independence, so it is no surprise that they can be contradictory at times—confused or confident, awkward or articulate, passive or passionate. But those of us who work with young adolescents know just how concerned, caring, and compassionate they can be.

So why, then, does the general public have such a poor impression of middle schoolers? Perhaps it's because we remember salient incidents that reinforce our beliefs. For example, when we see young adolescents being rude, it validates our perceptions, and we're more likely to remember it than when we see them being polite. Unfortunately, young adolescents themselves recognize this typecasting and are often disturbed by their public images.

We must actively communicate our students' and schools' successes. Enlist a staff member in your grade level, on your team, or in your department to take responsibility for sharing the school's and students' good news; this is essential to forming an accurate perception of your school and students within the wider community. Another staff member or a group of students can take on the task of posting newspaper or printed online articles in the hallways about any positive school or student event. Assign someone to write one article weekly or monthly for your local newspaper, highlighting some exciting growth or events at the school. Send a yearly invitation to legislators who represent your school: Ask them to visit classrooms and see the great work that teachers and students are doing. Call the local television station or news outlet and invite them to see your 'A' Day (see Chapter 5). Invite local realtors in for breakfast and have students share why yours is a great school to attend. Give a presentation to the school board of the school's accomplishments in the areas of attendance, attitude (citizenship), academics, arts, and athletics—or in any other areas of *belonging* or *becoming* you identify. Assign staff to post school news and happenings on social media. If you don't tell your story, someone else will (and you might not like what they say!).

PUTTING IT INTO PRACTICE

As an individual, team, small group, or entire staff, use these activities to spark discussions, reflect on your current practices or situations, listen to others, or set goals.

1. As staff, make a list of the different ways you celebrate your students (and yourselves!). How does your school ensure that all students are recognized in the different areas that help make a student successful? How can your school improve in this area?

2. Consider the following statement: "By celebrating what's right, we find the energy to fix what's wrong." Do you think that focusing on the positive can give the energy to fix what's not right, or should we concentrate on what's wrong if we want to fix it? Why or why not? How does this idea play out at our school? In our classrooms? Is there a difference? Should there be?

3. Collect as much data as you can on which students are being honored and celebrated at your school. Is it primarily athletes and honor-roll students? Is it balanced across gender, grade level, ethnicity, academic performance, etc.? Are students recognized for growth or primarily for achievement? Use the data to identify areas for improvement in your recognition and celebration plans.

4. Review this chapter's section "Considering How to Recognize and Reward." With a team or grade-level group, read and discuss some research findings about intrinsic and extrinsic motivation, praise, and rewards. See Chapter 9's endnotes 18 and 19 for two articles and two YouTube videos you might explore together. Identify practices and language changes that you can make to avoid dampening students' intrinsic motivation. Plan specific sessions

to hold the same discussion with students—perhaps in team meetings or advisory groups. Listen to their reflections about the value and effects of different kinds of rewards and recognitions. Ask students to contribute new ideas about how to celebrate *belonging* and *becoming*.

Conclusion

In Their Own Voices

When you ***belong****, you never have to sit alone at lunch.*

When I experience myself ***becoming*** *in some way, I feel that I am on top of the world.*

— The words of two middle grades students

Listen to students describe what it means to *belong* and *become* and why these matter to them and their peers.

To belong (in my school and in my classes) means...

- *You are accepted as a person.*
- *You have friends that you feel safe around.*
- *You're not alone when you leave class.*
- *You perform better because you know people and people know you.*
- *You fit in.*
- *You have someone to walk to class with.*
- *You are never alone at lunch or recess.*
- *You are energized.*
- *You have friends who support you, and you support them.*
- *People talk to you.*
- *You are happy with your work, friends, and education.*
- *You are welcomed and involved.*
- *People think of you as being kind and respectful.*
- *People don't spread stereotypes, rumors, or gossip about you.*

It matters to have a sense of **belonging** at school because...

- *It affects **everything**! It affects your motivation to do **anything**!*
- *You are confident.*
- *You will do better in school, which will help you to belong more.*
- *If you don't feel you belong, your confidence and social skills suffer.*
- *It's easier to focus on learning. Otherwise, you will spend all your time and energy stressing about not belonging.*
- *Without it, you have no energy for learning.*
- *When you don't belong, nothing else seems to matter at all.*
- *Without a sense of belonging, you are empty and depressed.*
- *When you don't belong, you don't care, you don't try, you don't want to finish your work.*
- *It is absolutely necessary for your overall happiness, self-esteem, and mental health.*

To become (in ways that students can do in school) means:

- *Achieving the best you can, even exceeding what is expected of you.*
- *Believing in your own actions.*
- *Believing that you can learn, think, and act responsibly on your own.*
- *Taking risks to go for more than just the minimum.*
- *Building from your mistakes.*
- *Finding friends that will include you.*
- *Achieving your own goals.*
- *Working hard and being nice.*
- *Getting prepared for high school.*
- *Persevering.*
- *Taking charge of your life and responsibility for your actions.*
- *Developing socially—reaching out to others and getting along with others.*
- *Being who you are.*

With the help of the school and the people in it, middle grades kids can **become:**

- *Harder workers who persevere and try.*
- *People who will make good choices.*

- *Better able to express themselves and speak up for themselves.*
- *More aware of and more caring of other people's feelings.*
- *Intelligent and experienced.*
- *People who are not content with just passing grades.*
- *The best that they can be.*
- *Whatever they want to be.*
- *Better people.*

This is our hope for our readers, our fellow adventurers in loving and educating young adolescents: that for every program you design, every lesson you plan, every new procedure you consider, or every goal you establish—for everything that you do now or think about doing—you will (individually and with your colleagues) ask,

WILL THIS HELP OUR STUDENTS *BELONG* OR *BECOME*—OR BOTH?

One of the best ways to find out how your plans, programs, processes, and procedures affect your students is to ask them. Remember, always, that students' voices tell you things you can't learn from any other source. They know things we educators don't know. And often, we won't find out these things until we ask them.

Remember, always, that students' voices tell you things you can't learn from any other source.

Shortly after the two of us had the epiphany about the all-encompassing concepts of *belonging* and *becoming,* and as we began to explore how to put that into words and action, we realized we needed to hear from students. We gathered groups of sixth through eighth graders; the groups were as heterogeneously mixed as possible. With each group, we held a short (15-minute) general discussion to start students thinking about *belonging* and *becoming*. We asked them to think about what the terms and concepts meant in the context of their school. We encouraged them to think about their own experiences with each of the concepts.

Then we sent them off on their own with an **anonymous** written survey and gave them about 30 minutes to reflect on the topics and express their ideas.

This was the perfect beginning for us, and we believe it would be for any other school's or teacher's journey with the partnership of *belonging* and *becoming*! What we learned from students has helped shape our own interests and directions both in this book and in our work with students. Even with our many years of experience as middle level educators, this endeavor brought us new insights into students' perceptions of the school community, students' beliefs about themselves and one another, the power of their voices, their positive mindsets and optimism, their hopes, and their wisdom. It gave us a fresh look at our choices and practices. The experience brought students an opportunity to dig into themselves, express their opinions, share their lives (some of it behind-the-scenes), and have a say.

We highly recommend that you explore these topics with your students—for your benefit and theirs. This can be done at a team, classroom, or grade level, or as all-school research. (And it **is** research—as valuable as any other school-improvement research you could do!) We've included some sample reflection surveys, "My Thoughts About Belonging" and "My thoughts About Becoming," (Appendix F-1 and F-2) on pages 280-283. But you can design surveys that fit your students or solicit this information in other ways. Ask about the things you need to learn from your students. We chose a process that combined discussion with individual reflection so students could warm up to the concepts with adult involvement while also being free to reflect—without influence from other students or pressure to give answers they thought might please the adults. We recommend that sessions tackle the two concepts of *belonging* and *becoming* separately. You might involve more students by forming different groups for each of the two topics. We also recommend that you take action on what you learn from the survey and then repeat the survey again during the year(s) to re-assess students' experiences of *belonging* and *becoming* in **their** school.

In addition to asking students to share what *belonging* and *becoming* mean to them, our survey asked students to reflect on some items related to the manifestations and experiences of *belonging* (or *not belonging*) and *becoming* (or *not becoming*). Below are some of the things students told us in these surveys:

Here's how someone can tell that he or she **belongs:**

- *They have someone to sit with at lunch.*
- *They are not alone at recess.*
- *They are not alone in the hall.*
- *They have people to talk to when they get to class.*
- *They are not constantly worrying about what someone might be posting or texting about them.*
- *They are confident around their classmates.*
- *They laugh.*

When you do NOT have a **sense of belonging**,

- *It is absolutely the most horrible feeling.*
- *You feel discarded.*
- *You think the whole world is against you.*
- *You feel insecure, sad, edgy, and hopeless.*
- *Your gut goes empty and your brain is just thinking of the worst things in life.*
- *You feel paranoid, not knowing what other people are saying about you.*
- *You feel that you have no place in school or life.*
- *It feels as if you've been abandoned in a forest, having to fend for yourself.*
- *You feel lonely, like nobody wants you.*
- *You think you are worthless—not a good person.*
- *It just feels like crap. There's no other way to describe it!*

Here's how I can tell if someone does NOT have a **sense of belonging:**

- *They look constantly disappointed.*
- *They sit alone at lunch.*
- *They are alone at recess.*
- *They avoid other kids.*
- *They don't talk to anyone.*
- *They don't care about their grades.*
- *They are the ones that get bullied.*

- *They look depressed.*
- *They walk with their heads down. They are always staring down.*

I can tell if I am **becoming** (in any of the ways I think I could **become** at school) by:

- *How much I feel at home.*
- *My success in my classes.*
- *How outgoing I feel.*
- *Improvement in my grades.*
- *Increased confidence in my ability to think, learn, and do my work.*
- *Improvement in my attitudes.*
- *Good experiences at my parent–teacher–student conferences.*
- *Noticing that people react to me positively.*
- *Whether I'm achieving my goals.*
- *Whether I'm doing even more than I expected.*
- *How much I am welcoming kids that are being left out or put down.*
- *My sense of control over my life and behavior, including on social media.*

When I experience myself **becoming** in some way, I feel:

- *A little brighter.*
- *Accomplished, proud, and maybe even excited.*
- *Motivated—like I can do anything.*
- *That I am on top of the world.*
- *Proud that I am appreciated and my work is noticed.*
- *That I am a better and more well-thought-of person.*
- *Happy and full.*
- *Higher self-esteem and self-confidence.*

When a student does NOT experience success at **becoming**,

- *They might feel like giving up on life.*
- *They have zero confidence.*
- *They have no self-belief.*
- *They cry.*
- *They withdraw.*
- *They can feel angry, depressed, or suicidal.*

Belonging and *becoming* are **not** passive verbs! They are not things teachers and schools **do to or for** their students. Of course, we can create communities, design activities and situations, train our teachers, lend support, and teach skills that help with both processes—that's what middle school is all about. But students must make choices about—and be actively involved in—their own *belonging* and *becoming*. As much as we'd like to, we can't wave a magic wand to make a student feel included, enjoy satisfying relationships with peers, be self-motivated, or be competent in schoolwork. Students are not pawns in these processes. *Belonging* is not the same as having adult acceptance. *Becoming* is not just doing everything the teacher asks or learning everything to the extent that the adults approve. We need to help our students understand that *belonging* and *becoming* are:

- Gradual (they take time).
- Current (they're happening now; they're not things that will happen only in the future; they're not things that are achieved with finality).
- Participatory (the student must take an **active** role).
- Fluid (the sense of *belonging* or *becoming* today will change and grow and take different shapes on different days and in different situations).

Part of the role of teachers is to help students find ways to be active in their own *belonging* and *becoming*. We urge you to watch for opportunities to do that. In addition, appreciate the major role that students have in helping one another with these processes. With many of the qualities, attitudes, and behaviors involved in *belonging* and *becoming*, students can actually be far more helpful and influential than adults. Confirm and re-confirm the message to students that **everyone** in the school should be involved in helping everyone *belong* and *become*.

Our survey asked students to reflect on and recall what they have done (and can do) to help other kids *belong* or *become* and to help themselves progress in *belonging* and *becoming*. We learned that many of the students were consciously taking an active role in *belonging* and *becoming* for themselves and others. We also found that they had no shortage of ideas and real deeds to recount. This helped us learn what behaviors we could teach, encourage, and strengthen. Students told us:

The best things kids can do to help other kids **belong** are:

- *Just be kind.*
- *Invite them into their group at lunch.*
- *Hang out with them at recess.*
- *Don't let anyone have to be alone in the hall.*
- *If you see someone sitting alone, move over and talk to them.*
- *Try to help them not feel awkward.*
- *Choose to work in a group with them.*
- *Just go for it. Talk to people.*
- *Sit at a table by them without being invited.*
- *Stand up to things that are not right that you see happening to someone.*
- *Do not judge them.*
- *Be respectful and careful not to post or text negative things about others.*
- *Stop just thinking about themselves and think about others.*

Something I've done to help someone else **belong** is:

- *Starting up a conversation.*
- *Volunteering to be their partner in an activity.*
- *Asking someone to sit with me when I saw him looking sad.*
- *Inviting them to sit with my group at lunch.*
- *Answering their questions.*
- *Showing them to class.*
- *Putting myself in their shoes.*
- *Talking positively about them to others.*
- *Including them in a project I was doing.*
- *Moving to someone's table at lunch (empty except for him).*
- *Getting my friends to include someone at recess.*

Something I've done to increase my **own sense of belonging** is:

- *Asked people to sit with me at lunch.*
- *Started saying "hi" and giving a smile to a lot more people.*
- *Joined a soccer team.*
- *Started being kinder to people.*

- *Took up an attitude of treating others the way I wanted to be treated.*
- *Tried to be more sociable, even though it was scary.*
- *Started getting my homework done sooner so I'd have time for making new friends.*
- *Just bit the bullet and sat at a lunch table with people I didn't know.*
- *Talked to people I don't know well.*
- *Tried to be more open-minded about who I could be friends with.*
- *Joined an after-school club.*
- *Worked at being positive and thankful for the things I already have.*
- *Asked to be in a group school project, knowing it would help me.*

The best things students can do to help other students to **become** are:

- *Listen in class and try hard—to be an example to other students.*
- *Help them belong, because that motivates them to become.*
- *Support their efforts by giving them attention and compliments.*
- *Don't make fun of them or insult them.*
- *Don't laugh at their questions or answers.*
- *Include them in groups and activities.*
- *Ask them questions to help them show what they know.*
- *Help them if they're having trouble with something.*
- *Ask them to help you with something.*
- *Encourage their ideas and efforts.*
- *Be kind.*

The best thing I have done to help another student **become** is:

- *Sitting with them at lunch.*
- *Being friendly and supportive.*
- *Introducing myself and helping them with the class.*
- *Pushing them a little past their comfort zone.*
- *Complimenting them.*
- *Helping to motivate them to do their best.*
- *Helping them ask for help.*
- *Asking them to explain something to me.*
- *Help them on things they are having trouble with.*

- *Talking to them when they're feeling put down.*
- *Sticking up for them when they're being bullied.*

The best things I can do to help myself to **become** are to:

- *Work to keep good relationships with my friends.*
- *Make a list of things to do because visualizing helps me achieve my goals.*
- *Never give up.*
- *Never hold grudges.*
- *Not be afraid to ask questions in class.*
- *Believe in myself.*
- *Look at myself in the third person and observe what I need to work on (like focusing in class or saying nice things to people).*
- *Persevere.*
- *Go for my full potential.*
- *Pay attention in class.*
- *Never exclude people.*
- *Make others feel good about themselves.*
- *Look ahead and see how something will help me in the future.*

The survey also gave students opportunities to reflect on things they observed in their school that were helping students *belong* and *become*, as well as things the school could do better. Students told us:

The best thing I've seen a teacher do to help a student **belong** is:

- *Let kids do learning activities that they think of themselves.*
- *Make students laugh and laugh with them.*
- *Help everyone in the class practice social skills.*
- *Mix up groups so students have a chance to make friends.*
- *Guide students into groups where they'll work best.*
- *Never let students choose their own seats.*
- *Always see that everyone is involved in every activity.*
- *Let students know that she accepts them all equally.*
- *Give someone a friend to tour the school with all day.*
- *Ask individual students how they are doing.*

- *Talk to every student every day.*
- *Just notice when students need help, even when they don't ask.*
- *Help students believe in themselves.*
- *Show trust in the students.*

These things work AGAINST everyone feeling a **sense of belonging** at school:

- *Exclusiveness of groups.*
- *A lot of attention to the popular people.*
- *Cliques.*
- *Name-calling.*
- *Unkind use of social media and texts.*
- *Students whispering behind other students' backs.*
- *Bullying.*
- *Students getting away with making fun of other students.*
- *The school not being open to suggestions or changes.*

To help ALL kids at my school feel that they **belong**, I would change this:

- *I would take away the invisible line that divides people into groups and cliques.*
- *Teachers should stop letting kids choose groups.*
- *We need bigger tables at lunch. The round tables hold few people and it's easy for kids to be excluded.*
- *I would make a school where everybody feels included.*
- *The adults in the school would recognize the students and talk to them.*
- *The school could be more inviting.*
- *There should be a welcoming committee that meets with new students for pizza or lunch and helps them make friends.*
- *I would find a way to put a stop these: mean nicknames, making fun, using negative words, and excluding others.*
- *I'd like to see that everyone has a group that they like and are comfortable.*
- *Add a class for all students to practice social skills and social media skills, and to learn about other people.*

Things that have happened in school that have MOST helped me to **become** are:

- *Good friends and good teachers.*

- *Learning to be supportive of other people.*
- *Setting high standards for myself.*
- *Helpful teachers and worthwhile assignments.*
- *Learning to ask for help.*
- *Teachers pushing me to try harder things.*
- *Being encouraged to learn new things outside of school.*
- *People helping me when I am confused.*
- *People treating me with respect.*
- *People being nice and kind.*
- *People encouraging me to be nice and kind.*
- *People including me and inviting me to join them.*
- *Putting me in a group of people that I don't usually hang out with so I could learn from them.*
- *Getting help with my problems and questions, no matter how "dumb" they are.*

The best things a teacher can do to help students to **become** are:

- *Listening—really listening.*
- *Encouraging them to learn beyond school.*
- *Challenging them to reach beyond what they thought they could do.*
- *Congratulating them on their achievements.*
- *Listening to what they have to say.*
- *Including them in decisions.*
- *Explaining things they don't understand, even if it takes a few tries.*
- *Telling them to believe they can improve.*
- *Assigning alternatives that match their learning level and pace.*
- *Exploring their talents.*
- *Not embarrassing them in front of others if they do something wrong.*
- *Not making them feel bad or stupid when they ask a question or don't know an answer.*

To help ALL kids at my school feel that they are **becoming**, I would change this:

- *I'd personally give more encouragement to help others succeed.*
- *All students should have help with social skills.*
- *Every student would receive a compliment a day.*

- *I would never let kids choose their own groups for group work in class.*
- *The school should offer a class where students could talk about their short-term and long-term goals.*
- *Make sure that the school has advisors for all kids to talk to.*
- *Add more group activities that help to make and improve friendships.*
- *See that all students have a chance to be heard.*
- *Include a daily goal with the morning announcements.*
- *Have the kinds of learning activities that involve everyone.*
- *I would ban: cliques, exclusion, pulling pranks, and laughing at others.*
- *Give more encouragement for people to think outside themselves.*
- *Make absolutely sure that teachers are there for students and support them.*
- *There shouldn't be any students in the school who feel nobody believes in them.*

We're awed by the students' honesty, their sensitivity to human needs, their insights into themselves and others. It was interesting to see how many of their responses combined aspects of *belonging* and *becoming*; this showed us how entwined the two are in their experience. We're delighted to see the school through the students' eyes (even if they reveal some flaws or weaknesses). They told us nothing that we didn't need to hear, that didn't teach us something new, or that didn't reaffirm something we did know. These students, without knowing it, gave us a list of topics and practices to consider, add, or re-examine, as well as several issues to discuss. Their insights taught us what to celebrate and what to work on.

For example, we could not ignore the number of times we read about having someone (or no one) to sit with at lunch, or be with at recess, or the idea that students need someone to talk to them. We saw the words *kind, inclusion, compliment, believe in myself, support, challenge* repeated throughout their reflections. We read, more than once, that students don't want to be in a culture where others are made fun of, gossiped about, or bullied. We noticed they feel that letting students choose their own groups for academic group work interferes with *belonging* and *becoming*. We saw that students asked for more teaching of social skills. We can get right to work on finding practices to address these needs. Wouldn't it be wonderful if we could have a school where nobody sits alone at lunch! Think of how far that would go toward helping young adolescents in the school feel a sense of *belonging* that removes impediments to their *becoming*! We would guess that this is an issue in **every** middle level school. What a goal to set! And if we get anywhere close to meeting it—what an accomplishment to celebrate!

We hope that you embrace the concepts of *belonging* and *becoming* as the heart of the mission and the work you do with young adolescents and that you will make this powerful duo a motto for your school or your classroom (or both)! We hope that this will give you new lenses through which to see your practices and programs. And we hope you'll begin by asking the students themselves—it is a practice that gives them a meaningful way to matter and make a difference. Listen to your students' reflections, take them seriously, and work to act on what you learn. And we hope that you'll give plenty of attention to the processes of *belonging* and *becoming* for yourself, your colleagues, and students' parents and caregivers. When you do, you'll accelerate your success at making your school and classrooms places where students can truly *belong* and *become*—not just when they get into high school, college, and adulthood—but starting right now!

Appendices

APPENDIX A

Characteristics of Young Adolescent Development

The source of these characteristics is The Successful Middle School: This We Believe (2021).[1] *by Penny A. Bishop and Lisa M. Harrison, from AMLE. Learn more at* **amle.org/SMS**.

Also, find an overview of research on this topic from AMLE, "Developmental Characteristics of Young Adolescents: Research Summary" (2022), by Kathleen M. Brinegar and Micki M. Caskey, available at **amle.org/YAD.**

Physical Development

- Changes in hormones signal the development of primary sex characteristics and secondary sex characteristics.
- Females typically begin puberty one or two years before males.
- Breast development and first menstruation starts for girls, while boys experience enlargement of testes and increased penis size.
- Pubic, underarm, and facial hair growth develops.
- Acne and body odor may start to develop due to oil and sweat glands beginning to function.
- Young adolescents' bones often grow more rapidly than muscles, which can cause lack of coordination and clumsiness.

- Young adolescents can experience physical growing pains of legs and joints when bones are not sufficiently protected by muscle and tendons.
- Growth spurts and fluctuations in basal metabolism can result in restlessness and fatigue.
- Growth in the size and thickness of the larynx creates voice changes. Both girls and boys experience these changes, though it is more pronounced in boys. Girls' voices typically drop around three tones, while boys' tones can change significantly more. It is also common for boys to experience "cracks" or sharp fluctuations in their voices as the change occurs.
- Growth is sporadic. For example, some young adolescents experience changes in hair growth and voice changes within a short period of time, while others experience these changes over the course of a couple of years. Collectively, changes can be seen as growth patterns.
- The onset of puberty is associated with higher incidents of peer group sexual harassment.
- Changes during puberty can cause transgender and gender-nonconforming youth great stress and anxiety. Some transgender youth take puberty blockers to prevent or delay the onset of puberty.

Cognitive Development

- Fundamental areas of the brain undergo significant development during early adolescence.
- Shifts from concrete thinking to an increased capability to engage in abstract thinking occur.
- Metacognition, or the ability to think about one's own thinking, starts to develop.
- Independent thought increases, as does the ability to debate different stances or positions.

- The ability to set personal goals and think about current and future needs is enhanced.
- Young adolescents are more interested to learn about topics they personally find relevant and interesting.
- The ability to engage in critical, analytical, and creative thinking increases, and students need opportunities to practice and develop these skills.
- Young adolescents enjoy using skills to solve real-life problems and prefer authentic learning experiences.
- Risk-taking increases and can be influenced by a tendency for sensation-seeking.
- Though young adolescents are influenced by stereotypes found in the media and learned in their homes, they have the ability to understand different perspectives and develop the ability to examine information objectively.
- By the end of early adolescence, most youth are able to perform cognitive control tasks at the same level as adults.

Social-Emotional Development

- While still seeking affirmation from their family and other important adults in their life, young adolescents have a strong desire to belong to a peer group.
- As friend groups become more important, exposure to positive and negative peer pressure increases.
- Most incidents of bullying occurred during early adolescence and can have a profound impact on students' well-being.
- Young adolescents can feel torn between fitting in with their peer groups while also trying to form their own individual identities.
- Young adolescents are often interested in popular culture and trends. In addition, social media usage increases as a way to connect with peers and the world at large.

- Though they continue to be influenced by family values, young adolescents increasingly model the behaviors of their peers, celebrity icons, and heroes.
- Fluctuation in emotions and behaviors occur, such as moments of anxiety and worry and instances of bravado and optimism.
- Young adolescents often feel their problems are unique to them, and their emotions sometimes appear exaggerated to others.
- As young adolescence seek independence, their propensity for challenging adult authority can increase.
- Romantic and sexual attraction often develops. This includes same-sex attraction, with 14 being around the average age that gay youth come out in the United States.
- A sizable minority of young adolescents engage in sexual behaviors.
- Young adolescents develop a deeper and more nuanced awareness and understanding of social injustices such as racism, sexism, and homophobia. This heightened awareness can be triggering and lead to racialized trauma for students from racially marginalized backgrounds.

Psychological Development

- During early adolescence, students often seek to find their own individuality, uniqueness, and autonomy. Central questions of exploration include *Who am I? How do I see myself? How do my peers and adults see me?* and *How will I affect the world?*
- Fluctuations in feelings of superiority and inferiority can occur as young adolescents engage in self-discovery.
- Young adolescents start to identify in multiple ways based on social context and environment. For example, they might act one way at home, and behave differently while with their peer groups in school or on social media.

- Young adolescents often desire autonomy, especially in personal matters such as hairstyles and fashion choices.
- Young adolescents often (inaccurately) assume they have less autonomy than their peers.
- Young adolescents may begin to develop a passion for at least one hobby, sport, or interest that brings them joy and a sense of purpose. Sometimes students need help identifying such interests.
- Young adolescents often experience a deeper awareness of their social identities—such as race, gender, social class, religion, sexuality, and immigration status. Having a strong and positive connection to their social identities is important for their social and academic well-being. Though this is true for all youth, this is particularly true for students with marginalized social identities.
- Young adolescents benefit from a nuanced and multifaceted understanding of identity that goes beyond stereotypical expectations of group norms.

APPENDIX B-1

Individual Development Profile

Suggestions for Use

1. Use the form in Appendix B-2 (or your own variation of it) to plot or describe information that gives an overview of an individual student's development in several categories at a particular time. Identify the student, the names of the teachers who contribute to the profile, and the date the profile was created. Be careful to keep this and other confidential notations about students in a secure, private place.

2. Choose a method to describe the student in each of the categories.

   A. You might use a research-based scale or series of steps. For example (all of these are readily available on the Internet):

      - Piaget's Stages of Cognitive Development
      - Erik Erikson's Stages of Psychosocial Development
      - Four Stages of Puberty (the Tanner stages)
      - Kohlberg's Stages of Moral Development along with Gilligan's Stages of the Ethics of Care*
      - Or other well-researched, reputable scales

   B. Or, use the AMLE list of "Characteristics of Young Adolescents" (reprinted in Appendix A of this book) as a guide to categories. Instead of identifying a stage, you might make observational notes about an individual student to generate a profile in each of the categories of development.

3. You might add other categories—such as those specifically related to *belonging* and aspects of *becoming* such as self-determination, autonomy, self-regulation, and competence.

4. As you work on this, you may find that you don't know as much as you could about certain categories. This gives an incentive to dig a little deeper in

observing or learning about the student. When you're finished, try to absorb the whole picture and let it sink in to give you a deeper understanding of that student. If you work on a team, you might share the profiles with other team members. They may have other information to add, and they'll benefit from getting a closer look at the student, too.

**Note: Carol Gilligan, a colleague of Kohlberg, had reservations about Kohlberg's conclusions in that his research used only male subjects. Her own observations and research led her to believe that females tend to follow a somewhat different path in moral development—one inclined more toward care and responsibility to others than toward decision making based on abstract, impartial reasoning and logic.*

APPENDIX B-2

Individual Development Profile (Template)

Student Name ***Date*** ***Teacher(s)***

Developmental Category	Scale Rating, Descriptors, Comments
Physical	
Cognitive	
Social	
Emotional	
Psychological	

Note: Add other categories, such as sense of belonging, executive function, academic tenacity, academic patterns, demonstration of competence, self-determination, and autonomy.

APPENDIX C

Take Away Science Class? Not So Fast, Please!

Dr. Betty Crocker

Because so many students at the middle school where I taught science were reading well below grade level, it was proposed to take them out of science classes in order to give them an additional hour of reading instruction. As the science department chair, I was concerned, prompting me to ask, "If they are already unsuccessful in a one-hour reading class, how will giving them an additional hour (that would be taught in a similar manner) improve their ability to read?"

Believing that success leads to increased success, I made the case that science was not an expendable class to be given up to gain extra time for reading instruction, but was instead an important subject for all students. I proposed that if students were not succeeding the way they were currently being taught, we needed to change the instruction style rather than doing more of the same. To put my money where my mouth was, I offered to take all the students in question if the other science teachers would take all my higher-performing students. And even though it resulted in a slight increase in students in every science class, they agreed.

All students who had scored twenty-four percent or lower in reading on the achievement tests we used at the time were invited to an informal meeting to explain what was happening and give them a choice in the decision. They were promised that assignments would be non-traditional and taught in a style that would help them be more successful, both in science and in reading. They were told that effort would be required and cautioned that a zero would not be allowed and would get them transferred out of the class. "You cannot make an F in this class. Seating is limited, so hold on to yours" was the motto of these new classes. Only three turned down the offer, and one of them asked to join after six weeks. One student dropped out, but after a month he apologized and asked to return. Scheduling changes were made to keep disruptions at a minimum, and the new program began.

Instruction was almost exclusively hands-on with limited writing. The structured format used for written work was designed and followed by all the science teachers. Since we knew struggling students needed precise information, we made a poster for each classroom that illustrated the format. Even the higher-achieving students liked this! Since reading skills were almost non-existent, reading from the text was replaced by a teacher-led conversation on the concept being introduced and was based on a KWL (Know, Want-to-know, Learned) chart. I discovered that these students had a lot of science knowledge but were very restricted in their ability to express or share this knowledge.

There are strong relationships and overlaps between science process skills and reading comprehension skills; observation and inferences (science) are akin to fact or opinion (reading); prediction (science) is akin to asking what happens next in the story (reading). Therefore, the science instruction focused on using correlated skills no matter which science concept was being addressed, and the relationship between what they were learning in science and how they could apply the skills to reading was emphasized.

I also gave direct instruction on such expected behaviors for school success as following rules and interacting positively with peers. (In spite of being in middle school, many students had not learned these unwritten rules and did not understand why they mattered).

As the students became more engaged in their learning, their reading skills began to improve, they began to get higher grades, and behavior problems dramatically decreased. Additionally, as time passed, teachers who had these students in other content areas began to ask what was happening in my class. It seemed that the positive impact flowed into other classes. And it was especially rewarding when some of my students returned after their first semester in high school to show me report cards with passing grades in several subjects!

APPENDIX D

Student Leadership Council

Dr. Laurie Barron

The Student Leadership Council was a new idea to intentionally solicit input and feedback from students (who really like giving their opinions!). Initially, the composition of the group (choosing which students should be included) was a little controversial. Teachers and administrators felt it was important that students in this group represent some of the strongest leadership on campus, including students who were using their leadership skills in both positive and not-so-positive ways. Leadership is leadership. Those leading negatively needed opportunities to refocus their leadership on something positive, and we believed that giving them a voice would help them direct their leadership tendencies in ways that would benefit everyone. There were some discussions about not giving a "difficult" student attention by an appointment to the Council. But in the end, we all knew we needed to do what was best to support our students, help all of them grow, and not just continually punish a student for his or her poor decisions.

We had 30 students on the Council. Teachers chose ten students per grade level representing all different types of students in the school. We wanted balance in gender, academic ability (including students with disabilities and gifted students), extra-curricular involvement, citizenship, and other areas. I (the principal) half-jokingly told teachers that we wanted five students per grade level that you hope your child brings home to marry one day and five students that you prayed your child would never bring home (and that you'd better invest in now in just in case your child chooses that student for a spouse one day!). You get the picture.

I recall the consideration of a student who, during the previous year, had more discipline referrals than any other student in the entire school (that's a lot, by the way). His teacher saw his leadership potential and insisted that he be on the Council. She fought to make sure he had a seat at the table. When placed on the Student Leadership Council the following year, not only did he have no discipline referrals, but he also helped to keep others from making poor decisions and receiving discipline referrals. During class change one afternoon, I was standing at a hallway intersection when the bell rang. Students began filling the halls, when, out of nowhere, several students began squirting water out of water bottles. (The had poked holes in the bottle tops in preparation for this escapade.) Before I could say anything, this young man quickly approached me and stopped my attempt to end the madness. (Picture 300 plus seventh graders in small hallways shooting water randomly through the air). He calmly said, "I've got this, Dr. Barron." In less than 20 seconds, he had taken water bottles away from all offenders (with no back talk or recourse whatsoever) and had all students in class before the tardy bell rang. I stood there, amazed. He wished me a good day and returned to class.

Leadership. He had it, and he needed to use it. Redirecting this one student's negative leadership to positively address school needs had a significant impact on our school, teachers, and students. This all happened because someone reached out to this student, built a relationship with this student, believed in this student, and helped him believe that he could have a positive influence on others. (He also prevented a few altercations, a potential food fight, and several instances of sagging pants). His opinion now mattered, and he knew it.

As a group, the students on the Student Leadership Council met each month to share concerns, suggestions, and celebration ideas contributed by their peers ranging from serious topics such as peer pressure and the overall operation of the school to less serious, yet no less important, topics to middle level students such as hall change and what is served for lunch. By alternating meeting times, students were able to meet as a grade level every other month (sometimes it is best to hear one grade's input separately from another), and then to meet as a full group in alternate months. This schedule removed students from class less frequently since every other month the meeting took place during their lunchtime. We chose not to meet after school because we didn't ever want someone excluded because he couldn't get a ride home or she would miss basketball practice.

This group once took a survey to help the cafeteria manager determine which (federal regulation approved) cookies to make available. These student leaders were small heroes when students' favorite cookies returned to the menu. We also gave this student leadership group opportunities to work with other school leadership groups such as the school's (staff) leadership team so they could see their voice truly matters. And, we invited others to see this group in action. Along with the school staff leadership team, the Student Leadership Council hosted the state superintendent of schools for lunch and visits to classrooms. These students had evidence that their voices mattered. Authentic audiences showed them and the remainder of the student body that their contributions were valued. At the same time, these experiences and responsibilities held them more accountable for their decisions and the actions resulting from those decisions. This group of students collaboratively led and served others to make a positive difference. They took on a true sense of ownership of their school and enjoyed the satisfaction of taking part in what happened in *their* school.

APPENDIX E

Students Take the Lead

Dr. Laurie Barron

Adapted from article originally published in AMLE Magazine, October, 2015

Okay, I admit it. I was a little worried about what they would ask for. If I've learned nothing else after 19 years in education, I certainly know that you should be ready to hear it when you ask for students' opinions.

I know the importance of giving students a voice and allowing students to lead and how important it is to make sure students know we take them seriously and that we value their perceptions, input, and opinions. However, I found that giving students a voice was a little easier for me to implement as a classroom teacher and even as a building-level principal. When I moved to the role of superintendent, my interaction with students understandably decreased, and I had trouble finding ways to seek out students' opinions in relevant and meaningful ways.

After seeing a colleague do something similar, our K-8 district began hosting student-led board work sessions two times per year; one session is hosted by our district's 4th-graders and the other by our 8th-graders. The work session is led by pairs of students sharing with board of trustees' members, administrators, teachers, and parents their ideas of how to help improve our schools and our district.

The process of preparing for and presenting to the board of trustees is a serious one; this takes time and commitment from students and their teachers to make the student-led session a reality (and a success). The work begins long before the board work session when students start preparing in their English language arts class. In collaboration students spend time learning and applying the content standards for reading, writing, listening, speaking, and viewing. They learn standards in a way that matters to them: by picking something that they don't like or that they want to improve about school and then working to convince others that they have a good idea. In doing this work, they learn and implement skills in researching, developing, and supporting a topic; reasoning and acknowledging opposing views;

understanding the conventions of written language; using appropriate vocabulary, figurative language, voice, and mood; using technology to produce writing; presenting findings with appropriate displays of evidence; and engaging the audience (they were impressively convincing in many instances), just to name a few.

One of the most difficult parts of the process is the teachers narrowing it down to 10 presentations for students to share at the public board work session. And while this process is a lengthy one, eighth-grade teacher Kara Gronley says it's well worth the effort because it "really provides a platform for student learning that gives them a meaningful and authentic audience. It gives them a real-world experience that causes change to happen. It allows for student buy-in due to their suggestions being implemented."

When the work session begins, there are typically 10 groups with two students each, for a total of 20 students presenting. In our cozy (and not large) boardroom, we set up five tables. Two groups of students sit at each table, and the other guests sitting at the tables are trustees, administrators, teachers, and parents. Before the students begin, I remind the audience (and myself) that the students are leading this meeting and that it is important for us, as their audience, to maintain a sense of wonder, not make assumptions, show our curiosity, and be open to all ideas students present. I also remind us all that we need to be a good audience and to listen like we mean it (which includes putting away cell phones!). Then, over the next two hours, students share their presentations at their table, and the adults rotate several times to different tables to hear as many presentations as possible.

Perhaps one of the most rewarding aspects of the evening is watching the students' ideas come to fruition. In our two years of hosting student-led board work sessions, these students have made quite an impact. Students have successfully rallied for having new soccer nets installed on the playing fields, lines painted on the pavement for basketball games, alterations to the dress code, new elective classes for journalism and drama, and improvements to the bell system. Their ideas (and persuasive delivery of them) also led to our school fielding our first-ever cross-country team last spring and a tree being planted in honor of the eighth-grade class, traditions that will remain far after these students' time with us. When last year's 8th graders actually planted the tree, many students helped dig the hole for the tree, and the entire eighth-grade class gathered when the tree was set in place as Lane Whiteman, the student whose idea it was to plant the tree, spoke to his classmates about why he felt planting the tree was important.

What I learned and continue to learn from these students is that their voice matters, not just because they get to share their input (which is so important for young adolescents who often feel undervalued and like everything keeps happening *to* them instead of *for* them), but also because in allowing them to express their opinions in an open forum, we are teaching them the invaluable lesson of how to appropriately share their input. These young people learn very quickly that sharing that "the dress code stinks" isn't likely to get them anywhere but that sharing specific examples of how they can be responsible with more dress code options might just get the powers-that-be to listen to (and maybe even implement) some of their ideas. No one has yet to ask for anything outlandish or silly, immature, or mean-natured. Students have taken the invitation to share their ideas very seriously, and they have not wasted the opportunity.

Perhaps one of our eighth-grade teachers Melissa Hardman says it best: "At this age, sometimes students begin to resent adults, and knowing adults are actually listening to their suggestions helps them believe in adults and gives students the power to make a difference in their school."

Another important point to remember is that students' perceptions, just like all other data, are important not only to listen to but also to seek out and review. Just as with other forms of data (think test scores . . .), different data gives us a more rich and valid understanding our culture and our progress. Who better to receive this data from than students themselves, the ones we are here to serve each day. Students need to know that this is *their* school, *their* district. As such, they must take responsibility for helping us to continuously improve. And if we give them this responsibility, we must give them some avenue to help make it possible.

Principal Kim Anderson says that these student-led sessions are impacting their school in ways she never imagined, showing students that "they do have a voice, and when they use it, change can happen. It is empowering and connected to life skills. They can carry these skills to the real world. And, this process is directly related to our state curriculum content standards!"

What could have been another typical board work session led by adults or a typical school assignment to write a persuasive essay has been turned into something that is helping to shape not just our schools and our district but the students and adults in them as well. I am honored to be a small part of that.

So, do I still worry sometimes about what ideas our students will come up with next? Not really. I'm far more concerned about what will happen if we ever stop asking them to help us lead and improve.

APPENDIX F-1

My Thoughts About BELONGING

Think of each of these items as it relates to school.
Answer as many as you can. Don't name any individual students or teachers.

1. **To belong** (in my school and in my classes) means:

2. Here's why it matters for a kid to have a **sense of belonging** at school:

3. Here's how I can tell if someone does NOT have a **sense of belonging**:

4. When someone does NOT have a **sense of belonging**, it feels:

5. The best thing I've seen a teacher do to help a student **belong** is:

6. The best things kids can do to help other kids **belong** are:

7. Something I've done to help someone else **belong** is:

8. Something I've done or could do to increase my **own sense of belonging** is:

9. To help ALL kids at my school feel that they **belong**, I would change this:

APPENDIX F-2

My Thoughts About BECOMING

Think of each of these items as it relates to school.
Answer as many as you can. Don't name any individual students or teachers.

1. These are some things I think middle school students can **become** with the help of their schools:

2. Here are signs of **becoming** that I already see for myself:

3. When I experience myself **becoming** in some way, I feel:

4. When a student does NOT experience success at **becoming**, the effects might be:

5. Things that have happened in school that have MOST helped me to **become** are:

6. The best thing I have done to help another student **become** is:

7. The best things I can do to help myself to **become** are:

8. I've seen these things keep kids from **becoming:**

9. To help ALL kids at my school feel that they are **becoming**, I would change this:

APPENDIX G

Brainstorming Guide: What You Already Do to Help Students Belong		
Attitudes, beliefs, and behaviors you model	*Ways you relate to students*	*Expectations you communicate to students*
Activities that intentionally teach emotional skills	*Activities that intentionally teach social skills*	*Activities that boost students' confidence in themselves as learners*
Activities that help students see one another's strengths and value	*Activities that give students opportunity to express their opinions*	*Activities that give students opportunity to make choices about their own learning*

APPENDIX H

Reflection: What Does Belonging Mean to You?

1. Describe or define *belonging* as you understand it, based on your own experiences.

2. List a few places or situations where you feel or have felt a sense of belonging.

3. How can you "tell" you belong in those places or situations? Dig into those feelings of belongingness and describe them.

4. List a few places or situations in which you feel or have felt a lack of belonging.

5. Think back to your student days. What factors contributed to your sense of belonging (or not belonging) at school or in a classroom?

6. List some signs you look for or have seen that suggest students in your classroom don't feel a sense of belonging.

7. Describe what and how you feel when you see a student (or perhaps a child of your own) struggle with belonging.

8. Describe your past experiences—successes and failures—with helping students feel they belong.

9. Describe the ways in which your own background, culture, and life experiences are similar to those of your students.

10. Describe the ways in which your own background, culture, and life experiences are different from those of your students.

APPENDIX I

Log of Teachable Skills and Practices That Increase Belonging		
The following skills and practices have been shown to increase belonging for students—on both the giving and receiving ends of the actions. Intentionally integrate these practices into your plans for lessons and activities. Indicate the dates that you provided an opportunity for your students to specifically practice each of the skills and what activities or lessons you presented.		
Skill or Practice	**Date**	**Lesson/Activity Notes**
Give and expect respect from classmates		
Create an inclusive classroom community by embracing diversity (racial, linguistic, cultural, etc.) and engaging with differences with curiosity and respect		
Actively resist and protect against the exclusion of anyone		
Practice kindness and helpfulness		
Work collaboratively in diverse teams to complete tasks, make decisions, debate constructively, and solve problems—academic topics, classroom-living topics, and social issues in the local community		
Take some responsibility for their own belonging		
Increase awareness and use of their own personal resources, skills, and abilities		
Increase social awareness in their communities and the wider world		
Grow in self-management and control of emotions in socially aware and meaningful ways that respect and honor differences		
Learn and practice organizational and planning skills		
Make choices about classroom life and their own learning		
Have a voice in classroom life and their own learning, and make efforts to hear from students who haven't had a voice		
Learn, practice, and improve skills of coping and flexibility		
Take part in making real and meaningful decisions		

(continued)

Log of Teachable Skills and Practices That Increase Belonging (*continued*)		
The following skills and practices have been shown to increase belonging for students—on both the giving and receiving ends of the actions. Intentionally integrate these practices into your plans for lessons and activities. Indicate the dates that you provided an opportunity for your students to specifically practice each of the skills and what activities or lessons you presented.		
Skill or Practice	**Date**	**Lesson/Activity Notes**
Build self-awareness skills, including how they may relate to identity and equity		
Build reflection skills that help them "check in" with themselves in terms of their assumptions about the world and identify any biases that they have or may be developing		
Gain academic confidence and a satisfying view of themselves as students		
Experience mastery and competence		
Have experience with autonomy		
Set, manage, and achieve goals		
Learn ways to bounce back from failure		
Engage actively in learning activities		
Enjoy learning and opportunities to make it relevant to their lives and interests		
Enjoy fun, humor, and excitement in the classroom		
Have meaningful and frequent participation in classroom events of all sorts		
Participate in creative endeavors, leadership, and responsibility		
Advocate for themselves as learners and for issues they believe in, and seek help when needed		
Give and receive kind, constructive feedback		
Learn about and practice growth mindset		

APPENDIX J

Student Survey on Teacher–Student Relationships

Instructions: Answer as many as of these questions as you can. Don't include your name or any student or teacher names.

Part 1

1. How can you tell that a teacher accepts or values you?
2. What teacher actions make you wonder whether the teacher likes you or not?
3. What helps you trust a teacher?
4. What makes it hard to trust a teacher?
5. What is the best action you've seen a teacher do in relating to students?
6. What helps you feel positive about a teacher?
7. What causes you to feel uncomfortable with a teacher?
8. What do you wish teachers would do *for sure?*
9. What do you wish teachers would NOT do *for sure?*

Part 2

1. Do you think your teacher(s) would notice if you are having trouble with something you are learning?
2. Do you think your teacher(s) would notice if you are upset about something going on at school?
3. How can you tell when a teacher is really interested in you?
4. How can you tell when a teacher is determined to help you succeed in school?

Part 3

What are one or two top pieces of advice you'd give a teacher about what students your age need?

Endnotes

PART I INTRODUCTION: FOUNDATIONS FOR BELONGING AND BECOMING

1. Bishop, P. A., & Harrison, L. M. (2021). *The successful middle school: This we believe* (p. 8). Association for Middle Level Education.

Chapter 1: Build a Common Understanding of Belonging and Becoming

1. Goodenow, C. (1993). The psychological sense of school membership among adolescents: Scale development and educational correlates (p. 80). *Psychology in the Schools, 30*(1), 70–90.
2. Baumeister, R. F., & Leary, M. R. (1995). The need to belong: Desire for interpersonal attachments as a fundamental human motivation. *Psychological Bulletin, 117*(3), 497–529.
3. Libbey, H. P. (2007). *School connectedness: Influence above and beyond family connectedness* (p. 52). University of Michigan ProQuest Information and Learning Company.
4. Allen, K. A. (2022, January 22). The science of school belonging. *Psychology Today.* https://www.psychologytoday.com/intl/blog/sense-belonging/202201/the-science-school-belonging
   Allen, K. A. (2020). *The psychology of belonging.* Routledge.
   Hagerty, B. M., Lynch-Sauer, J., Patusky, K. L., Bouwsema, M., & Collier, P. (1992). Sense of belonging: A vital mental health concept. *Archives of Psychiatric Nursing, 6*(3), 172–177. https://doi.org/10.1016/0883-9417(92)90028-H
5. Kuttner, P. J. (2023). The right to belong in school: A critical, transitional conceptualization of school belonging. *AERA Open, 9*(1), 1–12. https://journals.sagepub.com/doi/pdf/10.1177/23328584231183407

Souto-Manning, M. (2021). On the abolition of belonging as property. Toward justice for immigrant children of color. *Urban Education*. 59(1). https://doi.org/10.1177/00420859211017967

6. Allen, K. A. (2022, January 22). The science of school belonging. *Psychology Today*. https://www.psychologytoday.com/intl/blog/sense-belonging/202201/the-science-school-belonging#

   Allen, K. A. (2022, February 9). A deep dive into the benefits of school belonging: A recap of major research findings. *Psychology Today*. https://www.psychologytoday.com/intl/blog/sense-belonging/202202/deep-dive-the-benefits-school-belonging

   Allen, K. A. (2020). *The psychology of belonging*. Abington, UK: Routledge.

   Allen, K.A., & Bowles, T. (2012). Belonging as a guiding principle in the education of adolescents. *Australian Journal of Educational & Developmental Psychology, 12*, 108–119.

   Anderman, E. M. (2002). School effects on psychological outcomes during adolescence. *Journal of Educational Psychology, 94*(3), 795–809.

   Anderman, L. H. (2003). Academic and social perceptions as predictors of change in middle school students' sense of school belonging. *Journal of Experimental Education, 72*(1), 5–22.

   Furrer, C., & Skinner, E. (2003). Sense of relatedness as a factor in children's academic engagement and performance. *Journal of Educational Psychology, 95*(1), 148–162.

   O'Brien, K. A., & Bowles, T. (2013). The importance of belonging for adolescents in secondary school settings. *The European Journal of Social & Behavioural Sciences*, 5(2), 976–984.

   Romero, C. (2015). *What we know about belonging from scientific research*. Student Experience Network. https://studentexperiencenetwork.org/wp-content/uploads/2018/11/What-We-Know-About-Belonging.pdf

   Wingspread. (2004). Wingspread declaration on school connections. *Journal of School Health, 74*(7), 233–234.

7. Allen, K. A. (2022, January 22). The science of school belonging (para.16). *Psychology Today*. https://www.psychologytoday.com/intl/blog/sense-belonging/202201/the-science-school-belonging#

8. Allen, K. A. (2022, January 22). The science of school belonging. *Psychology Today*. https://www.psychologytoday.com/intl/blog/sense-belonging/202201/the-science-school-belonging#

Allen, K. A. (2022, February 9). A deep dive into the benefits of school belonging: A recap of major research findings. *Psychology Today*. https://www.psychologytoday.com/intl/blog/sense-belonging/202202/deep-dive-the-benefits-school-belonging

Baumeister, R. F., & Leary, M. R. (1995). The need to belong: Desire for interpersonal attachments as a fundamental human motivation. *Psychological Bulletin, 117,* 497–529.

Furrer, C., & Skinner, E. (2003). Sense of relatedness as a factor in children's academic engagement and performance. *Journal of Educational Psychology, 95*(1), 148–162.

Wingspread. (2004). Wingspread declaration on school connections. *Journal of School Health, 74*(7), 233–234.

9. Belsha, K. (2021, September 27). *Stress and short tempers: Schools struggle with behavior as students return.* Chalkbeat. https://www.chalkbeat.org/2021/9/27/22691601/student-behavior-stress-trauma-return

   Kurtz, H. (2022, January 12). *Threats of student violence and misbehavior are rising, many school leaders report.* Education Week. https://www.edweek.org/leadership/threats-of-student-violence-and-misbehavior-are-rising-many-school-leaders-report/2022/01

10. Furrer, C., & Skinner, E. (2003). Sense of relatedness as a factor in children's academic engagement and performance (p. 158). *Journal of Educational Psychology, 95*(1), 148–162.
11. Romero, C. (2015). *What we know about belonging from scientific research* (p. 2). Student Experience Network. https://studentexperiencenetwork.org/wp-content/uploads/2018/11/What-We-Know-About-Belonging.pdf
12. Wingspread. (2004). Wingspread declaration on school connections (p. 233). *Journal of School Health, 74*, 233–234.
13. Allen, K. A. (2022, January 22). The science of school belonging (para. 1). *Psychology Today*. https://www.psychologytoday.com/intl/blog/sense-belonging/202201/the-science-school-belonging#
14. Montana Administrative Rules. *Education standards of accreditation. Rule 10:55.602*(17). https://rules.mt.gov/gateway/RuleNo.asp?RN=10%2E55%2E602
15. Balfanz, R. (2020). *Putting middle grades students on the graduation path: A policy and practice*

brief. Association for Middle Level Education. https://www.amle.org/wp-content/uploads/2020/04/Executive_Summary_Balfanz.pdf

Balfanz, R. (2009). *Putting middle grades students on the graduation path*. Everyone Graduates Center.

Balfanz, R., Herzog, L., & MacIver, D. J., (2007). Preventing student disengagement and keeping students on the graduation path in urban middle-grades schools: Early identification and effective interventions. *Educational Psychologist, 42*(4), 223–235.

National Academies Press. (2011). *Early warning indicators: High school dropout, graduation, and completion rates*. National Academies Press. https://nap.nationalacademies.org/read/13035/chapter/7.

16. Ryan, R. M., & Deci, E. L. (2000a). Intrinsic and extrinsic motivation: Classic definitions and new directions. *Contemporary Educational Psychology, 25*(1), 54–67.

    Ryan, R. M., & Deci, E. L. (2000b). Self-determination theory and the facilitation of intrinsic motivation, social development, and well-being. *American Psychologist, 55*(1), 68–78.

    Ryan, R. M., & Deci, E. L. (2018). *Self-determination theory: Basic psychological needs in motivation, development, and wellness*. The Guilford Press.

17. Deci, E. L., & Ryan, R. M. (1985). *Intrinsic motivation and self-determination in human behavior* (p. 76). Plenum Press.

18. Bonnie, R. J., & Backes, E. P. (Eds.) (2019, May 16). *The promise of adolescence: Realizing opportunity for all youth*. National Academies Press. DOI: 10.17226/25388

19. Stepp, L. S. (2001). *Our last best shot: Guiding our children through early adolescence*. Penguin Radom House.

20. Balfanz, R. (2020). *Putting middle grades students on the graduation path: A policy and practice brief*. Association for Middle Level Education. https://www.amle.org/wp-content/uploads/2020/04/Executive_Summary_Balfanz.pdf

    Lounsbury, J. H. (2000). *Understanding and appreciating the wonder years*. Association for Middle Level Education. https://www.amle.org/the-importance-of-early-adolescence/

    Patterson, J. (2019). *Middle matters*. Education World. https://www.educationworld.com/teachers/middle-matters-middle-school-years-are-important-and-theres-tools-help

21. Bishop, P. A., & Harrison, L. M. (2021). *The successful middle school: This we believe* (p. 9). Association for Middle Level Education.
22. Clarkson, S., & Clarkson. S. (2016). *The lifegiving home: Creating a place of belonging and becoming* (p. 6). Tyndale Momentum.

Chapter 2: Understand Young Adolescents and Their World

1. Bishop, P. A., & Harrison, L. M. (2021). *The successful middle school: This we believe* (p. 55). Association for Middle Level Education.
2. Bishop, P. A., & Harrison, L. M. (2021). *The successful middle school: This we believe* (pp. 55–64). Association for Middle Level Education.
3. Chahal, R., Kirshenbaum, J. S., Miller, J. G., Ho, T. C., & Gotlib, I. H. (2020) Higher executive control network coherence buffers against puberty-related increases in internalizing symptoms during the COVID-19 pandemic. Biological Psychiatry: Cognitive Neuroscience and Neuroimaging, 6(1), 79–88. https://pubmed.ncbi.nlm.nih.gov/33097469/
4. Center on the Developing Child (2012). *InBrief: Executive function* (para. 2). https://developingchild.harvard.edu/resources/inbrief-executive-function/
5. Center on the Developing Child (2012). *InBrief: Executive function* (para. 3). https://developingchild.harvard.edu/resources/inbrief-executive-function/
6. Center on the Developing Child. (2012). *InBrief: Executive function* (paras. 4–7). Harvard University Center on the Developing Child. https://developingchild.harvard.edu/resources/inbrief-executive-function/
7. Chahal, R., Kirshenbaum, J. S., Miller, J. G., Ho, T. C., & Gotlib, I. H. (2020). Higher executive control network coherence buffers against puberty-related increases in internalizing symptoms during the COVID-19 pandemic. Biological Psychiatry: Cognitive Neuroscience and Neuroimaging, 6(1), 79–88. https://pubmed.ncbi.nlm.nih.gov/33097469/
8. Executive function. (2023). *Psychology Today*. https://www.psychologytoday.com/us/basics/executive-function
9. Wormeli, R. (2013, August) *Looking at executive function*. Association for Middle Level Education. https://www.amle.org/BrowsebyTopic/WhatsNew/WNDet/TabId/270/ArtMID/888/ArticleID/298/Looking-at-Executive-Function.aspx
10. Guare, R., Dawson, P., & Guare, C. (2013). *Smart but scattered teens: The "Executive Skills" program for helping teens reach their potential*. The Guilford Press.

11. Executive function. (2023). *Psychology Today*. https://www.psychologytoday.com/us/basics/executive-function
12. Lounsbury, J. H. (2000). *Understanding and appreciating the wonder years* (paras. 5–7). Association for Middle Level Education. https://www.amle.org/the-importance-of-early-adolescence/
13. Bishop, P. A., & Harrison, L. M. (2021). *The successful middle school: This we believe* (pp. 57–64). Association for Middle Level Education.
14. Bishop, P. A., & Harrison, L. M. (2021). *The successful middle school: This we believe* (p. 56). Association for Middle Level Education.
15. Bishop, P. A., & Harrison, L. M. (2021). *The successful middle school: This we believe* (p. 56). Association for Middle Level Education.
16. Bishop, P. A., & Harrison, L. M. (2021). *The successful middle school: This we believe* (p. 8). Association for Middle Level Education.

Chapter 3: Organize to Promote Belonging and Becoming

1. Bishop, P. A., & Harrison, L. M. (2021). *The successful middle school: This we believe* (p. 9). Association for Middle Level Education.
2. Bishop, P. A., & Harrison, L. M. (2021). *The successful middle school: This we believe* (p. 9). Association for Middle Level Education.
3. Bishop, P. A., & Harrison, L. M. (2021). *The successful middle school: This we believe* (pp. 8–9). Association for Middle Level Education.
4. *The successful middle school: This we believe*. Association for Middle Level Education. https://www.amle.org/wp-content/uploads/2021/01/AMLE_SMS_Summary_Color.pdf
5. Wilcox, K. C. (with Angelis, J. I.). (2007). *What makes middle schools work* (pp. 12–13). University at Albany School of Education: Albany Institute for Research in Education.
6. McCarty Perez, A. (2022). *The successful middle school schedule,* (p. vii). Association for Middle Level Education.
7. McCarty Perez, A. (2022). *The successful middle school schedule*. Association for Middle Level Education.
8. Williamson, R. (2009, March). The schedule as a tool to improve student learning (p. 4). *Middle Level Leader*. National Association of Secondary School Principals.

9. Bishop, P. A., & Harrison, L. M. (2021). *The successful middle school: This we believe* (p. 9). Association for Middle Level Education.

PART II: PRACTICES FOR BELONGING AND BECOMING

Chapter 4: Create Connections and Community

1. Clavis, M., & Lee, K. (2023). "What is community anyway?" *Stanford Social Innovation Review* (paras. 4–7). https://ssir.org/articles/entry/what_is_community_anyway
2. Osterman, K. F. (2000). Students' need for belonging in the school community. *Review of Educational Research, 70*(3), 323–367.
3. Osterman, K. F. (2000). Students' need for belonging in the school community. *Review of Educational Research, 70*(3), 324.
4. Allen, K. A., Kern, M. L., Vella-Brodrick, D., Waters, L., & Hattie, J. (2018). What schools need to know about fostering belonging: A meta-analysis (para. 1). *Educational Psychology Review, 30*(1), 1–34. https://doi.org/10.1007/s10648-016-9389-8
5. Allen, K. A., Kern, M. L., Vella-Brodrick, D., Waters, L., & Hattie, J. (2018). What schools need to know about fostering belonging: A meta-analysis (para. 1). *Educational Psychology Review, 30*(1),1–34. https://doi.org/10.1007/s10648-016-9389-8
6. Romero, C. (2015). *What we know about belonging from scientific research* (pp. 3–4). Student Experience Network. https://studentexperiencenetwork.org/wp-content/uploads/2018/11/What-We-Know-About-Belonging.pdf
7. Schaps, E. (2003). Creating a school community. *Educational Leadership, 60*(6), 31–33.
   Schaps, E., Battistich, V., & Solomon. (2003). Community in school as key to student growth: Findings from the Child Development Project. *Caring communities and education* (ch. 9). Developmental Studies Center.
8. Anderman, E. M. (2002). School effects on psychological outcomes during adolescence (p. 807). *Journal of Educational Psychology, 94*(3), 795–809.
9. Bishop, P. A., & Harrison, L. M. (2021). *The successful middle school: This we believe* (p. 9). Association for Middle Level Education.
10. Merrill, L., Lotero, A., Gilliard, R., & Black, K. (2021). *Learning and academic growth: Insights*

from an innovative research-practice partnership. The Research Alliance for New York City Schools. https://steinhardt.nyu.edu/sites/default/files/2021-07/SSN%20SEL%20FINAL.pdf

Balfanz, R., & Byrnes, V. (2020). *Connecting social-emotional development, academic achievement, and on-track outcomes.* Everyone Graduates Center at the Johns Hopkins University School of Education. https://www.cityyear.org/wp-content/uploads/2020/05/EGC_overview_FY20_05.20.pdf

11. Centers for Disease Control and Prevention. (2023). *School connectedness.* Centers for Disease Control and Prevention. https://www.cdc.gov/healthyschools/school_connectedness.htm

Allen, K. A. (2022, January 22). The science of school belonging. *Psychology Today*. https://www.psychologytoday.com/intl/blog/sense-belonging/202201/the-science-school-belonging#

Allen, K. A. (2022, January 15). Your sense of belonging in modern times: Considerations for schools, universities, workplaces, and communities. *Psychology Today*. https://www.psychologytoday.com/us/blog/sense-belonging/202201/your-sense-belonging-in-modern-times

Osterman, K. F. (2000). Students' need for belonging in the school community. *Review of Educational Research, 70*(3), 323–367.

Riley, K. (2017, June 20). *Re-creating schools as places of belonging: The art of possibilities.* Teaching Times. https://core.ac.uk/download/pdf/219542903.pdf

Romero, C. (2015). *What we know about belonging from scientific research.* Student Experience Network. https://studentexperiencenetwork.org/wp-content/uploads/2018/11/What-We-Know-About-Belonging.pdf

Wingspread. (2004). Wingspread declaration on school connections. *Journal of School Health, 74*, 233–234.

12. Bishop, P. A., & Harrison, L. M. (2021). *The successful middle school: This we believe* (p. 9). Association for Middle Level Education.

13. Allen, K., Gray, D. L., Arslan, G., Riley, K., Vella-Brocrick, D., & Waters, L. (2021). School belonging policy. In K. Allen, A. Reupert, & L. Oades (Eds.), *Building better schools with evidence-based policy* (ch. 19; pp. 139–146). Routledge. https://www.taylorfrancis.com/chapters/oa-edit/10.4324/9781003025955-19/school-belonging-policy-kelly-ann-allen-deleon-gray-g%C3%B6kmen-arslan-kathryn-ri-

ley-dianne-vella-brodrick-lea-waters?context=ubx&refId=b0b80b8e-420c-469e-a1-b7-5d5bc907a619

14. Bishop, P. A., & Harrison, L. M. (2021). *The successful middle school: This we believe* (p. 9). Association for Middle Level Education.
15. Arruda, W. (2024, January 3). Why belonging is the key to authentic leadership. *Forbes*. https://www.mckinsey.com/capabilities/people-and-organizational-performance/our-insights/the-organization-blog/its-not-about-the-office-its-about-belonging

    Coqual. (2020). *The power of belonging: What it is and why it matters in today's workplace: Key findings*. Center for Talent Innovation. https://coqual.org/wp-content/uploads/2020/09/CoqualPowerOfBelongingKeyFindings090720.pdf

    Kennedy, J. T., & Jain-Link, P. (2021, June 21). What does it take to build a culture of belonging? *Harvard Business Review*. https://hbr.org/2021/06/what-does-it-take-to-build-a-culture-of-belonging

    DeSmet. A., Downlig, B., Mugayar-Baldocchi, M., & Spratt, J. (2022). *It's not about the office, it's about belonging*. McKinsey & Company. https://www.mckinsey.com/capabilities/people-and-organizational-performance/our-insights/the-organization-blog/its-not-about-the-office-its-about-belonging

    DeVry University. (2022, June 13). *How to create a culture of belonging*. DeVry University. https://www.devry.edu/blog/how-to-create-a-culture-of-belonging.html
16. Coqual. (2020). *The power of belonging: What it is and why it matters in today's workplace: Key findings* (p. 2). Center for Talent Innovation. https://coqual.org/wp-content/uploads/2020/09/CoqualPowerOfBelongingKeyFindings090720.pdf
17. Arruda, W. (2024, January 3). Why belonging is the key to authentic leadership. *Forbes*. https://www.mckinsey.com/capabilities/people-and-organizational-performance/our-insights/the-organization-blog/its-not-about-the-office-its-about-belonging

    Carr, E. W., Reece, A., Kellerman, G. R., & Robichaux, A. (2019, December 16). The value of belonging at work. *Harvard Business Review*. https://hbr.org/2019/12/the-value-of-belonging-at-work

    Coqual. (2020). *The power of belonging: What it is and why it matters in today's workplace: Key findings*. Center for Talent Innovation. https://coqual.org/wp-content/uploads/2020/09/CoqualPowerOfBelongingKeyFindings090720.pdf

DeVry University. (2022, June 13). *How to create a culture of belonging*. DeVry University. https://www.devry.edu/blog/how-to-create-a-culture-of-belonging.html

Kennedy, J. T., & Jain-Link, P. (2021, June 21). What does it take to build a culture of belonging? *Harvard Business Review*. https://hbr.org/2021/06/what-does-it-take-to-build-a-culture-of-belonging

The Master Teacher. (2023, July 20). *Seven keys to sustaining a culture of belonging (for adults)*. The Master Teacher. https://masterteacher.net/seven-keys-to-sustaining-a-culture-of-belonging-for-adults/

18. Organization for Economic Cooperation and Development. (2019). *PISA results (Volume III): What school life means for students' lives.* OECD Publishing. https://doi.org/10.1787/acd78851-en.
19. Bishop, P. A., & Harrison, L. M. (2021). *The successful middle school: This we believe* (p. 9). Association for Middle Level Education.
20. Gray, C. (2023). *The successful middle school leader* (p. 26). Association for Middle Level Education.
21. Gray, C. (2023). *The successful middle school leader* (p. 27). Association for Middle Level Education.
22. Center on the Developing Child. (2023). *Resilience* (para. 3). Harvard University Center on the Developing Child. https://developingchild.harvard.edu/science/key-concepts/resilience/
23. Allen, K., Kern, M. L., Vella-Brodrick, D., Hattie, J. & Waters, L. (2018). What schools need to know about fostering school belonging: A meta-analysis. *Educational Psychology Review, 30*(1),1–34. http://dx.doi.org/10.1007/s10648-016-9389-8
24. Allen, K., Slaten, C. D., Arslan, G., Roffey, S., Craig, H., & Vella-Brodrick, D. A. (2021, June 25). *School belonging: The importance of student and teacher relationships.* Springer Link. https://link.springer.com/chapter/10.1007/978-3-030-64537-3_21
25. Wormeli, R. (2010). *Rick Wormeli: Redos, retakes, and do-overs, part one*. [Video File, 2:18]. https://www.youtube.com/watch?v=TM-3PFfIfvI
26. American Psychological Association (2020, October 29). *Positive student-teacher relationships benefit students' long-term health, study finds.* APA. https://www.apa.org/news/press/releases/2020/10/student-teacher-relationships

    Emslander, V., Holzberger, D., Ofstad, S. B., Fischback, A., & Scherer, R. (2023, September). *Teacher-student relationships and student outcomes: A systemic review of meta-analyses and second order meta-analyses.* Researchgate. DOI:10.31234/osf.io/qxntb

Giles, D. (2011). Relationships always matter: Findings from a phenomenological research inquiry. *Australian Journal of Teacher Education, 36*(6), 80–91.

Visible Learning (2019). *250+ Influences on student achievement.* Corwin Visible Learning. https://visible-learning.org/wp-content/uploads/2022/01/250-Influences.pdf

Jederlund, U., & von Rosen, T. (2022, May 12). Teacher–student relationships and student self-efficacy beliefs. *Education Inquiry, 14*(4), 529–553. https://www.tandfonline.com/doi/full/10.1080/20004508.2022.2073053

Kincade, L., Cook, C., & Goerdt, A. (2020). Meta-analyses and common practice elements of universal approaches to improving student–teacher relationships. *Review of Educational Research 20*(10), 1–39. https://sais.org/app/uploads/2023/06/RELATIONSHIPS-meta-analysis.pdf

Martin, A.J., & Dowson, M. (2009). Interpersonal relationships, motivation, engagement, and achievement: Yields for theory, current issues, and educational practice. *Review of Educational Research, 79*(1), 327–365.

Quin, D. (2016). Longitudinal and contextual associations between teacher-student relationships and student engagement: A systematic review. *Review of Educational Research, 87*(2), 345–387.

27. Bergin, C. (2022, March 7). *Positive teacher–student relationships lead to better teaching.* College of Education & Human Development, University of Missouri. https://education.missouri.edu/2022/03/positive-teacher-student-relationships-lead-to-better-teaching/
28. Libbey, H. P. (2007). *School connectedness: Influence above and beyond family connectedness.* University of Michigan ProQuest Information and Learning Company.
29. Furrer, C., & Skinner, E. (2003). Sense of relatedness as a factor in children's academic engagement and performance. *Journal of Educational Psychology, 95*(1), 148–162.
30. Allen, K. A., & Bowles, T. (2012). Belonging as a guiding principle in the education of adolescents. *Australian Journal of Educational & Developmental Psychology, 12*, 108–119.
31. Bishop, P. A., & Harrison, L. M. (2021). *The successful middle school: This we believe* (p. 9). Association for Middle Level Education.
32. Carnegie Council on Adolescent Development. (1995). *Turning points: Preparing American youth for the 21st century.* Carnegie Council on Adolescent Development.

Wingspread. (2004). Wingspread declaration on school connections. *Journal of School Health, 74,* 233–234.

33. Brist, T. L., (2023). *Successful middle school advisory* (p. 15). Association for Middle Level Education.
34. Berckemeyer, J. (2022). *Successful middle school teaming* (pp. 1–8, 121–133). Association for Middle Level Education.
35. Bishop, P. A., & Harrison, L. M. (2021). *The successful middle school: This we believe* (p. 11). Association for Middle Level Education.
36. Battistich, V., Solomon, D., Watson, M., & Schaps, E. (1997). Caring school communities. *Educational Psychologist, 32,* 137–151.

    Battistich, V., Watson, M., Solomon, D., Schaps, E., & Solomon, J. (1991). The Child Development Project: A comprehensive program for the development of prosocial character. In W. M. Kurtines & J. L. Gewirtz (Eds.), *Handbook of moral behavior and development, Vol. 1. Theory; Vol. 2. Research; Vol. 3. Application* (pp. 1–34). Lawrence Erlbaum Associates, Inc.
37. Bishop, P. A., & Harrison, L. M. (2021). *The successful middle school: This we believe* (p. 9). Association for Middle Level Education.
38. Ferguson, C. (2009). *Toolkit for Title I parent involvement* (sec. 2, p. 7). Southwest Educational Development Laboratory. https://sedl.org/connections/toolkit/

    Bachman, H. F., Anderman, E. M., Zyromski, B., & Boone, B. (2021). The role of parents during the middle school years: Strategies for teachers to support middle school family engagement. *School Community Journal 31*(1), 109–126.
39. Greene, J., & Voiles, D. (2023). *Positive contact: Redefining parent involvement* (paras. 16–17). Association for Middle Level Education. https://www.amle.org/positive-contact-redefining-parent-involvement/
40. Greene, J., & Voiles, D. (2023). *Positive contact: Redefining parent involvement* (paras. 18–20). Association for Middle Level Education. https://www.amle.org/positive-contact-redefining-parent-involvement/

    Kubesch, L. (2023). *From home visits to parent academies: Transforming engagement in middle level education.* Association for Middle Level Education. https://www.amle.org/from-home-visits-to-parent-academies-transforming-engagement-in-middle-level-education/

41. Bergman, S., & Brough, J. A. (2012). *Reducing the risk, increasing the promise* (p. 113). Eye on Education.
42. Jetten, J., Haslam C., & Haslam, S. A. (2011). The case for a social identity analysis of health and well-being. In J. Jetten, C. Haslam, & S.A. Haslam (Eds.), *The social cure: Identity, health and well-being* (pp. 3–4). Psychology Press.

Chapter 5: Believe in Students

1. Rosenthal, R., & Jacobson, L. (1992). *Pygmalion in the classroom: Expanded edition.* Irvington Publishing.
2. Cohen, G. L., & Garcia, J. (2014). Educational theory, practice, and policy and the wisdom of social psychology. *Policy Insights from the Behavioral and Brain Sciences, 1*(1), 13–20. https://doi.org/10.1177/2372732214551559
3. Hattie, J. (2023). *The visible learning research* (para. 3). Corwin Visible Learning. https://www.visiblelearning.com/content/visible-learning-research
4. Visible Learning (2019). *250+ Influences on student achievement* (pp. 1–2). Corwin Visible Learning. https://visible-learning.org/wp-content/uploads/2022/01/250-Influences.pdf
5. Visible Learning Plus (2019). *Influences overview.* Corwin Visible Learning. https://visible-learning.org/wp-content/uploads/2022/01/Influences-overview-Visible-Learning.pdf
6. Bishop, P. A., & Harrison, L. M. (2021). *The successful middle school: This we believe* (p. 9). Association for Middle Level Education.
7. Visible Learning (2019). *250+ Influences on student achievement* (pp. 1–2). Corwin Visible Learning. https://visible-learning.org/wp-content/uploads/2022/01/250-Influences.pdf
8. Osterman, K. F. (2000). Students' need for belonging in the school community. *Review of Educational Research, 70*(3), 323–367.
   Bandura, A. (1997). *Self-efficacy: The exercise of control.* Freeman.
   Harvard Graduate School of Education (2018). *Building a culture of self-efficacy.* Harvard Graduate School of Education. https://www.gse.harvard.edu/ideas/usable-knowledge/18/09/building-culture-self-efficacy
9. Terada, Y. (2023, August 4). *Powerful, evidence-backed ways to connect with students in the first week of school.* Edutopia. https://www.edutopia.org/article/evidence-backed-ways-to-connect-with-students-first-week

10. National Association of Secondary School Principals. (2006). *Breaking ranks in the middle: Strategies for leading middle level reform* (p. 68). National Association of Secondary School Principals.
11. Seligman, M. E. (2006). *Learned Optimism: How to change your mind and your life*. Vintage.
12. Seligman, M. E. (2006). *Learned Optimism: How to change your mind and your life*. Vintage.
13. Fox, E. (2012). *Rainy brain, sunny brain: How to retrain your brain to overcome pessimism and achieve a more positive outlook*. Basic Books.
    Sharot, T. (2011). *The optimism bias: A tour of the irrationally positive brain*. Pantheon.
    Seligman, M. E. (2006). *Learned Optimism: How to change your mind and your life*. Vintage.
    Silver, D., & Berckemeyer, J. (2023). *Deliberate optimism: Still reclaiming the joy in education*. Corwin.
14. Visible Learning (2019). *250+ Influences on student achievement* (pp. 1–2). Corwin Visible Learning. https://visible-learning.org/wp-content/uploads/2022/01/250-Influences.pdf
15. Bandura, A. (1995). Exercise of personal and collective efficacy changing societies. In A. Bandura (Ed.), *Self-efficacy in changing societies* (pp. 1–45). Cambridge University Press.
16. Curwin, R. (2012, December 26). *Believing in students: The power to make a difference* (paras. 11–15). Edutopia. https://www.edutopia.org/blog/believing-in-students-richard-curwin
17. Curwin, R. (2012, December 26). *Believing in students: The power to make a difference* (para. 15). *Edutopia.* https://www.edutopia.org/blog/believing-in-students-richard-curwin
18. Goethe, J. W. (1968). Johann Wolfgang von Goethe quotes about friendship. Litchfield Historical Society. *My Country*, *2*(3), 23.

Chapter 6: Supporting Academic and Personal Success

1. Bishop, P. A., & Harrison, L. M. (2021). *The successful middle school: This we believe* (p. 9). Association for Middle Level Education.
2. Alexander, W. M. (2011). The junior high school: A changing view. In T. W. Smith & C. K. McEwen (Eds.), *The legacy of middle school leaders: In their own words* (pp. 3–16). Information Age Publishing.
3. Kampakis, K. (2015, August 15). 10 truths middle schoolers should know (paras. 1–2). *Kari Kampakis.* http://www.karikampakis.com/2015/08/10-truths-middle-schoolers-should-know/.

4. Bishop, P. A., & Harrison, L. M. (2021). *The successful middle school: This we believe* (p. 8). Association for Middle Level Education.
5. Bishop, P. A., & Harrison, L. M. (2021). *The successful middle school: This we believe* (p. 9). Association for Middle Level Education.
6. Bishop, P. A., & Harrison, L. M. (2021). *The successful middle school: This we believe* (p. 9). Association for Middle Level Education.
7. Bishop, P. A., & Harrison, L. M. (2021). *The successful middle school: This we believe* (p. 9). Association for Middle Level Education.
8. Bishop, P. A., & Harrison, L. M. (2021). *The successful middle school: This we believe* (p. 9). Association for Middle Level Education.
9. Alley, K. M. (2019). Fostering middle school students' autonomy to support motivation and engagement. *Middle School Journal, 46*(5), 26–32. http://dx.doi.org/10.1080/00940771.2019.1603801

   Bernal-Romero, T., Melandro, M., De-Juanas, A., & Goyette, M. (2021). Understanding young individuals' autonomy and psychological well-being. *Educational Psychology, 12.* https://www.frontiersin.org/articles/10.3389/fpsyg.2021.750115/full
10. Bernal-Romero, T., Melandro, M., De-Juanas, A., & Goyette, M. (2021). Understanding young individuals' autonomy and psychological well-being (para. 3). *Educational Psychology, 12.* https://www.frontiersin.org/articles/10.3389/fpsyg.2021.750115/full
11. Bernal-Romero, T., Melandro, M., De-Juanas, A., & Goyette, M. (2021). Understanding young individuals' autonomy and psychological well-being. *Educational Psychology, 12.* https://www.frontiersin.org/articles/10.3389/fpsyg.2021.750115/full
12. Schlechy, P. (2011). *Engaging students: The next level of working on the work.* Jossey-Bass.
13. Hattie, J. (2019). *250+ Influences on student achievement.* Visible Learning. Corwin Visible Learning. https://visible-learning.org/wp-content/uploads/2022/01/250-Influences.pdf
14. Hattie, J. (2019). *250+ Influences on student achievement.* Visible Learning. Corwin Visible Learning. https://visible-learning.org/wp-content/uploads/2022/01/250-Influences.pdf
15. Visible Learning. (2023). *Glossary of Hattie's influences on student achievement.* Visible Learning. https://visible-learning.org/glossary/#9_Teacher_clarity
16. Harackiewicz, J. M., Durik, A. M., Barron, K. E., Linnenbrink-Garcia, L, & Tauer, J. M. (2008). The role of achievement goals in the development of interest: Reciprocal

relations between achievement goals, interest, and performance. *Journal of Educational Psychology, 100*(1),105–122. https://doi.org/10.1037/0022-0663.100.1.105

Wolters, C. A. (2004). Advancing achievement goal theory: Using goal structures and goal orientations to predict students' motivation, cognition, and achievement. *Journal of Educational Psychology, 96*(2), 236–250. https://doi.org/10.1037/0022-0663.96.2.236

17. Tucker, C. (2013, December 1). *Five musts for mastery*. Association for Supervision and Curriculum Development. https://www.ascd.org/el/articles/five-musts-for-mastery
18. Pink, D. (2009). *Drive: The surprising truth about what motivates us* (p. 109.) Riverhead.
19. Johnson, D. W., & Johnson, R. T. (2009). An educational psychology success story: Social interdependence theory and cooperative learning. *Educational Researcher, 38*(5). DOI:10.3102/0013189X09339057
20. Lalor, A. D. M. (2022, June 24). *Feedback that empowers students*. Edutopia. https://www.edutopia.org/article/feedback-empowers-students

    Hattie, J., & Timperley, J. (2007). The power of feedback. *Review of Educational Research (77)*1. https://doi.org/10.3102/003465430298487
21. Collaborative for Academic, Social, and Emotional Learning. (2019). *CASEL's framework for systemic social and emotional learning.* Collaborative for Academic, Social, and Emotional Learning. https://measuringsel.casel.org/wp-content/uploads/2019/08/AWG-Framework-Series-B.2.pdf
22. Dewey, J. (1913). *Interest and effort in education* (p. 1). University of Michigan Library.
23. Bell, S. (2010). Project-based learning for the 21st century: Skills for the future. *The Clearing House, 83*(2), 39–43.

    Caine, R., Caine, G., McClintic, C. L., & Klimek, K. J. (2015). *12 mind/brain learning principles in action.* Corwin.
24. Scherer, M. (2006, September). Celebrate strengths, nurture affinities: A conversation with Mel Levine. *Educational Leadership, 64*(1), 8–15.
25. Guskey, T. R. (2011). Educational leadership: Effective grading practices (p. 18). *Educational Leadership, 69*(3), 16–21.
26. Bishop, P. A., & Harrison, L. M. (2021). *The successful middle school: This we believe* (pp. 29–30). Association for Middle Level Education.

27. Pew Research Center. (2023). Teens, social media, and technology, 2023. Pew Research. https://www.pewresearch.org/internet/2023/12/11/teens-social-media-and-technology-2023/
Common Sense. (2023). *Constant companion: A week in the life of a young person's smartphone use.* Common Sense Media. https://www.commonsensemedia.org/sites/default/files/research/report/2023-cs-smartphone-research-report_final-for-web.pdf
28. Common Sense. (2023). *Constant companion: A week in the life of a young person's smartphone use* (p. 3). Common Sense Media. https://www.commonsensemedia.org/sites/default/files/research/report/2023-cs-smartphone-research-report_final-for-web.pdf
29. Anderson, J. (2022, August 19). *Teens in a digital world* (paras. 4, 25). Harvard Graduate School of Education. https://www.gse.harvard.edu/ideas/usable-knowledge/22/08/teens-digital-world
30. Weinstein, E., & James, C. (2022). *Behind their screens: What teens are facing (and adults are missing).* MIT Press.
31. U. S. Surgeon General. (2023). *Social media and youth mental health: The U.S. Surgeon General's advisory.* (2023). SurgeonGeneral.gov. https://www.hhs.gov/surgeongeneral/priorities/youth-mental-health/social-media/index.html
Weinstein, E., & James, C. (2022). *Behind their screens: What teens are facing (and adults are missing).* MIT Press.
32. Paruthi, S., Brooks, L. J., D'Ambrosio, C., Hall, W. A., Kotagal, S., Lloyd, R. M., Malow, B. A., Maski, K., Nichols, C., Quan, S. F., Rosen, C. l., Troester, M. M., & Wise, M. S. (2016). Recommended amount of sleep for pediatric populations: A consensus statement of the American Academy of Sleep Medicine. *Journal of Clinical Sleep Medicine, 12*(6):785-786. doi:10.5664/jcsm.5866
Alonzo, R., Hussain, J., Strange, S., & Anderson, K. (2021, April). Interplay between social media use, sleep quality, and mental health in youth: A systematic review. *Sleep Medicine Review, 56.* https://www.sciencedirect.com/science/article/abs/pii/S108707922030157X
Woods, H. C., & Scott, H. (2016, August). #Sleepyteens: Social media in adolescence is associated with poor sleep quality, anxiety, depression, and low self-esteem. *Journal of Adolescence, 51,* 41–49. https://www.sciencedirect.com/science/article/abs/pii/S0140197116300343

Perrault, A. A., Bayer, L., Bayer, L., Peuvrier, M., Afyouni, A., Ghisletta, P., Brockmann, C., Spirion, M., Vesely, S. H., Hallier, D. M., Pichon, S., Perrig, S., Schwartz, S., & Sterpenich V. (2019). Reducing the use of screen electronic devices in the evening is associated with improved sleep and daytime vigilance in adolescents. *Sleep,* 42(9). doi:10.1093/sleep/zsz125

33. Dweck, C. S. (2007). *Mindset: The new psychology of success*. Ballantine Books.
34. Dweck, C. S. (2007). *Mindset: The new psychology of success*. New Ballantine Books.
    Dweck, C. S. (2015). Carol Dweck revisits the "growth mindset." *Education Week Commentary, 35*(5), 20, 24.
35. Dweck, C. S. (2007). *Mindset: The new psychology of success*. New York, NY: Ballantine Books.
36. Dweck, C. S. (2015). Carol Dweck revisits the "growth mindset." *Education Week Commentary, 35*(5), 20, 24.
37. The Efficacy Institute. (2008). *Efficacy for students: Your tools for getting smart*. Efficacy Institute. http://www.efficacy.org/Portals/7/Products/Efficacy%20Secondary%20Workbook%20Demo.pdf
38. Krakovsky, M. (2007, March/April). The effort effect. *Stanford Alumni Magazine*. https://alumni.stanford.edu/get/page/magazine/article/?article_id=32124
39. Dweck, C. S. (2015). Carol Dweck revisits the "growth mindset." *Education Week Commentary, 35*(5), 20.
40. Yeager, D., S., Carroll, J. M., Dweck, C. S., et al. (2021) Teacher mindsets help explain where a growth-mindset intervention does and doesn't work. *Psychological Science, 33*(1). https://doi.org/10.1177/09567976211028984
41. Rattan, A., Good, C., & Dweck, C. S. (2012). "It's ok—Not everyone can be good at math": Instructors with an entity theory comfort (and demotivate) students. *Journal of Experimental Social Psychology, 48*(3), 731–737.
42. Silver, D. (2021). *Fall down 7 times, get up 8: Teaching kids to succeed* (pp. 92–93). Corwin.
43. Gross-Loh, C. (2016, December 16). How praise became a consolation prize (para. 11). *The Atlantic*. https://www.theatlantic.com/education/archive/2016/12/how-praise-became-a-consolation-prize/510845/
44. Gross-Loh, C. (2016, December 16). How praise became a consolation prize (para. 11). *The Atlantic*. https://www.theatlantic.com/education/archive/2016/12/how-praise-became-a-consolation-prize/510845/

45. Arduini-Van Hoose, N. (2020). Attribution theory. *Educational Psychology.* https://edpsych.pressbooks.sunycreate.cloud/chapter/attribution-theory/
46. Arduini-Van Hoose, N. (2020). Attribution theory. *Educational Psychology* (para. 7). https://edpsych.pressbooks.sunycreate.cloud/chapter/attribution-theory/
47. Brooks, R. (2012). *Dr. Robert Brooks definition of resiliency and the charismatic advisor.* [Video File, 0.15-0.39]. https://www.youtube.com/watch?v=3P1rpDGiVNU
48. Brooks, R. (2015, April 14). *Resilience: The common underlying factor* (para. 2). http://www.drrobertbrooks.com/resilience-common-underlying-factor/
49. Brooks, R. (2012). *Dr. Robert Brooks definition of resiliency and the charismatic advisor.* [Video File, 0.53-1.22]. https://www.youtube.com/watch?v=3P1rpDGiVNU
50. National Scientific Council on the Developing Child (2015). *Supportive relationships and active skill-building strengthen the foundations of resilience: Working paper no. 13.* www.developingchild.harvard.edu.
51. Hoffman, J. (2017). *Kids can cope: Parenting resilient children at home and at school.* Psychology Foundation of Canada. http://cemh.lbpsb.qc.ca/parents/ResilienceChildrenBooklet.pdf
52. Hoffman, J. (2017). *Kids can cope: Parenting resilient children at home and at school* (p. 4). Psychology Foundation of Canada. http://cemh.lbpsb.qc.ca/parents/ResilienceChildrenBooklet.pdf
53. Wormeli, R. (2011, November 1). *Redos and retakes done right* (para. 7). Association for Supervision and Curriculum Development. https://www.ascd.org/el/articles/redos-and-retakes-done-right
54. Wormeli, R. (2016, 25 September). *The right way to do redos.* Middleweb. https://www.middleweb.com/31398/rick-wormeli-the-right-way-to-do-redos/
55. Wormeli, R. (2010). *Rick Wormeli: Redos, retakes, and do-overs, part one.* [Video File]. https://www.youtube.com/watch?v=TM-3PFflfvI

    Wormeli, R. (2010). *Rick Wormeli: Redos, retakes, and do-overs, part two.* [Video File]. https://www.youtube.com/watch?v=wgxvzEc0rvs

CHAPTER 7: HONOR AND FOSTER STUDENT VOICE AND CHOICE

1. United Nations General Assembly. (1989). *General assembly resolution A (Article 12, Part 1).* http://www.un.org/documents/ga/res/44/a44r025.htm

2. St. John, K., & Briel, L. (2017, April). *Student voice: A growing movement within education that benefits students and teachers.* VCU Center on Transition Innovations. https://centerontransition.org/publications/download.cfm?id=61#:~:text
3. Quaglia Institute for School Voice and Aspirations. (2016). *School voice report 2016* (p. 6). Quaglia Institute. quagliainstitute.org/dmsView/School_Voice_Report_2016
4. Benner, M., Brown, C., & Jeffrey, A. (2019). *Elevating student voice in education.* Center for American Progress. https://www.americanprogress.org/issues/education-k-12/reports/2019/08/14/473197/elevating-student-voice-education/.

   Conner, J., Posner, M., & Nsowaa, B. (2022). The relationship between student voice and student engagement in urban high schools. *The Urban Review, 54*(1), 1–20.

   Kahne, J. Bowyer, B. Marshall, J. & Hodgin, E. (2022, June 1). Is responsiveness to student voice related to academic outcomes? Strengthening the rationale for student voice in school reform. *American Journal of Education,* 128(3), 361–524.

   Mitra, D. (2018). Student voice in secondary schools: The possibility for deeper change. *Journal of Educational Administration, 56*(5), 473–487.

   Mitra, D., Jerusha Conner, J., & Holquist, S. (2021). Conditions that enable and constrain student voice(s) in schools. In Michael A. Peters (Ed.), *Encyclopedia of Teacher Education.* Springer.

   Quaglia Institute for School Voice and Aspirations. (2016). *School voice report 2016* (p. 2). Quaglia. quagliainstitute.org/dmsView/School_Voice_Report_2016

   Ruddick, J., & Flutter, J. (2000). Pupil participation and pupil perspective: Carving a new order of experience. *Cambridge Journal of Education, 30*(1).

   St. John, K., & Briel, L. (2017, April). *Student voice: A growing movement within education that benefits students and teachers.* VCU Center on Transition Innovations. https://centerontransition.org/publications/download.cfm?id=61#:~:text

   Toshalis, E. & Nakkula, M. (2012). *Motivation, engagement, and student voice toolkit.* Students at the Center Hub. https://studentsatthecenterhub.org/wp-content/uploads/1_SATC_Motivation_Toolkit_051713.pdf
5. McCombs, B. L., & Whisler, J. S. (1997). *The learner-centered classroom and school: Strategies for increasing student motivation and achievement* (p. 33). San Francisco, CA: Jossey-Bass.
6. Levin, B. (2000). Putting students at the centre of education reform (p. 172). *Journal of Educational Change, 1*(2), 155–172.

7. Bishop, P. A., & Harrison, L. M. (2021). *The successful middle school: This we believe* (p. 9). Association for Middle Level Education.
8. Cook-Sather, A. (2002). Authorizing students' perspectives: Toward trust, dialogue, and change in education (p. 363). *Educational Researcher, 31*(4), 3–14.
9. Dobson, J., & Dobson, T. (2021). Empowering student voice in a secondary school. *Teacher Development, 24*(2), 103–119.
   Fletcher, A. (2015, June 20). *Tips for teachers: Meaningful student involvement everyday*. Soundout. https://soundout.org/tips-for-teachers-meaningful-student-involvement-everyday/
   Marzano Research (2008). *Tips from Dr. Marzano: Delivering on the promise.* Marzano Research. marzanoresearch.com/resources/tips/dotp_tips_archive
   Mitra, D. (2018). Student voice in secondary schools: The possibility for deeper change. *Journal of Educational Administration, 56*(5), 473–487.
   Quaglia Institute for School Voice and Aspirations (2017). *Our framework: 8 conditions.* Quaglia. https://www.quagliainstitute.org/uploads/originals/8-conditions-2022.pdf
   Toshalis, E. & Nakkula, M. (2012). *Motivation, engagement, and student voice toolkit.* Students at the Center Hub. https://studentsatthecenterhub.org/wp-content/uploads/1_SATC_Motivation_Toolkit_051713.pdf
10. Flutter, J., & Rudduck, J. (2004). *Consulting pupils: What's in it for schools?* London, England: Routledge Falmer.
11. Jones, M-A, & Bubb, S. (2021). Student voice to improve schools: Perspectives from students, teachers and leaders in "perfect" conditions. *Improving Schools, 24(3)*, 233–244. https://doi.org/10.1177/1365480219901064
12. Corwin & Quaglia School Voice. (2017). *Student Voice Survey.* Corwin. http://svsurveys.corwin.com/
13. Quaglia Institute for School Voice and Aspirations (2017). *Our framework: 8 conditions.* Quaglia. https://www.quagliainstitute.org/uploads/originals/8-conditions-2022.pdf
14. Cushman, K. (2009). *Fires in the middle school bathroom: Advice for teachers from middle schoolers* (p. 6.). The New Press.
15. Fletcher, A. (2003). *Meaningful student involvement: A guide to inclusive school change.* SoundOut. http://www.soundout.org/MSIGuide.pdf
16. Pink, D. (2011). *Drive: The surprising truth about what motivates us.* Penguin Group.
17. Asssor A. (2012). Allowing choice and nurturing an inner compass: Educational practices

supporting students' need for autonomy. In S. L. Christenson, A. L. Reschly, & C. Wylie (Eds.), Handbook of research on student engagement (pp. 421–439). Springer.

Assor, A., Kaplan, H., & Roth, G. (2002). Choice is good, but relevance is excellent: Autonomy-enhancing and suppressing teacher behaviours predicting students' engagement in schoolwork. *British Journal of Educational Psychology, 72*(2), 261–278.

Deci, E. L., & Ryan, R. M. (1987). The support of autonomy and the control of behavior. *Journal of Personality and Social Psychology, 53,* 1004–1037.

Patall, E., Cooper, H., & Robinson, J. C. (2008). The effects of choice on intrinsic motivation and related outcomes: A meta-analysis of research findings. *Psychological Bulletin, 134*(2), 270–300.

Patall, E. A., Cooper, H., & Wynn, S. R. (2010). The effectiveness and relative importance of choice in the classroom. *Journal of Educational Psychology* 102*(4),* 896–915.

Williams, J. D., Wallace, T. L., & Sung, H. C. (2015). An exploratory study of enactment variability and student reflection. *The Journal of Early Adolescence 36*(4). https://doi.org/10.1177/0272431615570057

Wolpert-Gawron, H. (2018, November 18). *Why choice matters to student leaning.* Mindshift. https://www.kqed.org/mindshift/52424/why-choice-matters-to-student-learning

18. Asssor A. (2012). Allowing choice and nurturing an inner compass: Educational practices supporting students' need for autonomy. In S. L. Christenson, A. L. Reschly, & C. Wylie (Eds.), Handbook of research on student engagement (pp. 421–439). Springer.

Wolpert-Gawron, H. (2018, November 18). *Why choice matters to student leaning.* Mindshift. https://www.kqed.org/mindshift/52424/why-choice-matters-to-student-learning

Wolpert-Gawron, H. (2018, November 20). *What giving students choice looks like in the classroom.* Mindshift. https://www.kqed.org/mindshift/52421/what-giving-students-choice-looks-like-in-the-classroom

19. Katz, I., & Assor, A. (2006). When choice motivates and when it does not. *Educational Psychology Review 19*(4): 429–442. October 2006.

20. Patall, E. A., Cooper, H., & Wynn, S. R. (2010). The effectiveness and relative importance of choice in the classroom. *Journal of Educational Psychology 102*(4), 896–915. DOI:10.1037/a0019545

Patall, E., Cooper, H., & Robinson, J. C. (2008). The effects of choice on intrinsic motivation and related outcomes: A meta-analysis of research findings. *Psychological Bulletin, 134*(2), 270–300. DOI: 10.1037/0033-2909.134.2.270

21. Iyengar, S. S., & Lepper, M. R. (2000). When choice is demotivating: Can one desire too much of a good thing? (p. 1003). *Journal of Personality and Social Psychology, 79*(6), 995–1006.
22. Gonzalez, J. (2016, October 30). *Is your lesson a "Grecian urn?"* (para. 7). Cult of Pedagogy. http://www.cultofpedagogy.com/grecian-urn-lesson/
23. Gonzalez, J. (2016, October 30). *Is your lesson a "Grecian urn?"* (para. 17). Cult of Pedagogy. http://www.cultofpedagogy.com/grecian-urn-lesson/

Chapter 8: Develop Student Leadership

1. Bishop, P. A., & Harrison, L. M. (2021). *The successful middle school: This we believe* (p. 9). Association for Middle Level Education.
2. Edwards, B. (2015, October). *The power of youth leadership*. Association for Middle Level Education. https://www.amle.org/the-power-of-youth-leadership/

   Fletcher, A. (2013, January 23). Teaching meaningful student involvement. *Adam F. C. Fletcher.* https://adamfletcher.net/teaching-meaningful-student-involvement/

   Martinez, B., Jurado, M., Perez-Fuentes, M., & Jurado, M. (2022). Addressing leadership effectiveness for student academic engagement a systematic review. *School Leadership and Management, (42)*3, 1–15. https://www.researchgate.net/publication/362818741_Addressing_leadership_effectiveness_for_student_academic_engagement_a_systematic_review

   Mindset. *Mindset for middle school.* (2024). Mindset Enterprises. https://www.mymindsetmatters.org/curriculum/full-lessons/leadership-curriculum-for-middle-school/

   Mozhgan, A., Parivash, J., Nadergholi, G., & Jowkar, B. (2011). Student leadership competencies development. *Procedia Social and Behavioral Sciences, 15,* 1616–1620.

   The Ripple effect: Rethinking middle school student leadership. (2023). Association for Middle Level Education. https://www.amle.org/the-ripple-effect-rethinking-middle-school-student-leadership/
3. Martinez, B., Jurado, M., Perez-Fuentes, M., & Jurado, M. (2022) Addressing leadership effectiveness for student academic engagement a systematic review. *School Leadership*

and Management, 42(3), 1–15. https://www.researchgate.net/publication/362818741_Addressing_leadership_effectiveness_for_student_academic_engagement_a_systematic_review

The Ripple effect: Rethinking middle school student leadership. (2023). Association for Middle Level Education. https://www.amle.org/the-ripple-effect-rethinking-middle-school-student-leadership/

4. Zelinko, P. (2024). *Teaching today's students to be the leaders of tomorrow* (para. 4). Association for Middle Level Education. https://www.amle.org/teaching-todays-students-to-be-the-leaders-of-tomorrow/
5. Cook-Sather, A. (2002). Authorizing students' perspectives: Toward trust, dialogue, and change in education. *Educational Researcher, 31*(4), 3–14.

   Fielding, M. (2006). Leadership, radical student engagement and the necessity of person-centered education. *International Journal of Leadership in Education, 9*(4), 299–313.

   Martinez, B., Jurado, M., Perez-Fuentes, M., & Jurado, M. (2022). Addressing leadership effectiveness for student academic engagement a systematic review. *School Leadership and Management, 42*(3), 1–15. https://www.researchgate.net/publication/362818741_Addressing_leadership_effectiveness_for_student_academic_engagement_a_systematic_review
6. DePass, M., Ehrlich, V., & Leis, M. (2019). *Transforming K-12 schools by investing in leadership development* (para. 1). [White paper]. Center for Creative Leadership. https://www.ccl.org/articles/white-papers/leadership-development-for-k-12-leaders/
7. Martinez, B., Jurado, M., Perez-Fuentes, M., & Jurado, M. (2022). Addressing leadership effectiveness for student academic engagement a systematic review. *School Leadership and Management*, (42)3, 1–15. https://www.researchgate.net/publication/362818741_Addressing_leadership_effectiveness_for_student_academic_engagement_a_systematic_review

   Matthews, M. (2015). Student leadership development: A literature review and focus group interview on leadership education. *University of Wyoming Doctoral Projects, Masters Plan B, and Related Works. Paper 8*. http://repository.uwyo.edu/cgi/viewcontent.cgi?article=1007&context=plan
8. Lewis, J., Hunter, M., & Green, A. (2009, February). *Teaching student leadership in an inner-city school* (para. 1). Association for Middle Level Education. https://www.amle.org/

BrowsebyTopic/WhatsNew/WNDet/TabId/270/ArtMID/888/ArticleID/136/Teaching-Student-Leadership-in-an-Inner-City-School.aspx

9. Van Velsor, E., & Wright, J. (2012) *Expanding the leadership equation: Developing next-generation leaders* [White Paper] (pp. 2–4). ERIC: Center for Creative Leadership. http://files.eric.ed.gov/fulltext/ED543117.pdf
10. Fletcher, A. (2013, January 23). Teaching meaningful student involvement (para. 1). *Adam Fletcher.* https://adamfletcher.net/teaching-meaningful-student-involvement/
11. Fletcher, A. (2003, November 14). *Meaningful student involvement: A guide to inclusive school change* (p. 4). SoundOut.org. https://soundout.org/
12. Komives, S. R., Dugan, J. P., Owen, J. E., Slack, C., & Wagner, W. (Eds.) (2011). *The handbook for student leadership development (2nd ed.)* (p. xvi). Jossey-Bass.
13. DePass, M., Ehrlich, V., & Leis, M. (2019). *Transforming K-12 schools by investing in leadership development* (para. 1). [White paper]. Center for Creative Leadership. https://www.ccl.org/articles/white-papers/leadership-development-for-k-12-leaders/

    Van Velsor, E., & Wright, J. (2012) *Expanding the leadership equation: Developing next-generation leaders* [White Paper]. ERIC: Center for Creative Leadership. http://files.eric.ed.gov/fulltext/ED543117.pdf
14. Edwards, B. (2015, October). *The power of youth leadership.* Association for Middle Level Education. https://www.amle.org/the-power-of-youth-leadership/

    Matthews, M. (2015). Student leadership development: A literature review and focus group interview on leadership education. *University of Wyoming Doctoral Projects, Masters Plan B, and Related Works. Paper 8.* http://repository.uwyo.edu/cgi/viewcontent.cgi?article=1007&context=plan

    Rosch, D., & Meixner, C. (2011). Powerful pedagogies. In S. R. Komives, J.P. Dugan, J. E. Owen, C. Slack, & W. Wagner (Eds.), *The handbook for student leadership development* (pp. 307–337). San Francisco, CA: Jossey-Bass.
15. Komives, S. R., Dugan, J. P., Owen, J. E., Slack, C., & Wagner, W. (Eds.) (2011). *The handbook for student leadership development (2nd ed.).* Jossey-Bass.
16. Fletcher, A. (2003, November 14). *Meaningful student involvement: A guide to inclusive school change* (pp. 10-11). SoundOut. https://soundout.org/
17. Lewis, J., Hunter, M., & Green, A. (2009, February). *Teaching student leadership in an inner-city school.* Association for Middle Level Education. https://www.amle.org/

BrowsebyTopic/WhatsNew/WNDet/TabId/270/ArtMID/888/ArticleID/136/Teaching-Student-Leadership-in-an-Inner-City-School.aspx

Miller, M. (2022, June 21). *20 Leadership activities for middle school students.* Teaching Expertise. https://www.teachingexpertise.com/classroom-ideas/leadership-activities-for-middle-school/

Wheeler, L. (2022, October 12) *5 tips for creating effective student leadership groups.* Edutopia. https://www.edutopia.org/article/5-tips-creating-effective-student-leadership-groups

18. Meridian School District. (2023, March 29). *Leadership students build a culture of belonging at Meridian Middle School* (paras. 1–6, 8, 10–11). Meridian School District. https://www.meridian.wednet.edu/news/2023/03/29/leadership-students-build-a-culture-of-belonging-at-meridian-middle-school/

Chapter 9: Celebrate Belonging and Becoming

1. Budgen, S. H. (2023, April 20). *The power of celebration: An exploration of how the simple act of celebration can impact student outcomes and well-being.* Open University. https://www.open.ac.uk/blogs/learning-design/?p=1591

Farr, V. (2003). *The role of celebration in building classroom-learning communities* (Paper No.771) [Doctoral dissertation, East Tennessee State University]. Electronic Theses and Dissertations. https://dc.etsu.edu/etd/771/

Hoffman, A. & Field, S. (1995). Promoting self-determination through effective curriculum development. *Intervention in School and Clinic. 30*(3),134–141.

Mishra, S. (2020). Social networks, social capital, social support and academic success in higher education: A systematic review with a special focus on "underrepresented" students. *Educational Research Review.* https://doi.org/10.1016/j.edurev.2019.100307

Younghans, M. (2016, August 30). *Recognizing student success: Creating a positive culture for students.* National Association of Secondary School Principals. https://www.nassp.org/2016/08/30/recognizing-student-success-creating-a-positive-culture-for-students/

2. Hummel, C. E. (1994). *Tyranny of the urgent, revised edition.* InterVarsity Press.
3. Budgen, S. H. (2023, April 20). *The power of celebration: An exploration of how the simple*

act of celebration can impact student outcomes and well-being. Open University. https://www.open.ac.uk/blogs/learning-design/?p=1591

Farr, V. (2003). *The role of celebration in building classroom-learning communities* (Paper No. 771) [Doctoral dissertation, East Tennessee State University]. Electronic Theses and Dissertations. https://dc.etsu.edu/etd/771/

4. Bandura, A. (1997). *Self-efficacy: The exercise of control.* Freeman.
5. Deci, E. L., Koestner, R., & Ryan, R. M. (2001). Extrinsic rewards and intrinsic motivation in education: Reconsidered once again (p. 14). *Review of Educational Research, 71*(1), 1–27.
6. Lepper, M., Greene, D., & Nisbett, R. E. (1973). Undermining children's intrinsic interests with extrinsic reward: A test of the "over justification" hypothesis. *Journal of Personality and Social Psychology, 28*(1), 129–137.
7. Deci, E. L., with Flate, R. (1995). *Why we do what we do: Understanding self-motivation.* Gross/Putnam Books.

   Deci, E. L., Koestner, R., & Ryan, R. M. (2001). Extrinsic rewards and intrinsic motivation in education: Reconsidered once again (p. 14). *Review of Educational Research, 71*(1), 1–27.

   Kohn, A. (2018). *Punished by rewards, Twenty-fifth anniversary edition: The trouble with gold stars, incentive plans, A's, praise, and other bribes.* Boston, MA: Houghton Mifflin.

   Ryan, R. M., & Deci, E. L. (2018). *Self-determination theory: Basic psychological needs in motivation, development, and wellness.* The Guilford Press.
8. Pink, D. (2011). *Drive: The surprising truth about what motivates us* (p. 58). Penguin Group.
9. Kohn, A. (2018). *Punished by rewards, Twenty-fifth anniversary edition: The trouble with gold stars, incentive plans, A's, praise, and other bribes.* Houghton Mifflin.
10. Morehead, J. (2012, June 19). *Stanford University's Carol Dweck on the growth mindset and education* (para. 23). OneDublin. https://onedublin.org/2012/06/19/stanford-universitys-carol-dweck-on-the-growth-mindset-and-education/
11. Assor, A., Kaplan, H., & Roth, G. (2002). Choice is good, but relevance is excellent: Autonomy-enhancing and suppressing teacher behaviours predicting students' engagement in schoolwork. *British Journal of Educational Psychology, 72*(2), 261–278.

    Deci, E. L., with Flate, R. (1995). *Why we do what we do: Understanding self-motivation.* Gross/Putnam Books.

Deci, E. L., & Ryan, R. M. (1985). *Intrinsic motivation and self-determination in human behavior.* Plenum Press.

Dweck, C. S., & Leggett, E. L. (1988). A social-cognitive approach to motivation and personality. *Psychological Review, 95*(2), 256.

Ryan, R. M., & Deci, E. L. (2018). *Self-determination theory: Basic psychological needs in motivation, development, and wellness*. The Guilford Press.

12. Deci, E.L., Koestner, R. & Ryan, R.M. (1999). A meta-analytic review of experiments Examining the effects of extrinsic rewards on intrinsic motivation (p. 653). *Psychological Bulletin, 125*(6), 627–668.
13. Amabile, T. (1996). *Creativity in context.* Westview Press.
14. Center on Educational Policy. (2012). *Student motivation – An overlooked piece of school reform* (p. 3). Center on Education Policy. https://files.eric.ed.gov/fulltext/ED532666.pdf
15. Kohn, A. (2018). *Punished by rewards, Twenty-fifth anniversary edition: The trouble with gold stars, incentive plans, A's, praise, and other bribes.* Houghton Mifflin.
16. Henderlong, J., & Lepper, M. (2002). The effects of praise on children's intrinsic motivation: A review and synthesis. *Psychological Bulletin, 128*, 774–795. https://www.researchgate.net/publication/11182972_The_Effects_of_Praise_on_Children%27s_Intrinsic_Motivation_A_Review_and_Synthesis
17. Black, S., & Allen, J. D. (2018). Insights from educational psychology part 7: Rewards, motivation, and performance. *The Reference Librarian*, 59(4), 205–218. https://www.tandfonline.com/doi/full/10.1080/02763877.2018.1499164
18. Lemov, D. (2016, January 25). *On praise: Carol Dweck and beyond.* Teach Like a Champion. https://teachlikeachampion.org/blog/coaching-and-practice/praise-carol-dweck-beyond/
19. Dweck, C. S. (2008). The perils and promises of praise. *Educational Leadership, 65*(2), 34–39. https://www.ascd.org/el/articles/the-perils-and-promises-of-praise-summer-2008

    Dweck, C. (2014, January 30). *A study on praise and mindsets.* YouTube.com [Video file] https://www.youtube.com/results?search_query=carol+dweck+a+-study+on+praise+and+mindsets

    Dweck, C. (2013, November 7). *Process praise.* YouTube.com [Video file]. https://www.youtube.com/results?search_query=carol+dweck+process+praise

20. Center on Educational Policy. (2012). *Student motivation – An overlooked piece of school reform* (p. 8). Center on Educational Policy. https://files.eric.ed.gov/fulltext/ED532666.pdf
21. Center on Educational Policy. (2012). *Student motivation – An overlooked piece of school reform* (pp. 8–9). Center on Educational Policy. https://files.eric.ed.gov/fulltext/ED532666.pdf

APPENDIX A

1. Bishop. P. A., & Harrison, L. M. (2021). Characteristics of young adolescent development. In *The successful middle school: This we believe* (pp. 57–64). Association for Middle Level Education.

About the Authors

Laurie and Patti both have the distinguished honor of being named as MetLife/NASSP National Middle Level Principals of the Year. Although a decade separates their respective honors, they both agree that there is one constant for middle school students: No two are ever alike.

LAURIE BARRON

Dr. Laurie Barron was a leading force behind the turnaround of Smokey Road Middle School. When she took over in 2004, she was the fourth principal to lead the school in five years. However, by demonstrating her commitment to the success of students and staff members, she was able to tackle the rampant discipline problems, high absenteeism, and low student achievement.

"NASSP's experience has taught us time and again that nothing is more challenging or essential to school improvement than changing the school's culture," said NASSP Executive Director JoAnn Bartoletti. "With genuine concern for her students' welfare, Laurie Barron established at Smokey Road Middle School a model climate of what the *Breaking Ranks* school improvement framework requires—a personalized environment where every student is known and feels valued."

Currently in her 29th year in education, Laurie served six years as a high school English teacher and coach, two years as a middle school assistant principal, and nine years as a middle school principal in Newnan, Georgia. She also served as a part-time assistant professor at the university level. Currently, she is in her 12th year as the superintendent of the Evergreen School District in Kalispell, Montana. She served eight years as a board member for the Association for Middle Level

Education and was named as one of the University of Georgia Alumni Association's "40 Under 40" recipients.

Laurie is a National Board Certified Teacher and was honored as a Teacher of the Year and STAR Teacher. Her work as the principal of Smokey Road Middle School in Newnan, Georgia, led to her selection as the 2012 Georgia Middle School Principal of the Year, 2013 MetLife/NASSP National Middle Level Principal of the Year, and Smokey Road Middle School's selection as one of five middle schools in the nation to be named a 2011 MetLife Foundation–NASSP Breakthrough School.

Laurie holds a BSEd in English Education from the University of Georgia, an MEd in Supervision and Administration from the University of West Georgia, and an EdS and EdD in Educational Leadership from the University of Sarasota. She also studied abroad at Oxford University. She holds a National Superintendent Certification through AASA. Additionally, Laurie was the 2018 School Administrators of the Montana G.V. Erickson Award recipient, given to a member of the School Administrators of Montana who has made the greatest contribution to the betterment of education in Montana. She was named the 2019 Empowered Superintendent of the Year by the Montana Educational Technologists Association, and she was the 2021 Montana Superintendent of the Year. In 2022, Laurie was honored with the Distinguished Alumni Lifetime Achievement Award from the University of Georgia College of Education.

Laurie co-authored *We Belong: 50 Strategies to Create Community and Revolutionize Classroom Management*; *Middle School: A Place to Belong and Become*; and *What Parents Need to Know about Common Core and Other College- and Career-Ready Standards*. She has also authored numerous education articles.

Laurie is also a national speaker, consultant, and leadership coach who provides motivation and professional learning to teachers and administrators through promoting strategic planning and school improvement, positive school culture, inclusive teaching and learning environments, student engagement and voice, shared leadership, data-informed decision making, and standards-based assessment. Most importantly, Laurie believes that building relationships with staff and students, while celebrating what staff and students do right, is the key to success in any school.

Today, Laurie is living the dream with her husband Daniel in northwest Montana, where together they enjoy spending time with family watching Georgia Bulldogs football, snow skiing, camping, rafting, hiking, and watching their daughter Emma play college soccer.

PATTI KINNEY

In first grade, Patti decided to become a teacher when she realized that she wanted to be the person "who told kids what to do!" Fortunately, she eventually learned that the job entailed a great deal more than that! She began her career as an elementary music specialist and then taught fifth and sixth grade in an elementary school. She later taught sixth and seventh grade when her district made the transition to middle school in the mid-80s. During this time, she was also involved in staff development work for the district, taught a variety of instructional and management skills classes, and took a one-year sabbatical leave to teach in the education department of Southern Oregon University. As an assistant principal and later principal of Talent Middle School, she was highly involved in the process to transform this former 7–8 junior high school into a 6–8 middle school. In 2000, the school was named one of "100 Highly Successful Middle Schools" in a national research study sponsored by NASSP.

Patti is a past president of the Association for Middle Level Education and of the Oregon Middle Level Association. In 2007, she was awarded the Oregon Middle Level Association's first Distinguished Service Award, which was also named in her honor. Patti was named Oregon Assistant Principal of the Year in 1996, Oregon Principal of the Year in 2002, and in 2003, she was selected as the Met-Life/NASSP National Middle Level Principal of the Year. From 2007 through 2014, she served as Associate Director of Middle Level Services for the National Association of Secondary School Principals (NASSP) located in Virginia.

Patti currently speaks, presents, and consults on middle level issues at the national and international levels. She has authored the book *Fostering Student*

Accountability through Student-led Conferences and co-authored five books: *We Belong: 50 Strategies to Create Community and Revolutionize Classroom Management*; *Middle School: A Place to Belong and Become*; *What Parents Need to Know about Common Core and Other College- and Career-Ready Standards*; *Voices of Experience: Perspectives from Middle Level Leaders;* and *The What, Why, and How of Student-Led Conferences*. She has written regularly for NASSP's *Principal Leadership* magazine. Patti earned a B.A. in elementary education, an M.A. in outdoor education from Southern Oregon University, and an administrative license from the University of Oregon. In 2020, she married Dan Bolton, 62 years after they had been in the same first-grade classroom in Cottage Grove, Oregon, where they currently live.

www.ingramcontent.com/pod-product-compliance
Lightning Source LLC
LaVergne TN
LVHW081227250625
814604LV00002B/4

* 9 7 8 1 5 6 0 9 0 0 8 5 6 *